Didi-Huberman and the image

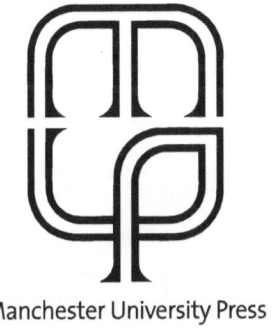

Manchester University Press

Didi-Huberman and the image

Chari Larsson

Manchester University Press

Published by Manchester University Press
Oxford Road, Manchester M13 9PL
www.manchesteruniversitypress.co.uk

British Library Cataloguing-in-Publication Data
A catalogue record for this book is available from the British Library

ISBN 978 1 5261 4926 8 hardback
ISBN 978 1 5261 6710 1 paperback

First published 2020
Paperback published 2022

The publisher has no responsibility for the persistence or accuracy of URLs for any external or third-party internet websites referred to in this book, and does not guarantee that any content on such websites is, or will remain, accurate or appropriate.

Typeset by Newgen Publishing UK

Contents

List of figures   *page* vii
Acknowledgements   xi

Introduction   1
1 The archaeological art historian   24
2 The materiality of images   48
3 Timely anachronisms   69
4 The *empreinte*   98
5 Making monsters   121
6 Thinking images   142
Conclusion   162

Bibliography   174
Index   189

Figures

1   Aby Warburg, *Bilderatlas Mnemosyne* at the reading room
    of the Kulturwissenschaftliche Bibliothek Warburg.
    Photograph, 1927. Germany. © Warburg Institute,
    London   *page* 11
2   Fra Angelico, *Annunciation with Saint Peter Martyr, c.*
    1440–44. Fresco. Florence, Museo di San Marco. © Photo
    Scala, Florence – courtesy of the Ministero Beni e Att.
    Culturali e del Turismo   15
3   Jan Vermeer, *View of Delft from the Rotterdam Canal,*
    1658–60. Oil on canvas. The Hague, Mauritshuis.
    © Photo Scala, Florence   50
4   Jan Vermeer, *View of Delft from the Rotterdam Canal*
    (detail), 1658–60. Oil on canvas. The Hague, Mauritshuis.
    © Photo Scala, Florence   50
5   Jan Vermeer, *The Lacemaker, c.* 1669–70. Oil on canvas,
    24 cm × 21 cm. Paris, musée du Louvre. © Photo Scala,
    Florence   52
6   Jan Vermeer, *The Lacemaker* (detail), *c.* 1669–70. Oil
    on canvas, 24 cm × 21 cm. Paris, musée du Louvre.
    © Photo Scala, Florence   53
7   Fra Angelico, fake marble panels below the *Madonna
    delle Ombre* (*Madonna of the Shadows*), *c.* 1450. Florence,
    Museo di San Marco. © Photo Scala, Florence   58
8   Fra Angelico, *Madonna delle Ombre* (*Madonna of the
    Shadows*). Fresco. Florence, Museo di San Marco.
    © Photo Scala, Florence – courtesy of the Ministero
    Beni e Att. Culturali e del Turismo   58
9   Albrecht Dürer, *Death of Orpheus,* 1494. Drawing,
    289 × 225 mm. Hamburg, Kunsthalle. Photo © Warburg
    Institute, London. Reproduced under a creative
    commons licence   85

10   Anonymous, Northern Italian, *Death of Orpheus, c.* 1470–80.
     Engraving, 145 cm × 214 cm, Hamburg, Kunsthalle.
     © Warburg Institute, London. Reproduced under a
     creative commons licence   86
11   Anonymous, Venice, *Death of Orpheus*, 1497.
     Woodcut from Ovid, *Metamorphoses*. © Warburg Institute,
     London. Reproduced under a creative commons licence   86
12   Anonymous, *Death of Orpheus*, detail of vase from Nola,
     c. 475–50 BC. 31.5 cm. Paris, musée du Louvre.
     © Warburg Institute, London. Reproduced under
     a creative commons licence   87
13   Anonymous (member of the *Sonderkommando* of
     Auschwitz), *Cremation of Gassed Bodies in Open-Air
     Incineration Pits, in Front of the Gas Chamber of
     Crematorium V in Auschwitz*, August 1944. The State
     Museum Auschwitz-Birkenau in Oświęcim
     (negative no. 281)   122
14   Anonymous (member of the *Sonderkommando* of
     Auschwitz), *Cremation of Gassed Bodies in Open-Air
     Incineration Pits, in Front of the Gas Chamber of
     Crematorium V in Auschwitz*, August 1944. The State
     Museum Auschwitz-Birkenau in Oświęcim
     (negative no. 280)   123
15   Anonymous (member of the *Sonderkommando* of
     Auschwitz), *Women Pushed towards the Gas Chamber of
     Crematorium V in Auschwitz*, August 1944. The State
     Museum Auschwitz-Birkenau in Oświęcim
     (negative no. 282)   124
16   Anonymous (member of the *Sonderkommando* of
     Auschwitz), August 1944. The State Museum Auschwitz-
     Birkenau in Oświęcim (negative no. 283)   125
17   László Nemes, *Son of Saul*, 2015   132
18   László Nemes, *Son of Saul*, 2015   133
19   Aby Warburg, *Bilderatlas Mnemosyne* (1927–29),
     plate 79. Photograph. London, Warburg Institute
     Archive. Photo: Warburg Institute   156
20   Jean-Luc Godard, *Histoire(s) du cinéma*, 1988–98,
     episode 1B, 'Une histoire seule'   163

21 Jean-Luc Godard, *Histoire(s) du cinéma*, 1988–98,
    episode 1B, 'Une histoire seule'   163

22 Jean-Luc Godard, *Histoire(s) du cinéma*, 1988–98,
    episode 1B, 'Une histoire seule'   164

Acknowledgements

This book has been influenced and inspired by many people. I would like to thank Amelia Barikin, Andrea Bubenik, Rex Butler and Sally Butler for providing institutional support in the manuscript's embryonic stages at the University of Queensland. Early drafts were read by Elisabeth Bronfen and Keith Moxey, whose encouragement was crucial in the manuscript's development.

I would like to acknowledge my dear friends and colleagues at Griffith University's Queensland College of Art. This manuscript was completed with the expert guidance of Susan Best, Elisabeth Findlay and Rosemary Hawker.

I have had the opportunity to develop many of my ideas and arguments at numerous conferences and lectures, for which many thanks are due to Helen Hughes, Giles Fielke, Toni Ross and Raymond Spiteri. With helpful conversation and other acts of generosity, other friends have helped me along the way: Amy Carkeek, Natalya Hughes, Neroli Jager, Tim Riley Walsh and Richard Whan.

I would like to express my sincere appreciation and gratitude to my editor at Manchester University Press, Emma Brennan. Emma's support through the entire lifecycle of the project was both humbling and instructive. Thanks are due also to the anonymous reviewers for their generous suggestions about the revisions of the manuscript.

It was a privilege to be awarded a publication subsidy by the Australian Academy of the Humanities, for which I give thanks.

Finally, I am grateful for the love and support of my family, Scott, Rex and Chris. This book is dedicated to you.

Introduction

Georges Didi-Huberman's *The Surviving Image* concludes with a quotation drawn from a speech delivered by art historian Aby Warburg to mark the reopening of the German Institute of Art History in Florence in 1927. Warburg completed his paper with the rallying cry: '*Si continua – coraggio! – ricominciamo la lettura!*' ('To be continued to our next – courage! – Let's begin the reading again!'). Warburg's comments led Didi-Huberman to pithily observe, 'This was his way of saying that in every age, indeed in every moment, art history needs to be reread and begun anew.'[1] Didi-Huberman's remarks were made in relation to Warburg's legacy, but might easily be redirected to describing his own project.

Why a monograph on Didi-Huberman, and why now? As we approach the significant milestone of 130 years since art history's modern inception, a series of questions arise: What is the current shape of art history? How does this assume alternative forms in different geographies? Like other disciplines, it is no longer possible, or desirable, to speak of a singular, unified framework. How, then, has Didi-Huberman contributed to the ongoing reworking of a discourse notoriously slow to absorb and respond to broader shifts in the humanities? This book is based on the premise that Didi-Huberman's work is crucial for art historians and theorists of visual culture as he takes us back to basic questions: What does it mean to look? What does it mean to know? What does it mean to write? These questions lie at the heart of what art historians do, yet how frequently do we pause and self-consciously reflect on our practice?

Didi-Huberman is a prolific writer and his work is sprawling, ambitious, fragmentary. Since the 1990s, Didi-Huberman has taught at the École des hautes études en sciences sociales (EHESS). His research draws from multiple disciplines, such as philosophy, anthropology and psychoanalysis, and traverses diverse historical periods ranging from the Renaissance to modern and contemporary art. In 2015, Didi-Huberman was awarded the prestigious Theodor W. Adorno Prize. Didi-Huberman's writing reflects a deep and sustained dialogue with some of the key orientations of poststructuralism, and he has regularly engaged with the great intellectual projects of Georges Bataille, Aby Warburg and Walter Benjamin.

Didi-Huberman is important because of what he has accomplished. His research project now spans forty years and fifty books and has become an inescapable reference point in France. His aims may be summarised as threefold: firstly, to critique the foundations of art history. What normative assumptions and conventions do we bring to the discipline? If art history was 'born' in the Renaissance, what legacies continue to inform and direct our understanding and practice? Secondly, what is the philosophy of time underpinning these conventions? Art history has traditionally been measured and categorised through careful periodisation. These periods were organised in a linear direction. If a Hegelian narrative of progress can no longer be convincingly maintained in the contemporary era, how may we begin to imagine alternative modes of time and temporality?

Finally, Didi-Huberman is committed to rethinking the expectations of how we write about images. His writing is extremely literary and he has long experimented with different forms of art writing. These three concerns have been developed systematically over the decades in a programmatic attempt to analyse the 'unseen' or 'unwritten' rules of the discipline. Disciplinary critique, nevertheless, only amounts to half of Didi-Huberman's programme. The other half is consumed with renewal, developing new theoretical orientations and modes of thinking. But what does this renewal look like, and what lessons can we learn?

Didi-Huberman and the image attempts to bring clarity to Didi-Huberman's formidable body of work. I argue that what is at stake in his work is the deeply visual tradition of art history rethinking its relationship with representation. Representation, mimesis and imitation are notoriously slippery terms, and are frequently used interchangeably. Didi-Huberman's principal achievement is to criticise, destabilise and correct the monolith that is representation and has become a proxy in art-historical thinking. Specifically, this is the idealism that underpins mimesis. In its broadest sense, idealism privileges the notion that ideas are primary, while non-ideas, such as physical and material things, are secondary. As art historians, we can recognise this line of thought descending from Plato, who derided images as secondary and derivative as opposed to the higher Forms.

Interest in Didi-Huberman's work is naturally greatest in his native France. His writing has been the subject of two edited volumes, *Penser par les images: autour des travaux de Georges Didi-Huberman* and *Devant les images: penser l'art et l'histoire avec Georges Didi-Huberman*.[2] The French literary journal *Europe* dedicated an issue to his work in 2018.[3] Didi-Huberman is credited with the growth of interest in Warburg in France. Philippe-Alain Michaud's *Aby Warburg et l'image en movement*, for instance, was a response to Didi-Huberman's seminars on Warburg during the late 1990s.[4] Over the past two decades he has curated a series of exhibitions in Paris at the Centre Pompidou, the Palais de Tokyo and most recently in 2016 at the Jeu de Paume.[5] These exhibitions have given visual form to the theoretical undercurrents that have informed his research.

In the English-speaking world, the literature examining Didi-Huberman's work is scattered through journal articles and book chapters. Nigel Saint's chapter 'Georges Didi-Huberman: Images, Critique and Time' in *Modern French Visual Theory* provides an incisive entry point to his research project.[6] The implications of Didi-Huberman's investigation of anachronistic models of time and temporality in *Devant le temps* and *L'image survivante* are emerging in art-historical scholarship. Keith Moxey has taken up Didi-Huberman's provocation that images are capable of generating their own time, consequently disrupting Hegelian precepts of linearity and progress.[7] In a similar vein, Alexander Nagel and Christopher Wood examined the deliberate use of anachronisms or the juxtaposition of historical styles in Renaissance painting. The authors write, 'Our own project responds to Warburg's provocation, amplified in Didi-Huberman's exegesis, by attempting to draw a nonevolutionary "metaphorics" of time from the historical works themselves.'[8] In 2018, *Angelaki* dedicated an entire issue to his work with a focus on Didi-Huberman's most recent research.[9]

Didi-Huberman's contribution to Holocaust discourse with the publication of *Images malgré tout* (2003) has become an important reference point for the broader community of Holocaust scholars, historians, photographic historians and trauma theorists. In this, arguably his most important book, Didi-Huberman intervened in philosophical debates relating to the visuality of the Holocaust that have dominated philo-sophical discourse since the 1980s.[10] More recently, Andrzej Leśniak has undertaken an analysis of Didi-Huberman's cycle of books titled *L'œil de l'histoire*, of which six volumes have been completed at the time of writing.[11] Despite these contributions, Didi-Huberman's reception continues to remain uneven in Anglo-American communities. His name 'pops up' frequently, though it is usually confined to the context of a specific topic. There has yet to be an attempt to consider his work in its entirety, or an attempt to map his intellectual development through the decades. This book aims to address this gap and is based on the con-viction that to return Didi-Huberman to his philosophical and institu-tional context will provide an ideal vantage point to assess his full body of work. In spite of the breadth and diversity of Didi-Huberman's sub-ject matter, there is a remarkable thematic unity that unites his writing.

Didi-Huberman and the image is designed to be an introduction to Didi-Huberman's project. It has not been my intention to produce an uncritical reading of Didi-Huberman's research and I must signal to the reader early on in this book that the material is not without its challenges. I will attempt to address these with the question: why the belated reception of Didi-Huberman's work? Frustratingly, there is no single or straightforward answer. His project questions the pillars that art-historical practice has rested on: the linearity of history, period-isation, origins, continuity, progress and authorship. This renders his work virtually unrecognisable to many art historians. James Elkins encapsulates this sentiment:

> I worry about Georges Didi-Huberman, because there is interesting material there that is *almost* unusable by, in, or as art history. Aside from problems that arise from particular claims he makes, or from the rhetorical and narrative form he chooses, there is also the question of the structure which would be left – that would be recognizable by art historians – if we were to take everything he says seriously.[12]

With faint echoes of the difficulty Michel Foucault initially posed to disciplinary categorisation decades ago, he does not sit comfortably as either philosopher or art historian. Instead, he borrows ideas from philosophy to renew art history. Didi-Huberman does not identify with a specific epoch or medium, instead adopting a transhistorical and transdisciplinary approach to his investigation of images.

Supplementing this, Didi-Huberman suffers from an 'image problem' of being associated with French 'theory' and is aggregated with other French philosophers and writers under the label of poststructuralism. If the 'heady' days of French theory have well and truly passed, Didi-Huberman is irrevocably *late*. The last four decades of the twentieth century were dominated by the 'heroic' figures of Jean-François Lyotard, Gilles Deleuze, Jacques Derrida and Michel Foucault. With their deaths, many assumed that French theory has died as well. The notion that deconstruction was once the avant-garde of Anglophone literature departments now seems a somewhat quaint and distant memory. In the wake of theory's 'death', we are now, apparently, 'posttheory'. This has done little to cultivate an intellectual environment receptive to a younger generation of French scholars. By virtue of his 'Frenchness', and his belated position in the roll-call of French 'theorists', Didi-Huberman is at odds with the 'posttheory' mood and intellectual land-scape in Anglo-American universities.[13]

As Sylvère Lotringer demonstrated long ago, the notion of French 'theory' was an American construction, and no such equivalent exists in France.[14] One of the aims of this book is to map out the broader intel-lectual history and Didi-Huberman's position in it. Didi-Huberman, for his part, reenergises older, seemingly *passé* ideas that deserve revisiting. His ongoing negotiation with Foucault's archaeology, for instance, draws attention to an undertheorised period of Foucault's intellectual development. Furthermore, France has a long, prestigious philosoph-ical and literary tradition of placing images at the centre of its inquiry. Didi-Huberman self-consciously lays claim to this tradition and the deeply rich cross-disciplinary fertilisation between disciplines:

> Les textes théoriques les plus marquants sur l'image, en France, por-tent presque tous, en conséquence, la marque de ce profond ancrage poétique: c'est Georges Bataille écrivant sur Lascaux, Maurice Blanchot sur 'Les deux versions de l'imaginaire', Michel Foucault sur les *Ménines*, Roland Barthes sur la photographie. Même la tradition plus strictement philosophique – je pense aux écrits de Gilles Deleuze sur Francis Bacon, le cinéma ou la théorie de l'image selon Beckett; ou bien à ceux de Jacques Derrida sur le sublime, l'aveuglement, la dimension tactile – adopte la liberté des poètes pour malmener, devant les images, toute pensée esthétique qui chercherait un peu trop son propre mode de définition *stricto sensu*.[15]

The most striking theoretical texts on the image, in France, almost all carry, therefore, deep poetic roots: it is Georges Bataille writing on Lascaux, Maurice Blanchot on 'The Two Versions of the Imaginary', Michel Foucault on *Las Meninas*, Roland Barthes on the photograph. Even the more strictly philosophical tradition – I am thinking here of Gilles Deleuze's writing on Francis Bacon, cinema or Beckett's theory of the image; or of those by Jacques Derrida on the sublime, on blindness, on the tactile dimension – adopts the freedom of poets to manhandle, before images, all aesthetic thought that might be trying a little too hard to find its own *narrow definition*.

Didi-Huberman's work can be difficult. It assumes a familiarity with the central concerns of recent French intellectual history. His work unfolds through a sustained dialogue with specific figures such as Hegel, Nietzsche, Freud, Derrida, Deleuze, amongst others. Frequently, Didi-Huberman extracts ideas from philosophers and puts them to work, expecting the reader to be fully abreast of the philosophical context he is working in. There is a long history in France of implicit referencing as an acceptable academic practice, but for the English-language scholar, the experience can be disconcerting. This is combined with an ongoing engagement with the French essayistic tradition commencing with Michel de Montaigne in the late 1500s. Small essays are frequently published by Les Éditions de Minuit. Working against the mainstream art-historical commitment to objective realism, these essays are poetic, experimental and in recent years, increasingly personal. Didi-Huberman will freely adopt a range of tones and cadences. Within his corpus, individual books do not necessarily function as unified entities. Considered diachronically, Didi-Huberman's writing is essayistic as he returns to previous ideas and arguments, expanding and developing core concerns. To read one translated text in isolation is to miss the richness of a broader line of inquiry.

In the earliest days of his career, Didi-Huberman unleashed a series of interrogations towards various methodological positions occupied by American art historians. In a succession of essays written in the late 1980s and 1990s, he subjected the work of respected art historians Michael Baxandall, Svetlana Alpers and Michael Fried to forensic cross examinations.[16] The hostility Didi-Huberman displayed towards the methodological approaches of other scholars is no longer there, yet the damage was done, and until recent years he has remained relatively isolated from academic communities outside of Europe. This in turn raises further awkward questions concerning institutionalised power. Didi-Huberman has only published in the influential art journal *October* once, back in 1984.[17] This absence is a potent rejoinder to Didi-Huberman's early career aggression, and points to the influence wielded by art historians that formed the core of the *October* editorial board: Yve-Alain Bois, Benjamin H. D. Buchloh, Hal Foster and Rosalind Krauss. Since the 1970s, the four American-based authors have dominated international discourse on modern and contemporary art. Accentuating the silence is Didi-Huberman's lack of engagement with other influential theorists of images such as W. J. T. Mitchell. As part of the embrace of visual culture underway in American universities from the late 1980s, Mitchell published an important series of books seeking to theorise images.[18] Despite this, their respective projects remain clearly separate, with Mitchell aligning his research with the German proponents of *Bildwissenschaft*, most prominently Gottfried Boehm.[19]

Didi-Huberman's work is often abstracted from its institutional context. He is the direct descendent of a rich intellectual lineage centred at EHESS.[20] This institution has provided support to multiple generations of scholars who have established a reputation for exploring new forms of 'unconventional' art history. From the outset, EHESS provided the freedom and the flexibility to break from iconographic art history practised at the Sorbonne by André Chastel and his followers. Didi-Huberman has observed, 'Dans le domaine de l'histoire de l'art, l'Université – je parle d'un temps dominé par les disciples directs d'André Chastel – a longtemps barré la route à tout ce qui pouvait se faire d'intéressant dans le domaine de la réflexion sur les images.'[21] ('In the domain of art history, the University – I speak of a period dominated by the direct disciples of André Chastel – for a long time blocked the path to all that was interesting in the field of consideration of images.') Alongside Didi-Huberman, this includes Daniel Arasse (1944–2003), Giovanni Careri (1958–) and André Gunthert (1961–) as part of the group of art historians having taught or currently teaching at EHESS and whose doctoral theses were supervised by Louis Marin and Hubert Damisch.

A further premise of this book is to emphasise the fact that art-historical discourses have assumed different shapes in different national territories. Contemporaneous with Didi-Huberman's archaeological investigation of the discipline's origins and foundational assumptions, significant changes were underway in other geographies. Didi-Huberman emerged as an early career scholar when the 'new' and 'radical' art history was altering the landscape of Anglophone art history. In Britain, the discipline was being placed under intense scrutiny, where the notion of a 'New Art History' was gaining momentum. This was codified with the text *The New Art History* of 1986.[22] Associated with the social and feminist art histories of T. J. Clark, Michael Baxandall and Griselda Pollock, the new art history was subsequently expanded to embrace postcolonial, psychoanalytical and broader gender-studies approaches in the ensuing decades. At the same time, historiographical questions came to the fore in the United States, driven by scholars such as Michael Ann Holly, Keith Moxey and Mark A. Cheetham.[23] Another important trajectory was the emergence of visual culture studies in the mid-1990s in North America. At the time, the boundaries, aims and methodological approaches of visual culture studies were the subject of vigorous debate.[24] By the mid-2000s, visual culture was generally understood as a strategy for studying the visual in culture through a range of material that art history had once disavowed. This was encapsulated by W. J. T. Mitchell's coining of the phrase the 'visual turn' and the 'widely shared notion that visual images have replaced words as the dominant mode of expression in our time'.[25]

It is crucial to highlight that Didi-Huberman's project has been shaped by an institutional and intellectual heritage that is uniquely French. As Ralph Dekoninck argues, it is possible to identify a distinct discursive body of thought in France that is different from both its German and Anglophone counterparts.[26] By failing to read Didi-Huberman in this context, his claims are sometimes rendered somewhat opaquely. In 1988, Norman Bryson's anthology *Calligram* included French thinkers such as Julia Kristeva, Louis Marin and Yves Bonnefoy and introduced, as Bryson put it: 'a form of writing that is not art history as we in the English-speaking world know it'.[27] Didi-Huberman's concerns differ, and his project, especially in the early years, must be framed as an attempt to move beyond the linguistic preoccupations of his predecessors. This helps us understand why Erwin Panofsky and the Austro-German art history tradition figure so prominently during this early period of his intellectual development. In Panofsky's iconological method, he detects a semiotic 'system' that purports that images are a visual language that can 'read'.

Representation and its discontents

The emergence of visual culture and image studies in recent decades has re-energised long philosophical and aesthetic histories pertaining to representation and images. The term 'representation' enjoys a long and complex history. Christopher Prendergast offers a useful definition. Firstly, representation is used in the sense of re-presenting, to make present again. This is the act of re-presenting a once present object, and draws from the Latin *repraesentare*, literally the 'bringing to presence again'. The second meaning is understood as a 'standing in' or substitution. A linguistic sign, for example, 'stands in' for something else.[28]

In art's history, representation is frequently conflated with mimesis. Depending on the context, mimesis is translated from the Greek as 'imitation', 'copy' or 'representation', hence contributing to the term's elasticity.[29] Put briefly, in Book Ten of the *Republic* Plato outlines his ideas about the illusory nature of images. While individual forms had a transient, material existence, their *Forms* appeared eternally. This led Plato to establish a hierarchy, where Forms were more real than their physical manifestation. Plato declared:

> The art of representation is therefore a long way removed from truth, and is able to reproduce everything because it has little grasp of anything, and that little is of a mere phenomenal appearance.[30]

Art was merely an imitation of an imitation, what he denounced as a 'third remove from reality'.[31] Plato's formulation of mimesis has underwritten the history and philosophy of images and served to establish binary oppositions: essence versus appearance, original versus copy, truth versus illusion, signified verses the signifier. As Stephen Halliwell has observed, 'The concept of mimesis lies at the core of the entire history of Western attempts to make sense of representational art and its values.'[32]

Across his body of work Didi-Huberman develops, in a sustained manner, an innovative rethinking of the question of the image and its relationship to representation. In the second half of the twentieth century, it was through the impact of linguistics, phenomenology and psychoanalysis that these terms were critiqued under the broad rubric of poststructuralism. This anti-representationalism may be understood as a shared commitment to extending Nietzsche's campaign of overturning

Platonism. In his essay on Deleuze called 'Theatrum Philosophicum' Foucault declared: 'The philosophy of representation – of the original, the first time, resemblance, imitation, faithfulness – is dissolving.'[33] It is this critique that connects the loosely aggregated philosophical projects advanced by Gilles Deleuze, Jacques Derrida and Michel Foucault.

Viewed in relation to this intellectual heritage, Didi-Huberman's project is a timely update to the previous generation of philosophers, who each, in their various ways, sought to complicate Platonic understandings of representation.[34] It is therefore logical that his project would be concerned with interrogating the idealist legacy conferred to art history from the Renaissance to the twentieth century. At the heart of his research lies the question: an image is a form of representation, but what is the philosophical framework supporting this? Didi-Huberman's work is important because he reminds us that representation is by no means a finished or closed system. Furthermore, his project rightly serves as a cautionary reminder that the richness of the term may become flattened and homogenised under a singular, unitary framework.[35] Considered in this context, Didi-Huberman's work is exemplary for a thinking through and beyond the theoretical work associated with poststructuralist critiques of representation.

Didi-Huberman's revisionism reminds us that the foundations of art history are constructed on the Platonic tradition his predecessors were intent on critiquing. This also helps us understand why Warburg's *Bilderatlas Mnemosyne* (*Mnemosyne Atlas*) occupies such a central position in his research since the early 2000s and the publication of *L'image survivante* (*The Surviving Image*). The *Mnemosyne Atlas* was left incomplete at the time of Warburg's death in 1929 and was an attempt to map through images the 'afterlife of antiquity' (Figure 1). In its 'final version', the *Atlas* consisted of sixty-three panels. These panels were covered with black cloth. Drawing from his photo library, contemporary news images, maps and even postage stamps, Warburg would assemble and reassemble collections of images. For Didi-Huberman, the *Atlas* is a vehicle capable of disrupting both epistemological and aesthetic paradigms derived from Plato. Consider the following passage:

> The great Platonic tradition promised an epistemic model founded on the preeminence of the Idea: True knowledge supposes, in this context, that an intelligible sphere was extracted beforehand from – or purified of – the sensible space of images, where phenomena

appear to us ... In short, this would be the standard form of all rational knowledge, of all science.[36]

The *Atlas*, in Didi-Huberman's hands, is viewed as a disruption to the entire tradition reaching back from Plato, through to Alberti and the modernism of Clement Greenberg and Michael Fried.[37] Warburg was intent on discovering the unseen connections and relationships through juxtaposing images. Working against the illustration of a higher 'truth', the possible combinations of images are theoretically inexhaustible, unpredictable and unstable. At odds with the Platonic tradition that privileged the purity of the Idea, the *Atlas* is considered by Didi-Huberman as an *impure* form of knowledge. Undermining the separation between the intelligible and the sensible, the *Atlas* was a vehicle for epistemological pollution. This is not just a simple binary reversal, but in Didi-Huberman's words, the *Atlas* 'deconstructs, with its very exuberance, the ideals of uniqueness, of specificity, of purity, of logical exhaustion'.[38] The *Atlas* does not illustrate, it *demonstrates* in its ongoing construction of new possible forms of knowledge.

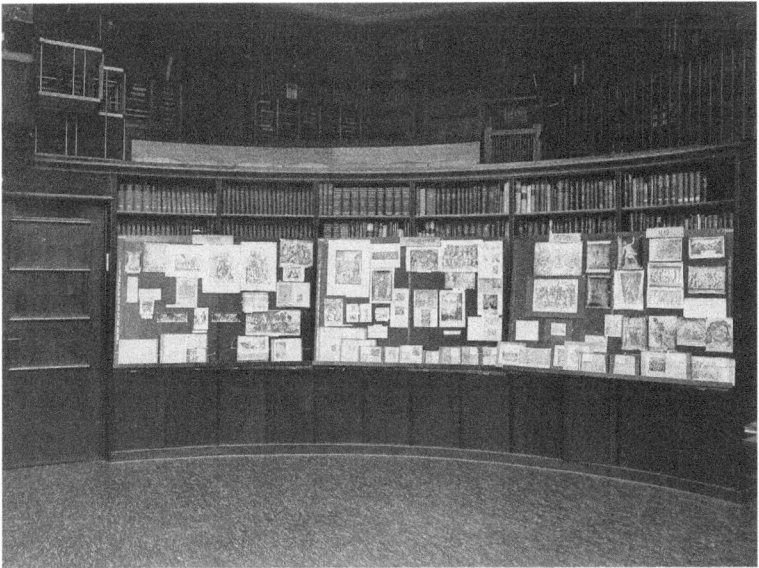

Figure 1 Aby Warburg, *Bilderatlas Mnemosyne* at the reading room of the Kulturwissenschaftliche Bibliothek Warburg

With this anti-Platonism in mind, one of the most lively strains in the domain of contemporary image theory is the notion that images do not merely reproduce a prior reality, but are actively creating this reality. Images are generally not considered 'passive', waiting for us to 'awaken' them. Instead, it is understood that images are autonomous, have agency, and perhaps can even 'think'. Horst Bredekamp is one of the most outspoken proponents and has argued that images 'do not merely represent, but veritably *construct*, do not simply illustrate, but actively *bring forth*, that which they show'.[39] At the heart of Bredekamp's claim is the claim that images are not inert, passive recipients of the spectator's gaze. An important historical precursor to this line of thought was David Freedberg's *The Power of Images*. In Freedberg's analysis, images could exert a power over the subject capable of eliciting responses ranging from fear and destruction to sexual desire.[40] The image's power was measured by the intensity of the spectator's response.

In a similar vein, Hans Belting took up the question of the power 'of images before art'. Like Freedberg, Belting attempted to broaden the canon's scope and to articulate a history of images based on people's interactions with them. For Belting, the aesthetic values of the humanist Renaissance sublimated earlier holy or cult images. The representational logic of the icon was different from mimesis in the Renaissance: the icon was not the creation of a painter of a model but *was* its model. Thus, by an 'image', Belting meant a representation that 'not only represented a person but also was treated like a person, being worshipped, despised, or carried from place to place in ritual processions'.[41] Extending this line of thought and the tendency to treat images as if they were human beings, W. J. T. Mitchell has observed that the magical qualities attributed to images are just as powerful in the present as they were in earlier historical periods. He asks:

> Why do they behave as if pictures were alive, as if works of art had minds of their own, as if images had a power to influence human beings, demanding things from us, persuading, seducing, and leading us astray?[42]

These concerns come to the fore in Didi-Huberman's writing, particularly with respect to his retrieval of Warburg. Two Warburgian concepts are important for Didi-Huberman: the first is *Nachleben*, or afterlife. The second is *Pathosformel*, or pathos formula and the notion that certain emotional gestures return after a period of time with an intensity. Didi-Huberman identifies a montage 'impulse' in Warburg's incomplete *Mnemosyne Atlas* (1925–29) project, where images become capable of developing new relationships, or lines of flight.[43] Didi-Huberman writes:

> The objects of Warburgian history – images – are thus not entirely objects. To reduce them to that status is to deny their 'life', that is to say, their capacity to metamorphize and to move about in a milieu in which their own substance actually participates.[44]

As the quotation implies, rather than being inert objects of the past, images are instead endowed with the capacity to think, remember and generate new lines of enquiry.

The belief that images are active and have agency has led Keith Moxey to suggest that the distinction between subject and object is undergoing a thorough revaluation.[45] This has important implications for the authorial speaking subject and its relationship with the art object or image. The art historian has traditionally been charged with the role of deciphering and explaining. If the authority of the art historian is no longer assured, the hierarchical relationship between the subject and image becomes increasingly difficult to maintain.

If we were to reach further back in intellectual history, the question of the subject's authority has been a central issue in French thought in the wake of Nietzsche.[46] The concept of the modern subject as the privileged locus of discourse was most famously expressed by Foucault in the final pages of *The Order of Things*. Here, Foucault conflated Nietzsche's death of God with the dissolution of the subject:

> Rather than the death of God – or, rather, in the wake of that death and in a profound correlation with it – what Nietzsche's thought heralds is the end of his murderer; it is the explosion of man's face in laughter, and the return of masks; it is the scattering of the profound stream of time by which he felt himself carried along and whose pressure he suspected in the very being of things; it is the identity of the Return of the Same with the absolute dispersion of man.[47]

For Didi-Huberman, the displacement of the subject's authority over the art object or image has epistemological consequences: what does it mean to know, when the historical privilege accorded to the interpreting subject is no longer on firm ground? In his earliest works, Didi-Huberman is closer to Derrida than Foucault when attempting to answer this question. Consider, for instance, his description of Fra Angelico's *The Annunciation* in the convent of San Marco in *Confronting Images* (Figure 2). Painted around 1440, the fresco is located in a small white-washed cell and depicts the scene of the Annunciation. Didi-Huberman leads the reader through a conventional iconographical reading of the scene. Fra Angelico has represented the moment where the Angel Gabriel visits the Virgin Mary and tells her she will become the mother of God. Eschewing the mimetic privileging of the visible and the legible, Didi-Huberman argues the fresco is better understood with regard to the paradox of the mystery of the Incarnation, where a mimetic reading falls short and seeing does not necessarily equate to knowing. It is not a matter of replacing the visible with the invisible, or knowledge with not-knowledge, as this would be to reinforce the binary and 'a way of keeping knowledge in its privileged position as absolute reference'.[48] Instead, he argues for a labyrinthian structure, 'in which knowledge loses its way and becomes a great displacement'.[49] In Derridean terms, what Didi-Huberman attempts to bring into view is the *undecidability* of the oppositions.

A cursory sketch of Didi-Huberman's intellectual development will orientate the reader to his most significant texts and establish this book's chronological chapter structure. Born in 1953 in Saint-Étienne, Didi-Huberman enrolled in philosophy and art history at the University of Lyon, where he studied with phenomenologist Henri Maldiney. Didi-Huberman spent the next decade working as a playwright at the Théâtre National de Strasbourg while preparing his doctoral thesis at EHESS and attending the lectures of Hubert Damisch and Louis Marin. His first text, *L'invention d'hystérie* (*Invention of Hysteria*) was an adapted version of his doctoral thesis.[50] Didi-Huberman explored the intersection of the birth of modern psychiatry and photography in the closing decades of the nineteenth century at the infamous Salpêtrière hospital. Under the directorship of Jean-Martin Charcot, the Salpêtrière developed a photographic service. These images provided visual evidence of Charcot's concept of hysteria. Didi-Huberman explicitly follows Foucault when he asks: 'What are the historical frameworks whereby hysteria is invented and perpetuated by the institution?' Didi-Huberman examined the series of books *Iconographie photographique*

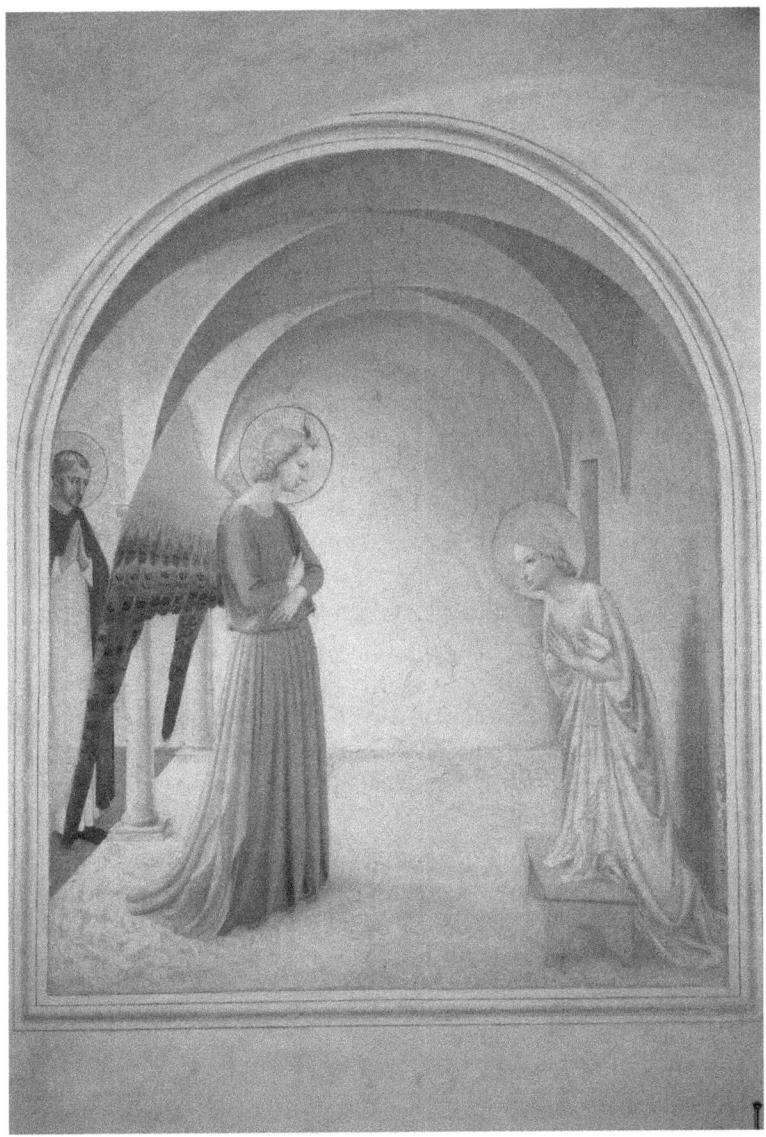

Figure 2 Fra Angelico, *Annunciation with Saint Peter Martyr*, c. 1440–44

de la Salpêtrière that documented, through the use of photography, the successive stages of hysterical episodes.[51] Against the neutral, scientific gaze the camera laid claim to, Didi-Huberman demonstrated how the images were the result of a highly fabricated performative collusion between Charcot, the patient and the photographer.

Foucault's ongoing influence in Didi-Huberman's work is discussed in Chapter 1. Didi-Huberman's gaze shifts from the psychiatric institution to the historical development of art history as epistemology emerges as a central concern. In particular, this is a response to Foucault's argument that is advanced in *The Archaeology of Knowledge* and the requirement to understand the disciplinary configurations, or discursive formations of thought. The discursive formations are what establish the state of knowledge in a disciplinary field. Didi-Huberman's project must therefore be measured in terms of the Foucauldian heritage he lays claim to: how is art history possible? What are the conditions of its emergence? If the disciplinary configurations have been constructed along Enlightenment lines of reason, knowledge and objective truth, what has been silenced, omitted and neglected from this narrative of continuous progress? This chapter investigates Didi-Huberman's archaeological project, as he responds to the challenge issued by Foucault for disciplinary renewal based on disruption and rupture.

Following the publication of *L'invention d'hystérie*, Didi-Huberman spent the years between 1984 and 1988 in Italy, taking up fellowships at the Academy of France in Rome (Villa Medici) and the Berenson Foundation de la Villa I Tatti in Florence. In one interview, he cited this period in Italy as especially formative in his intellectual development:

> J'ai découvert les outils philologiques nécessaires à cette discipline: des bibliothèques telles qu'il n'en existe pas en France. Et, surtout, j'ai découvert de nouveaux objets, aussi étrange que cela puisse paraître lorsqu'on parle du passé.[52]
> I discovered the philological tools necessary for the discipline: libraries that did not exist in France. And above all, I discovered new objects, as strange as that may sound when we are speaking of the past.

Italy proved to be a major turning point, providing the necessary institutional and cultural distance to develop his major 'breakthrough' text of 1990, *Devant l'image* (*Confronting Images*). This text firmly established the terms of Didi-Huberman's project as an archaeological critique of the foundations of humanist art history in the tradition of Vasari, Kant and Panofsky. It introduced the key concerns that were to sustain his research programme well into the next decade. Closely following was the publication *Fra Angelico* (1990), which may be regarded as a tangible application of the theoretical arguments developed in *Confronting Images*. *Fra Angelico* signalled Didi-Huberman's proximity to Derrida by exposing the hidden representational biases of art's history, with its privileging of idealism at the expense of other possible modes of representation. Didi-Huberman retrieves older theological forms of representation that pre-existed Vasari and the 'birth' of art's history.

A major thematic concern that emerges in this book is the question of representation itself. In particular, I am interested in tracing the numerous ways Didi-Huberman puts representation under pressure. Chapter 2 concentrates on investigating Didi-Huberman's denouncement of mimesis as one of the great 'totem-notions'[53] that persist in underwriting art's history from the Renaissance onwards. His interest in the image's materiality comes to the fore with the case study on Fra Angelico's *marmi finti*, or the fictive marble panels in the corridor of the San Marco convent. This facilitates a rethinking of the entire philosophical and historical tradition in which the history of art has been understood with its dependence on Platonism and Renaissance humanism. In this chapter, key terms such as *dissemblance*, the *pan* and presencing will be examined as part of Didi-Huberman's broader critique of representation, mimesis and the idealism that has sustained these terms and their usage.

The next decade marks a shift in Didi-Huberman's focus from issues relating to representation to an increasing preoccupation with time and temporality. Chapter 3 takes up the question of time in relation to Didi-Huberman's assessment of Walter Benjamin and Aby Warburg. If the image can no longer be imagined in purely mimetic terms, the temporal logic sustaining this history increasingly comes under pressure. Two texts are instrumental in this transition. The first is *Devant le temps* (2000), where Didi-Huberman moves the concept of anachronism to the fore of his enquiry. The second is *L'image survivante* (2002) (*The Surviving Image*), Didi-Huberman's major contribution to the current revival of interest in Aby Warburg. Ten years in development, it is the longest and most extensive monograph of an art historian's body of work ever to be completed. Didi-Huberman retrieves Warburg's enigmatic formulation of *Nachleben* (afterlife) and argues it is crucial in formulating an anachronistic history, made up of ghosts, survivals and phantoms. *Nachleben* lends itself to a ghostlike understanding of time, where a plurality of pasts coexist, haunting the present. Read alongside *Confronting Images, Devant le temps* and *The Surviving Image* are a formidable critique of art history, its philosophical and methodological frameworks and temporal assumptions.

Chapter 4 builds on the previous themes exploring the image's materiality by way of the *empreinte* or imprint. Didi-Huberman's attentiveness to the material, sensible and sensual aspects of the image is foregrounded against the disciplinary preoccupation with idealism. The role of the imprint is curious for art history, because it exists as a blind spot. Excluded by Vasari and demoted in his artistic hierarchy, the imprint occupies a shadowy role in the discipline's development. This chapter draws on the medieval theology of Thomas Aquinas to establish Didi-Huberman's distance from semiotic or language-based understandings of indexes, imprints and moulds.

Chapter 5 turns its attention to Didi-Huberman's contribution to Holocaust discourse. *Images malgré tout* signalled a major shift in his research project as Didi-Huberman directed his attention to Holocaust discourse and its trenchant distrust of images and their relationship to history. The text commenced as a catalogue essay for a 2001 photographic exhibition *Mémoire des camps* at the Hôtel de Sully that included photographs secretly taken by inmates from inside the Nazi concentration camp Auschwitz-Birkenau in August 1944.[54] This essay was developed into a book in 2003, which included the original catalogue essay as well as a series of rebuttals to his fiercest critics. *Images malgré tout* was significant because it marked a distinct 'turn' in the discourse of Holocaust unrepresentability that has dominated French intellectual thought since the 1980s. The English-language translation, *Images in Spite of All* (2008), rapidly expanded Didi-Huberman's reach to a broader, interdisciplinary audience. In recent years his arguments have influenced Holocaust scholars, photographic historians, film and theorists of visual culture. This chapter will consider the impact of Didi-Huberman's arguments on a younger generation of filmmakers who have taken up the challenge of representing the Holocaust.

The final chapter investigates the role that montage plays in Didi-Huberman's work. The most recent phase of Didi-Huberman's research is distinguished by a series of books titled *L'œil de l'histoire* (*The Eye of History*). At the time of writing six volumes have been published.[55] With a nod to Georges Bataille's *L'histoire de l'œil* (*Story of the Eye*), the series is dedicated almost exclusively to investigating the relationship between images and history. The convergence between politics and knowledge is described by Didi-Huberman in the following terms: 'Depuis cette polémique sur *Images malgré tout*, j'étais presque contraint d'intégrer une sorte de perspective politique à la perspective épistémologique.'[56] ('Since the polemic over *Images in Spite of All*, I was forced to join a kind of political perspective to the epistemological perspective.') In this series of texts, Didi-Huberman recovers the historical avant-garde's use of montage as a tool for disruption. This chapter will position Didi-Huberman's work in a long philosophical arc from Descartes through Foucault and Deleuze seeking to decouple the subject from thought. Didi-Huberman reactivates some of the great avant-garde montage projects of the early twentieth century to explore a mode of representation capable of generating its own theoretical and intellectual undertaking.

This book is not intended to be exhaustive. I do hope, however, that returning Didi-Huberman's texts and key terms to their philosophical, historical and institutional frameworks will in turn open his work to a broader community of scholars. Here, I will draw a parallel with Michael Ann Holly's assessment of Erwin Panofsky:

> It is necessary also to investigate the writings of art historians whose ideas embody the paradigms of their time and to read them in conjunction with works by the historians and philosophers who elaborated the paradigms in their own fields.[57]

Holly's comments are just as relevant today as when she made them in 1983. For Didi-Huberman, the paradigms of his time are distinguished with questions concerning the destruction of metaphysics, subjectivity and notions of origin, truth and knowledge. He takes up these subjects repeatedly over the course of his career. Didi-Huberman writes prolifically and his project remains unfinished. Despite this, it is not too early to begin historicising it.

Notes

1 Georges Didi-Huberman, *The Surviving Image: Phantoms of Time and Time of Phantoms*, trans. Harvey L. Mendelsohn (University Park: Pennsylvania State University Press, 2017), 339.

2   Laurent Zimmerman (ed.), *Penser par les images: autour des travaux de Georges Didi-Huberman* (Nantes: Cécile Defaut, 2006); Thierry Davila and Pierre Sauvanet (eds), *Devant les images: penser l'art et l'histoire avec Georges Didi-Huberman* (Paris: Les Presses du Réel, 2011).

3   Muriel Pic (ed.), 'Qu'est-ce que s'orienter dans les images?', *Europe*, 1069 (2018), 3–173.

4   Philippe-Alain Michaud, *Aby Warburg et l'image en mouvement* (Paris: Macula, 1998); Philippe-Alain Michaud, *Aby Warburg and the Image in Motion*, trans. Sophie Hawkes (New York: Zone Books, 2004).

5   Georges Didi-Huberman, *L'empreinte* (Paris: Éditions du Centre Georges Pompidou, 1997). Georges Didi-Huberman, *Soulèvements* (Paris: Gallimard/Jeu de Paume, 2016).

6   Nigel Saint, 'Georges Didi-Huberman: Images, Critique and Time', in Nigel Saint and Andy Stafford (eds), *Modern French Visual Theory: A Critical Reader* (Manchester: Manchester University Press, 2013), 219–38.

7   Keith Moxey, *Visual Time: The Image in History* (Durham: Duke University Press, 2013).

8   Alexander Nagel and Christopher S. Wood, 'Toward a New Model of Renaissance Anachronism', *Art Bulletin*, 87:3 (2005), 403–15. Also see Alexander Nagel and Christopher S. Wood, *Anachronic Renaissance* (New York: Zone Books, 2010).

9   Stijn De Cauwer and Laura Katherine Smith, 'Critical Image Configurations', *Angelaki*, 23:4 (2018), 1–2.

10   Georges Didi-Huberman, *Images malgré tout* (Paris: Les Éditions de Minuit, 2003); Georges Didi-Huberman, *Images in Spite of All: Four Photographs from Auschwitz*, trans. Shane B. Lillis (Chicago: University of Chicago Press, 2008).

11   Andrzej Leśniak, 'Images Thinking the Political: On the Recent Works of Georges Didi-Huberman', *Oxford Art Journal*, 40:2 (2017), 305–18.

12   See James Elkins and Robert Williams, *Renaissance Theory* (New York: Routledge, 2008), 246.

13   On the 'death' of 'theory', see Terry Eagleton, *After Theory* (New York: Basic Books, 2003); Valentine Cunningham, *Reading after Theory* (Oxford: Blackwell, 2001); Colin Davis, *After Poststructuralism: Reading, Stories and Theory* (New York: Routledge, 2006).

14   Sylvère Lotringer and Sande Cohen, *French Theory in America* (New York: Routledge, 2001), 1.

15   Georges Didi-Huberman, 'En ordre dispersé', *Trivium*, no. 1 (2008), http://journals.openedition.org/trivium/351.

16   For Didi-Huberman's critique of Baxandall's social art history, in particular the 'period eye', see *Devant le temps: histoire de l'art et*

anachronisme des images (Paris: Les Éditions de Minuit, 2000), 17. For his critique of Svetlana Alpers's *The Art of Describing*, see Georges Didi-Huberman, *Confronting Images: Questioning the Ends of a Certain History of Art*, trans. John Goodman (University Park: Pennsylvania State University Press, 2005), 240–4. For his interrogation of Michael Fried's arguments presented in his essay 'Art and Objecthood', see Georges Didi-Huberman, *Ce que nous voyons, ce qui nous regarde* (Paris: Les Éditions de Minuit, 1992); Michael Fried, 'Art and Objecthood', *Artforum*, 5:10 (1967), 12–23.

17 Georges Didi-Huberman, 'The Index of the Absent Wound (Monograph on a Stain)', *October*, 29 (1984), 63–81. Translated from the French: Georges Didi-Huberman, 'L'indice de la plaie absente (monographie d'un tache)', *Traverses*, 30–31 (1984), 151–63.

18 See W. J. T. Mitchell, *Iconology: Image, Text, Ideology* (Chicago: University of Chicago Press, 1986); W. J. T. Mitchell, *Picture Theory: Essays on Verbal and Visual Representation* (Chicago: University of Chicago Press, 1994); W. J. T. Mitchell, *What Do Pictures Want? The Lives and Loves of Images* (Chicago: University of Chicago Press, 2005).

19 See Gottfried Boehm and W. J. T. Mitchell, 'Pictorial versus Iconic Turn: Two Letters', *Culture, Theory and Critique*, 50:2 (2009), 103–21. For a comparison of the two traditions, see Keith Moxey, 'Visual Studies and the Iconic Turn', *Journal of Visual Culture*, 7:2 (2008), 131–46.

20 For a history of the development of art history at EHESS, see Jean-Claude Bonne, 'Art et image', in Jacques Revel and Nathan Wachtel (eds), *Une école pour les sciences sociales: de la VIe section à l'Ecole des hautes études en sciences sociales* (Paris: Les Éditions du Cerf, 1996), 353–65.

21 Didi-Huberman, 'En ordre dispersé'.

22 A. L. Rees and Frances Borzello (eds), *The New Art History* (London: Camden Press, 1986).

23 See, for instance, Mark A. Cheetham, Michael Ann Holly and Keith Moxey, *The Subjects of Art History: Historical Objects in Contemporary Perspectives* (Cambridge: Cambridge University Press, 1998).

24 Svetlana Alpers *et al.*, 'Visual Culture Questionnaire', *October*, 77 (1996), 25–70. For an excellent summation of the development of visual culture, see Deborah Cherry, 'Art History, Visual Culture', *Art History*, 27:4 (2004), 479–93.

25 Mitchell, *What Do Pictures Want?*, 5.

26 Ralph Dekoninck, 'Art History in France: A Conflict of Traditions', in Matthew Rampley *et al.* (eds), *Art History and Visual Studies in Europe: Transnational Discourses and National Frameworks* (Leiden: Brill, 2012), 315–33.

27   Norman Bryson, *Calligram: Essays in New Art History from France* (Cambridge: Cambridge University Press, 1988), xiv.

28   Christopher Prendergast, *The Triangle of Representation* (New York: Columbia University Press, 2000), 5–6.

29   J. O. Urmson, *The Greek Philosophical Vocabulary* (London: Duckworth, 1990), 107–8.

30   Plato, *The Republic*, trans. Desmond Lee, 2nd edn (London: Penguin Classics, 1987), 10:598.

31   *Ibid.*, 10:597.

32   Stephen Halliwell, *The Aesthetics of Mimesis: Ancient Texts and Modern Problems* (Princeton: Princeton University Press, 2002), vii.

33   Michel Foucault, 'Theatrum Philosophicum', in Donald F. Bouchard (ed.), *Language, Counter-Memory, Practice: Selected Essays and Interviews*, trans. Donald F. Bouchard and Sherry Simon (Ithaca, NY: Cornell University Press, 1977), 172.

34   See, for instance Foucault, 'Theatrum Philosophicum'; Jacques Derrida, 'Economimesis', *Diacritics*, 11:2 (1981), 3–25; Gilles Deleuze, 'Plato and the Simulacrum', *October*, 27 (1983), 45–56.

35   For an analysis of how the term has evolved over time and across geographies, see Jacqueline Lichtenstein and Elisabeth Decultot, 'Mimesis', in Barbara Cassin *et al.* (eds), *Dictionary of Untranslatables*, trans. Emily Apter, Jacques Lezra and Michael Wood (Princeton: Princeton University Press, 2014), 659–75.

36   Georges Didi-Huberman, *Atlas, or the Anxious Gay Science*, trans. Shane B. Lillis (Chicago: University of Chicago Press, 2018), 4.

37   *Ibid.*

38   *Ibid.*, 5.

39   Horst Bredekamp, *Image Acts: A Systematic Approach to Visual Agency*, trans. Elizabeth Clegg (Berlin and Boston: De Gruyter, 2018), x.

40   David Freedberg, *The Power of Images: Studies in the History and Theory of Response* (Chicago: University of Chicago Press, 1989).

41   Hans Belting, *Likeness and Presence: A History of the Image before the Era of Art*, trans. Edmund Jephcott (Chicago: University of Chicago Press, 1994), xxi.

42   Mitchell, *What Do Pictures Want?*, 7.

43   The term is drawn from Deleuze and Guattari's description of the rhizome with its emphasis on multiple non-hierarchical entry and exit points in *A Thousand Plateaus*. See Gilles Deleuze and Félix Guattari, *A Thousand Plateaus: Capitalism and Schizophrenia*, trans. Brian Massumi (Minneapolis: University of Minnesota Press, 1987), 3–28.

44   Didi-Huberman, *The Surviving Image*, 336.

45   Moxey, 'Visual Studies and the Iconic Turn'.

46 See Alan D. Schrift, *Nietzsche's French Legacy: A Genealogy of Poststructuralism* (New York and London: Routledge, 1995), 24–32.

47 Michel Foucault, *The Order of Things: An Archaeology of the Human Sciences*, trans. Anonymous (New York: Vintage, 1994), 385.

48 Didi-Huberman, *Confronting Images*, 20.

49 *Ibid.*, 21.

50 Georges Didi-Huberman, *Invention de l'hystérie. Charcot et l'iconographie photographique de la Salpêtrière* (Paris: Macula, 1982); Georges Didi-Huberman, *Invention of Hysteria: Charcot and the Photographic Iconography of the Salpêtrière*, trans. Alisa Hartz (Cambridge, MA: MIT Press, 2003).

51 D. M. Bourneville and P. Regnard, *Iconographie photographique de la Salpêtrière: service de M. Charcot* (Paris: Aux Bureaux du Progrés Médical, 1877–80).

52 Georges Didi-Huberman, 'Des gammes anachroniques', interview by Robert Maggiori, *Plaquette du journal Libération* (November 2000), 8.

53 Didi-Huberman, *Confronting Images*, see 53–138, especially 73–6.

54 See Clément Chéroux (ed.), *Mémoire des camps: photographies des camps de concentration et d'extermination Nazis, 1933–1999* (Paris: Marval, 2001).

55 Georges Didi-Huberman, *Quand les images prennent position*, L'œil de l'histoire 1 (Paris: Les Éditions de Minuit, 2009); Georges Didi-Huberman, *Remontages du temps subi*, L'œil de l'histoire 2 (Paris: Les Éditions de Minuit, 2010); Georges Didi-Huberman, *Atlas ou le gai savoir inquiet*, L'œil de l'histoire 3 (Paris: Les Éditions de Minuit, 2011); Georges Didi-Huberman, *Peuples exposés, peuples figurants*, L'œil de l'histoire 4 (Paris: Les Éditions de Minuit, 2012); Georges Didi-Huberman, *Passés cités par JLG*, L'œil de l'histoire 5 (Paris: Les Éditions de Minuit, 2015); Georges Didi-Huberman, *Peuples en larmes, peuples en armes*, L'œil de l'histoire 6 (Paris: Les Éditions de Minuit, 2016).

56 Georges Didi-Huberman, 'Georges Didi-Huberman: "... Ce qui rende le temps lisible, c'est l'image"', interview by Susana Nascimento Duarte and Maria Irene Aparício, *Cinema: Journal of Philosophy and the Moving Image*, 1 (2010), 119.

57 Michael Ann Holly, *Panofsky and the Foundations of Art History* (Ithaca, NY: Cornell University Press, 1984), 27.

1

The archaeological art historian

Across the breadth of his project Didi-Huberman has repeatedly declared his debt to Michel Foucault's *The Archaeology of Knowledge*. In his first text, *Invention of Hysteria*, Didi-Huberman observed, 'Archaeology tries to define not the thoughts, representations, images, themes, preoccupations that are concealed or revealed in discourses; but those discourses themselves, those discourses as practices obeying certain rules.'[1] In the preface to the English edition of *Confronting Images*, he broadens his gaze from the birth of modern psychology at the Salpêtrière to consider the field of art history. Here, Didi-Huberman delineates the goals of his project: 'To effect a true critique, to propose an alternative future, isn't it necessary to engage in an *archaeology*, of the kind that Lacan undertook with Freud, Foucault with Binswanger, Deleuze with Bergson, and Derrida with Husserl?'[2] This statement clearly signals his revisionist intent. It also simultaneously aligns his work with some of the great revisionist projects of the twentieth century. Fast forward to an interview of 2010, in which he declared his ongoing proximity to Foucault: 'De toute façon, Michel Foucault est très présent dans mon travail. De plus en plus. Parce que Foucault le dit très bien, que savoir c'est trancher. Savoir c'est savoir trancher.'[3] ('In every way, Michel Foucault is very much present in my work. More and More. Because Foucault said very well: to know is to cut. To know something is to know how to cut it.') Finally, 'Foucault created relationships between practices and discourses, and I just added another element, images.'[4]

Didi-Huberman's statements point to an ongoing engagement with Foucault's legacy, particularly in relation to Foucault's *Archaeology*. This presents an immediate challenge as Foucault's text curiously remains one of the most resistant to interpretation, particularly amongst art historians and theorists of visual culture. Instead, Foucauldian themes such as power, representation and sexuality have long occupied the discipline's attention. In his discussion of Foucault's influence on visual art, Roy Boyne concisely summarised this:

> Foucault's writing on art is both interesting and symptomatic of some of his wider concerns. It is, however, his innovative and controversial histories of the body, of sexuality, of the self and, overarching all of this, his approach to the understanding of power, that probably hold most significance for the field of art.[5]

In this chapter, I will argue that Didi-Huberman's proximity to Foucault's *Archaeology* shines a light on an under-investigated period of Foucault's intellectual development.

Theorists and art historians such as Geoffrey Batchen, Jonathan Crary and John Tagg have interrogated the question of photography's relationship to power.[6] In Didi-Huberman's own work, the relationship between photography and institutional power forms the basis of his argument in *Invention of Hysteria*. Drawing on themes central to Foucault's texts of the 1960s, *The Invention of Madness* and *The Birth of the Clinic*, Didi-Huberman examined the intersection between photography and psychiatry deployed by celebrated French neurologist, Jean-Martin Charcot. Charcot famously leveraged photography, with its documentary claims to truth, to document the symptoms of hysteria in the closing decades of the nineteenth century at the Salpêtrière hospital. Directly evoking the clinical gaze described by Foucault, Didi-Huberman described the camera as possessing a 'mute gaze, without gesture. It feigns to be pure.'[7] Didi-Huberman is describing the intersection between epistemology, power and the medical gaze described by Foucault, with 'deep structures of visibility in which field and gaze are bound together by *codes of knowledge*.'[8] These codes of knowledge become 'naturalised' as cultural conventions, anticipating Foucault's analysis of the formations of knowledge six years later in *Archaeology*.

Foucault is perhaps best remembered by art historians and theorists of visual culture for his analysis of Velázquez's *Las Meninas* (1656) in the opening chapter of *The Order of Things*. Foucault's essay signalled the possibility of an alternative to the existing historiographical approaches still dominated by Erwin Panofsky's iconological methodology. Foucault did not rely on familiar art-historical tropes such as the search for hidden meanings. There was no emphasis given to conventional disciplinary concerns such as biography, influence or genius. He conducted no archival research to give weight to his analysis, nor did he attempt to recreate the broader social and economic context. In the wake of the chapter's translation and dissemination amongst English-language art historians, Svetlana Alpers lambasted the discipline, asking: 'Why should it be that the major study, the most serious and sustained piece of writing on this work in our time, is by Michel Foucault?'[9] For Alpers, Foucault's reading of *Las Meninas* was a historiographic wake-up call: the disciplinary reliance on Panofsky-inspired iconography as the incumbent methodological tool had blinded art historians to the self-reflexive representational strategies deployed by Velázquez.[10]

One of the most important disciplinary critiques explicitly pursued along archaeological lines was conducted by feminist art historian Griselda Pollock, who, in her seminal text *Vision and Difference*, argued that art history was a discourse invented by men who had inaugurated and continued to support it. In respect to the influential role Foucault played in the feminist critique of art history, Pollock noted:

> Foucault's analyses of historical writing, of discursive formations and their practical institutionalization, provided a necessary instrument for feminist probing of the archive, of evidence, of the selective resources of historical research which secure masculine hegemony in the recirculation by one generation of a previous generation's ideological structurings of knowledge.[11]

Despite this early momentum, Foucault's archaeology continues to remain one of the most underexamined aspects of his thought, especially amongst art historians who never recognised what historian Paul Veyne described as the 'practical usefulness' of Foucault's archaeological method.[12] Didi-Huberman's focus on this phase of Foucault's intellectual development reinvigorates this period of French intellectual history and draws attention to the potential of archaeology as a method for disciplinary critique.

Archaeology itself has suffered from a bad reputation. In their influential book *Michel Foucault: Beyond Structuralism and Hermeneutics*, Hubert L. Dreyfus and Paul Rabinow described archaeology as a methodological impasse and structurally condemned to failure. They write, 'After *Archaeology*, Foucault spent some time rethinking and recasting his intellectual tools.'[13] This dismissal by Dreyfus and Rabinow is problematic, as it negated the most productive aspects of an archaeological approach. It also served to cement the general perception that *Archaeology* was the most theoretically impenetrable of Foucault's texts from the 1960s, compared to the rich visual language deployed in *The Birth of the Clinic* and *Discipline and Punish*. As Gary Gutting has argued in archaeology's defence, 'Properly understood, archaeology is a technique for revealing how a discipline has developed norms of validity and objectivity.'[14]

With regard to developing an archaeological history, Foucault instructs, what one is trying to uncover are disciplinary practices in so far as they give rise to a corpus of knowledge, as they assume the status and role of a science. In turn, it is this internalised formation of knowledge that a discipline normalises as 'natural' and 'true'. Foucault carefully defines the concerns of an archaeological analysis:

> Archaeology tries to define not the thoughts, representations, images, themes, preoccupations that are concealed or revealed in discourses; but those discourses themselves, those discourses as practices obeying certain rules.[15]

Foucault seeks to identify the conditions that make knowledge possible. Instead of asking 'what do these works mean?', we should examine how historical frameworks have emerged, and what they reveal about the deep underlying ideological and philosophical structures of art history. Archaeology is a technique for revealing how a discipline has developed and maintained conventions which structure knowledge.

Towards the end of *Archaeology*, Foucault argued that the scope for archaeologies be expanded beyond the life sciences, and 'might develop in different directions', and he nominates painting as a possible orientation for future archaeology.[16] Foucault's gesture is a broad invitation for scholars working in the humanities to consider archaeology as a mode for revision. Didi-Huberman has taken Foucault's invitation seriously and sought to undertake an archaeological critique, seeking to understand how these cultural codes of knowledge have emerged and developed over time. The questions that dominate the first phase of Didi-Huberman's research are direct responses to the historiographic questions an archaeological approach raises: how is the discipline possible? If the foundations of its knowledge stretch back to Giorgio

Vasari, how do these assumptions continue to covertly inform disciplinary practice?

Archaeological critique: mimesis as 'totem-notion'

Didi-Huberman commences *Confronting Images* with a case study to introduce the reader to his chief concerns. He takes us to a fresco in the San Marco convent in Florence, painted by Fra Angelico in the 1440s (Figure 2). The fresco is bathed in natural light, which streams in through the easterly facing window and tends to obscure the fresco. Slowly, the details begin to emerge, signs that can be 'read' as it slowly becomes legible and therefore readable. The fresco reveals itself as an Annunciation. Didi-Huberman, however, challenges an iconological reading of the fresco with its privileging of what is *visible* and thereby *legible*. Instead, he claims that Fra Angelico's decision to saturate the fresco in white, combined with the natural light, evokes the mystery of the Incarnation, the miracle of the Word becoming flesh. What is at stake here is an older, theological understanding of images drawn from the writings of Tertullian and the founding Church Fathers.[17] Fra Angelico, Didi-Huberman argues, has presented an image that is deeply suspicious of idolatry *as well as* acknowledging the miracle of the Incarnation, where the divine Word is made flesh and given visible form. With its origins residing in the early theological treatises of Christianity, this paradox was obscured by the humanists of the Renaissance.

The question of representation emerges as a core concern for Didi-Huberman and his ongoing investigation of the historiographical assumptions that underpin it. He argues that the Renaissance notion of *imitatio* obscures other representational systems. Central to this premise is that mimesis, or imitation, continues to function as a foundational cornerstone for understanding and evaluating images. He muses, 'It has been said only too often: what was reborn in the Renaissance was the *imitation* of nature. Such is the great totem-notion.'[18] Didi-Huberman's point that the discipline is ill-equipped to discuss modes of representation that depart from classical understandings of mimesis. The presence of the Divine is felt through representation's *failure*, not its success.

The discipline of art history, for Didi-Huberman, is ripe for archaeological analysis. 'Born' in the humanist treatises of Giorgio Vasari, the discipline is defined by a system of representational rules and conventions that have largely been in place since the Renaissance. As such, Didi-Huberman returns to the foundational disciplinary texts to examine the assumptions that he argues extend well into the twentieth century, most visibly in the work of Erwin Panofsky. This has been the idealism latently informing historiographical practice since Vasari, and codified by Panofsky via Kant. Didi-Huberman claims that art history has internalised this idealist formulation of representation as the 'truth' model for all representation:

> The art historian, in his every gesture, however humble or com-plex, however routine, is always making *philosophical choices*. They silently aid and abet him in resolving dilemmas; they are his abstract éminence grise, even and especially when he doesn't know this. Now nothing is more dangerous than to be unaware of one's own éminence grise.[19]

In this statement, Didi-Huberman draws attention to art history's dis-cursive structures. His investigation is a deep archaeological analysis of how mimesis is treated as a normative and transcendental concept and leads to a general preoccupation with what is shown and how it relates to the truth. Mimesis becomes conflated with the Idea, and hence reason.

Didi-Huberman's critique underscores his general preoccupation with what Derrida would describe as the 'transcendental signifier' and a general metaphysical valuing of presence as opposed to absence which is deemed to be derivative or secondary. Idealism in the his-tory of philosophy broadly speaking gives priority to the mental over matter and the material. In the 'Double Session', Derrida observed that Platonism stands 'more or less immediately for the whole history of Western philosophy including the anti-Platonisms that regularly feed into it'.[20] A hierarchy is created where the image follows reality and reality is 'anterior and superior to it'.[21] Derrida's comments are useful for framing Didi-Huberman's concerns during this early period of his intellectual development. Didi-Huberman seeks to remind the reader that what gets omitted in this rationalisation of representation are the qualities of the image that are not legible or conform to an iconograph-ical reading. The spectator's subjective experience before the image is subordinated to the disciplinary emphasis on neutrality and objectivity.

As is well known, Vasari's *Lives of the Most Eminent Painters, Sculptors, and Architects* has been an inescapable reference point for art historians concerned with the history of Italian Renaissance art. Commencing in the 1990s, increasing scholarly attention has been directed towards reassessing Vasari's aims and methods.[22] Didi-Huberman's critique differentiates itself from this body of commentary, as he concentrates on Vasari's exhortation of mimesis at the expense of other possible frameworks for understanding representation. Published in 1550 and updated in 1568, *Lives* is generally considered the first text on the visual arts extensive and consistent enough to be described a 'proper' art history. Vasari established a clear hierarchical taxonomy of quality that was measured by the degree of mimetic likeness. Didi-Huberman claims that Vasari's idealism and his privileging of the Idea over the material, sensual image, continues to extend its influence right up well into the twentieth century as this framework has served to 'fold all resemblance into the model of the mimetic drawing of the Renaissance'.[23]

Vasari developed a theory of the technical development of Italian art between 1250 and 1550, memorably writing in his preface that the arts 'progress step by step from modest beginnings, and finally to reach the summit of perfection'.[24] The visual arts evolved in three successive stages culminating in the triumphant achievements of Leonardo, Raphael and Michelangelo. A work's success was measured by the degree of likeness to nature. Consider Vasari's gentle praise of Giotto, who 'was always going for new ideas to nature itself, and so he could rightly claim to have had nature, rather than any human master, as his teacher'.[25] Vasari's narrative of technical improvement climaxes with his appraisal of Michelangelo:

> Michelangelo has triumphed over later artists, over the artists of the ancient world, over nature itself, which has produced nothing, however challenging or extraordinary, that his inspired genius ... has not been able to surpass with ease.[26]

Michelangelo pursued a beauty by way of the imagination that sought to surpass or exceed nature. This is a very Platonic hierarchy, with Michelangelo privileging the idea, or form, over nature.

Didi-Huberman's critique culminates with Erwin Panofsky's 1924 text *Idea*. Here, Panofsky traced the Platonic idea of art in late antiquity, through to the Renaissance and early modern period. Panofsky described the idealism underpinning Renaissance theories of beauty and imitation:

> In his own mind there dwells a glorious prototype of beauty upon which he, as a creator, may cast his inner eye. Although the absolute perfection of this inner model cannot enter into the work he creates, the finished work will reveal a beauty that is more than a mere copy of an attractive 'reality' (which is presented only to the easily deceived senses), yet something else than the mere reflection of a 'truth' essentially accessible only to the intellect.[27]

The Platonic hierarchy is firmly maintained, and the image is subordinated to a higher 'truth' model. Didi-Huberman maintains that to properly understand the behaviour of images, we must move beyond the notion of all forms of representation being associated with mimesis. For Didi-Huberman, resemblance and imitation became conflated with an ideational truth, eventually becoming normalised as a 'natural' value of Renaissance representational systems.

Didi-Huberman's argument directly intersects here with Foucault's: epistemic regularities determine what can and cannot be enunciated. These regularities are convention driven. They shape the contours of knowledge within a discipline. Didi-Huberman develops an archaeological critique, arguing 'I would like to propose that post-Vasarian art history – the history of art whence we come and which is still practiced – is partly of Kantian inspiration, or more accurately neo-Kantian … even when it does not know this.'[28] Didi-Huberman seizes on key passages in Kant's 1781 work *Critique of Pure Reason* to develop his line of thought. Consider, for example, Kant's description of Plato and the idea, and its relationship to reason:

> Plato made use of the expression *idea* in such a way that we can readily see that he understood by it something that not only could never be borrowed from the senses, but that even goes far beyond the concepts of the understanding, since nothing encountered in experience could ever be congruent to it. Ideas for him are archetypes of things themselves, and not, like the categories, merely the key to possible experiences. In his opinion they flowed from the highest reason, through which human reason partakes in them … But Plato was right to see clear proofs of an origin in ideas not only where

human reason shows true causality, and where ideas become efficient causes, namely in morality, but also in regard to nature itself.[29]

Since Vasari, the image has been theorised as an operation of the intellect, originating in the senses, yet through the faculty of human reason rises above the human senses. There are some pertinent points to draw from Didi-Huberman's argument. Firstly, Didi-Huberman's reading of Kant is extremely narrow, a point he explicitly acknowledges: 'The Kantian aesthetic is a veritable treasure-house of thought, one whose internal developments need not be pursued here.'[30] For Didi-Huberman, the privileging of the faculty of human reason entrenches a positivist bias towards what can be measured, read (*lisible*) and seen (*visible*). Secondly, his analysis of the ideological conventions underpinning art history is, as Matthew Rampley has observed, a sustained critique of the Austro-German tradition.[31] For Didi-Huberman, Panofsky represents the cumulative end of this tradition, at the expense of the silencing of other voices, such as Aby Warburg's.

To further understand Didi-Huberman's claims, it is possible to draw a parallel with Heidegger's observations deployed in his lecture courses and essays on Nietzsche in the 1930s. In 'Nietzsche's Overturning of Platonism', Heidegger described Nietzsche's reversal through reference to the *Republic* and the Platonic division between the supersensuous and sensuous worlds, or 'truth' to mere semblance.[32] For Plato, the supersensuous is the idea. The sensuous world, or the world of appearances, lies below. Heidegger's point is that Nietzsche's reversal of Platonism must avoid merely replicating the same structure: it is not enough to overturn the supersensuous with the sensuous.

Heidegger criticised Platonism, Christianity and Kant for casting the supersensuous into a separate world separate from the world of mankind. Importantly, Heidegger emphasised that Kant's Platonism enshrined a dualism in the *Critique of Pure Reason*:

> Nothing of the substance and structure of the Christian view of the world changes by virtue of Kant; it is only that all the light of knowledge is cast on experience, that is, on the mathematical-scientific interpretation of the 'world.' Whatever lies outside of the knowledge possessed by the sciences of nature is not denied as to its existence but is relegated to the indeterminateness of the unknowable.[33]

Heidegger observes that with Kant, the supersensuous is now a 'postulate' of the realm of practical reason and positivism takes over to occupy the sensuous world. He continued, 'If the supersensuous world is altogether unattainable for cognition, then nothing can be known about it, nothing can be decided for or against it.'[34] Heidegger's comments have important consequences for Didi-Huberman: what gets lost or repressed are the qualities and characteristics of the image that sit outside of reason, mimesis (the visible) and eschew meaning (the legible).

The discipline of art history was to adopt this neo-Kantianism commitment to reason and scientific judgement. Panofsky's iconology, developed through his reading of Kant, was based on an *a priori* system that structured the relationship between the mind and the world. The result is an experience that exists above experience. Subjectivity and psychology were effectively bracketed.[35] For Didi-Huberman, 'the natural consequences of the "Kantian tone" adopted by the history of art is, then, abruptly that *the unconscious does not exist in it*'.[36]

The stakes are therefore high: how to shift away from a mimetic understanding of representation based on Platonic idealism articulated by Vasari, codified by Kant and internalised by Panofsky's iconology? Didi-Huberman's solution was to turn to Sigmund Freud, who in the earliest years of the twentieth century put into crisis traditional notions of representation through his analysis of symptom formation. Didi-Huberman returns us to another symbolic 'birth'. Not Vasari's art history, but the 'father' of modern psychology, Freud.

An aesthetics of the symptom

In 1990, Didi-Huberman was searching for alternative models of representation that would help break with conventional theories of representation and the logocentrism. His solution lay in Freud's accounts of hysterical symptoms and dream formation, and functions as the cornerstone of Didi-Huberman's ongoing critique of mimesis.

Let's begin, however, with an anecdotal detour. Not with Freud, but Honoré de Balzac's *Le chef-d'œuvre inconnu* (*The Unknown Masterpiece*). Originally published in 1831, Balzac's novella continues to occupy a privileged position in French art history.[37] It is possible to detect an anti-mimetic impulse in Didi-Huberman's work as early as

1985 in *La peinture incarnée suivi de 'Le chef-d'œuvre inconnu' de Balzac*. Here, drawing on Balzac's short story, Didi-Huberman introduces the symptom and establishes its distance from conventional forms of representation. The term, however is cursorily sketched, with Didi-Huberman's full debt to Freud developed later in *Confronting Images*.

The tragedy of Balzac's central protagonist Frenhofer and his inability to represent the body of the 'perfect' woman Catherine Lescault has traditionally been interpreted in allegorical terms as concerning the limits of artistic creativity and representation, reality and artifice. Set on the Paris Left Bank in December 1612, Balzac's narrative unfolds around the old painter Frenhofer's mysterious portrait of his mistress Catherine Lescault. After ten years working in complete isolation, Frenhofer finally reveals his masterpiece to his younger artistic counterparts Porbus and Poussin. Proudly, he declares 'This is the woman I love!'[38] In Frenhofer's mind his masterpiece has ceased to be a representation, and had *become* his mistress. The schism between the copy and its model had been successfully overcome, and the canvas had come alive: 'Where's the art? Gone, vanished! Here's true form – the very form of a girl.'[39] No longer a mere representation, Frenhofer's portrait was now a living, breathing woman: 'It isn't a canvas, it's a woman! A woman with whom I weep and laugh and talk and think.'[40]

If one definition of mimesis is imitation, Frenhofer's portrait is condemned as an artistic failure. Far from a perfect rendering of the ideal woman, Porbus and Poussin can see only frenzied skeins of paint, except for a foot in the corner of the canvas, 'but a delightful foot, a living foot!'[41] The tip of the foot is alive, emerging from the chaos of painterly abstraction. Frenhofer finally sees the portrait through the eyes of his colleagues, as a material 'wall of paint'.[42] It is indeed a canvas, not a woman. Frenhofer burns his paintings and dies during the night.

The Unknown Masterpiece inhabits one of the great fault lines traversing the history of representation. Frenhofer's failure has conventionally been interpreted in Platonic terms, as a testament to the irreconcilable gulf separating the original from its copy. Following this line of thought, a 'successful' mimetic painting would have been indistinguishable from its model. As Elizabeth Mansfield explains, 'Poussin's bafflement – and Frenhofer's madness – spring from the same source: a desire to make visible the ideal, to paint what is too beautiful to picture.'[43] In his book *The Invisible Masterpiece*, Hans Belting remarks in respect of Frenhofer's tragedy, 'Perfect art was a shadow, a mere ghost of classical times, and not even Orpheus was able to bring it back into the world because he lost it when he tried to look at it.'[44] Ontologically condemned by Plato, the image always retains a derisory or secondary status. Frenhofer's failure reflects the desire and ultimate failure of mimesis to achieve absolute equivalence with its ideal form.

Frenhofer himself draws an analogy between his plight and the Greek myth of Pygmalion. Pygmalion's love towards his sculpture is typically interpreted in terms of fear and anxiety generated by the spectator's desire towards the image. Frenhofer muses, 'It's ten years now, young man, that I've been struggling with this problem. But what are ten short years when you're contending with nature? How long did Lord Pygmalion take to create the only statue that ever walked!'[45] Like Pygmalion, Frenhofer so loved his mistress he sought to incarnate her, to turn the canvas and paint into a living, breathing being. 'Her eyes seemed moist to me, her flesh was alive, the locks of her hair stirred … She breathed!'[46] Yet there exists a crucial difference forever separating Frenhofer and Pygmalion. The goddess Athena granted Pygmalion's wish, and his marble became flesh. Frenhofer, however, died in anguish, reminding us of the ultimate futility of the mimetic ambition of making absence present. Frenhofer's portrait is forever fated, unable to achieve equivalence with its model.

Despite this, is there another way of interpreting Frenhofer's 'failure' beyond Platonic terms? There are several clues in Balzac's novella alerting us to the possibility of a breach or rupture with mimesis. Frenhofer's goals lay beyond notions of imitation, rejecting Plato's condemnation of the art of representation and its departure from the ideal form. Early in the text, whilst correcting Porbus's portrait of *Mary of Egypt*, Frenhofer exclaims: 'It's not the mission of art to copy nature, but to express it!'[47] Furthermore, the logic of mimesis is predicated on the assumption that there is an original model. Paradoxically, there is no model. Balzac gives no indication that Catherine Lescault actually exists. Unlike the other female character in the text, Gillette, Lescault is physically absent from the unfolding drama. Later, unveiling his canvas, Frenhofer exclaims, 'You're in the presence of a woman, and you're still looking for a picture.'[48] Frenhofer sought to incarnate Lescault, to transform the canvas into flesh. His canvas is alive, the body of a living, breathing woman.

Hysterical looking: Freud and Charcot

How may we begin to think of Frenhofer's act of presencing an absent origin? It is necessary to turn to one of the major theoretical undercurrents of Didi-Huberman's writing, the concept of the symptom. In *Confronting Images* Georges Didi-Huberman announced that he would undertake 'an aesthetics of the symptom':

> So it is necessary to propose a phenomenology, not only of the relation to the visible world as empathetic milieu, but of the relation to meaning as structure and specific work (which presupposes a semiology). And thus be able to propose a semiology, not only of symbolic configurations, but also of events, or accidents, or singularities of the pictorial image (which presupposes a phenomenology). That's what an aesthetics of the symptom, in other words, an aesthetic of the sovereign accidents in painting, would tend toward.[49]

What is a symptom? And how can the history of this term – the ways it has been deployed and theorised – help us answer this question? Borrowed from psychology, the symptom signals a self-conscious departure from traditional art history terminology such as the iconographic symbol and detail. Didi-Huberman reaffirmed this point recently, arguing that the symptom was critical in circumventing Panofsky's iconography and its structuralist overtones:

> In this sense, I might say that the word *symbol*, via the Freudian approach to the symptom, allowed me to avoid the iconographic simplifications with which art history is all too often satisfied – even in the work of Panofsky and the structuralists whose work he inspired.[50]

What, then, does 'an aesthetics of the symptom' offer art history? Drawn from Freud's early writings on hysteria, the symptom performs a powerful role in Didi-Huberman's epistemological revision. In an early text, *La peinture incarnée*, the symptom is introduced as a critical tool in his critique of representation and mimesis. Didi-Huberman writes: 'Symptôme, et non plus mimesis.'[51] ('Symptom, rather than mimesis.') The symptom is distinctly at odds with art history's privileging of mimesis. In a conversation with psychoanalyst Patrick Lacoste,

Didi-Huberman reinforced this point: 'C'est ce rebut, cet inobservé central, ce contre-régime de la représentation figurée, que je qualifie de "symptôme".'[52] ('It's this scrap, this unnoticed something in the centre, this counter-regime of figurative representation, which I call the "symptom".')

I believe that the conditions of symptom formation are important for understanding how Didi-Huberman puts the symptom to work. In *Invention of Hysteria*, he observes key differences between Charcot's and Freud's theorisation of symptom formation. For Freud, the symptom was a privileged function of the unconscious, first appearing in Freud and Breuer's early studies of hysteria. Freud emphasised the difficulty in establishing a direct causal relation between the original trauma and visible hysterical symptoms. This insight was derived from his observations of the celebrated French neurologist Charcot, whose techniques Freud studied in Paris for several months in 1885 and early 1886. Freud attended Charcot's famous Tuesday lectures at the Salpêtrière, observing that Charcot 'was not a reflective man, not a thinker: he had the nature of an artist – he was, as he himself said, a "*visuel*", a man who sees.'[53] Freud described Charcot's process of working:

> He used to look again and again at the things he did not under-stand, to deepen his impression of them day by day, till suddenly an understanding of them dawned on him. In his mind's eye the apparent chaos presented by the continual repetition of the same symptoms then gave way to order: the new nosological pictures emerged, characterized by the constant combination of certain groups of symptoms.[54]

According to Freud, Charcot emphasised the *visibility* of the physical symptom and the idea that it could be clearly read and deciphered. Didi-Huberman extends Freud's observation in *Invention of Hysteria*, accentuating the performative aspect of the symptom formation. Didi-Huberman highlighted the performative aspect of this process, writing that Charcot 'provided a form and a *tableau* of hysteria.'[55] The hysterical performances became so institutionalised that Charcot's 'best' patients began 'enacting' their hysterical symptoms on demand.

Charcot's methods were enhanced with the use of photography. During his time at the Salpêtrière, Charcot oversaw the development of the multi-volume *Iconographie photographique de la Salpêtrière*, which documented female patients in various stages of hysterical attack. The photographic image recorded the visible signs of hysteria in order to record and analyse the symptoms. Charcot developed a taxonomy where each individual symptom was able to be classified. Consequently, hysterical disorders were organised in terms of their visual appearance so that every gesture could be recorded, categorised and 'read'. Later, Freud emphatically warned of the risks of these types of homogenising approaches to symptom interpretation. Freud argued for the *singularity* of the symptom's interpretation, maintaining that 'Neurotic symptoms, then, just like errors and dreams, have their meaning and, like these, are related to the life of the person in whom they appear.'[56] A plurality of possible symptoms could present themselves based on the patient's individual experiences.

Freud eventually sought to distance himself from Charcot's analysis of the physical manifestation of the hysterical symptom, rejecting the possibility that there was a direct causal relationship that could be represented by the hysteric. In *Invention of Hysteria*, Didi-Huberman highlights Freud's distance from Charcot's methods, arguing that Freud observed a gap or schism between the symptom and its source. Didi-Huberman writes: 'Freud understood this as the *indirection of representation*, obliging him to follow signifiers not simply by their traces but by the modulations of their detours – this is what it means to interpret.'[57] Freud argued that what mattered was less the visible manifestations of the symptom, but understanding the unconscious processes underlying them. If Charcot developed a direct causal relationship between the visible representation of the symptom and its source, Freud endlessly deferred attribution to a single point of origin or trauma.

The differences between Freud's and Charcot's methods contain enormous epistemological consequences. In Charcot's hands, '*the symptom became sign*.'[58] In an interview describing the opportunity afforded by the symptom, Didi-Huberman recollected: 'elle m'a permis, paradigme freudien aidant, d'explorer les voies d'un au-delà de la sémiologie structuraliste'[59] ('it allowed me, helped by the Freudian paradigm, to explore the paths beyond structuralist semiology'). The symptom provided an alternative to the totalising and homogenising ambitions of a structuralist-inspired art history.

For Freud, the symptom is a consequence of the process of repression, whereby the ego withdraws from inappropriate impulses or memories. In *Inhibitions, Symptoms and Anxiety*, Freud outlined this process in relation to the ego's defence struggle against the id. Freud defined the symptom as 'a sign of, and a substitute for, an instinctual satisfaction which has remained in abeyance; it is a consequence of the process of repression.'[60] Repression occurs when the ego rejects the inappropriate impulse, which is incompatible with the ego's ethical standards. Despite this psychic defence mechanism, the repressed impulse returns, albeit manifested in a disguised or displaced form. As a result, the symptom is the physical manifestation of unresolved conflict between the ego and the id. If the relationship between signs and their signification was natural for Charcot, Freud effectively decoupled the sign from its signifier, demonstrating the arbitrary nature of the relationship. Anticipating Ferdinand de Saussure's later research, Freud demonstrated that the signifier and the signified are completely out of sync. If Charcot sought synthesis and stability, Freud promoted oppositional conflict. For Freud, the psychic processes driving the symptom's formation are inherently dialectical. The symptom is driven by the conflict between the ego and the id with no opportunity for synthesis or resolution.

The structure of the symptom's unresolved conflict is an important entry point to Didi-Huberman's general antagonism to Hegel and the dialectic. It becomes a critical theme throughout his entire body of work. Didi-Huberman pursues a mode of dialectical inquiry that is not strictly Hegelian because it is entirely without synthesis. In addition to the psychic conflict underlying the symptom, Freud introduces the concept of *overdetermination* to emphasise the plurality of possible causes driving the process of symptom formation. Freudian overdetermination is vital for the advancement of Didi-Huberman's argument, as it consists of unresolved dialectical conflict. Freud observed, '*a hysterical symptom develops only where the fulfilments of two opposing wishes, arising each from a different psychical system, are able to converge in a single expression*'.[61] He continued:

A symptom is not merely the expression of a realized unconscious wish; a wish from the preconscious which is fulfilled by the same symptom must also be present. So that the symptom will have *at least* two determinations, one arising from each of the symptoms involved in the conflict.[62]

Freud effectively decoupled the symptom from a single traumatic origin. The symptom is rather the visible manifestation of many possible causes. Furthermore, by decoupling the physical symptom from its direct cause, Freud opened the way for a sustained critique of representation. The signifier no longer lays claim to the signified but dissolves in a 'chain' of signifiers. With no single point of origin, the symptom undermines the mimetic reliance on the origin and copy.

This has significant consequences for Didi-Huberman, because throughout his work it is possible to detect a mistrust of origins. By eliding a single, original cause, the symptom, by way of its very structure, complicates notions of originality. For Didi-Huberman, this enables him to advance, through Freud, an account of representation that sidesteps Platonic understandings of mimesis. As we shall see, this is further developed through Freud's account of dream formation.

Freud's early research into hysteria was to lead directly to his theorisation of dreams. In an 1899 letter to his friend Wilhelm Fliess, Freud directly linked the formation of hysterical symptoms with dream-work and the concepts of condensation and displacement. Freud confided to his friend, 'I want to reveal to you only that the dream schema is capable of the most general application, that the key to hysteria as well really lies in dreams.'[63] Given Freud's explicit linking of the process of symptom formation with the dream, it is necessary to examine his theorisation of dream interpretation. Freud's observations were distinctly at odds with other popular theories circulating at that time that treated dreams as things that were legible and able to be decoded.[64] Freud's insights, gleaned from his observations of hysteria, were transferrable to the field of dream analysis. Freud alerts the reader to the futility of imposing a single interpretation onto the dream, arguing that 'If we attempted to read these characters according to their pictorial value instead of according to their symbolic relation, we should clearly be led into error.'[65] As with the symptom, Freud warns of attempting to 'decrypt' or 'read' the dream.

Freud's key point of departure from other theories of dream formation lay in his distinction between the manifest and latent dream content. Rather than assigning a specific meaning to the manifest dream content, Freud emphasised the processes leading to its formation in the latent dream-thoughts, writing 'The dream-thoughts and the dream-content are presented to us like two versions of the same subject-matter in two different languages.'[66] It is these processes that formulate the dream-work. Freud's distinction between the manifest and latent content negates any direct correlation between the dream and its origin, evoking the process of overdetermination we saw in symptom formation.

Freud privileged the distorting operations of the dream-work constituted by processes of displacement, condensation and overdetermination. In *The Interpretation of Dreams*, Freud recounts one of his own dreams, the dream of the *botanical monograph* to stress the overdetermination or non-linear causality of the terms *botanical* and *monograph*:

> I had written a monograph on an (unspecified) genus of plant. The book lay before me and I was at the moment turning over a folded coloured plate. Bound up in the copy there was a dried specimen of the plant.[67]

Freud highlights the rhizomatic connections of both dream terms *botanical* and *monograph*. For instance, he links *botanical* with Dr Gärtner and his '*blooming*' wife, a patient named Flora, and the story of a lady who had forgotten her flowers. The dream-thoughts branch from the forgotten flowers to his wife's favourite flowers, which in turn are linked to the artichoke, the recollection of a trip to Italy, and so on. Subsequently, each dream-thought divides into multiple associations. *Monograph* is associated with Freud's specialised area of study and his expensive hobbies. The terms 'botanical' and 'monograph', wrote Freud, 'found their way into the content of the dream because they possessed copious contacts with the majority of the dream-thoughts … they constituted "nodal points" upon which a great number of the dream-thoughts converged'.[68] The dream terms *botanical* and *monograph* are the points of intersection where multiple dream-thoughts intersect. As Freud establishes in the case study, 'the elements of a dream determined by the dream-thoughts many times over'.[69] It was a matter of commencing with the manifest dream, and working backwards to examine the chain of associations, the nodal points of the rhizoid structure of the latent dream-thoughts.

Against this semiotic readability of the sign, Didi-Huberman accentuates the dynamism and movement of the symptom. Unlike the sign, the symptom is not a stable visual object. It is the point of instability, contention and crisis in the image. Didi-Huberman emphasises the difference between the sign and the symptom: 'le signe est un objet, le symptôme est un mouvement. Le signe est manipulable, le symptôme échappe, glisse entre les doigts. Le signe s'érige, le symptôme décrit une chute.'[70] ('[T]he sign is an object, the symptom is a movement. The sign can be manipulable, the symptom escapes us, slides between our fingers. The sign stands up, the symptom describes a fall.') Rather than a stable, readable image, the symptom is in perpetual motion, governed by a rhizomatic chain of associations, infinitely deferring synthesis.

Freud's theorisation of overdetermination is crucial for Didi-Huberman's critique of mimesis as it developed the notion of a slippage in the mimetic dependency on the transparency of the sign. To the extent that the hysterical symptom is disguised and displaced, it signals a gap or space between the physical manifestation of the symptom and its origin. We have seen that the process of overdetermination is the same for both dream and symptom. Overdetermination eliminates any vestiges of one-to-one correspondence between the dream-thoughts and the dream content. The link between the dream and resemblance is unable to be fixed as it dissolves in a chain of associations. The dream is incapable of representing as the signifier no longer has any direct relationship with the signified. Rather, the signifier points to a chain of associations or nodal points. The process of overdetermination places mimetic representation, and the logic underpinning it, into crisis.

Freud uses the example of a rebus, or picture puzzle, to emphasise the mutation in representation:

> Suppose I have a picture-puzzle, a rebus, in front of me. It depicts a house with a boat on its roof, a single letter of the alphabet, the figure of a running man whose head has been conjured away, and so on. Now I might be misled into raising objections and declaring that the picture as a whole and its component parts are nonsensical. A boat has no business to be on the roof of a house, and a headless man cannot run. Moreover, the man is bigger than the house; and if the whole picture is intended to represent a landscape, letters of the alphabet are out of place in it since such objects do not occur in nature. But obviously we can only form a proper judgement of the rebus if we put aside criticisms such as these of the whole composition and its parts and if, instead, we try to replace each separate element by a syllable or word that can be *presented* by that element in some way or other.[71]

It is crucial to highlight that there are differences in the translations of Freud's famous passage from German to French and English. In the original German, Freud deploys the term *Darstellbarkeit*, which is omitted in James Strachey's translation in favour of *represented*. This tends to flatten the complexity of the German *Darstellbarkeit*, and shifts it closer to conventional understandings of mimesis as an unproblematic and uncontested form of representation. Didi-Huberman retains Freud's use of the term *Darstellbarkeit* in *Devant l'image*. In the English-language translation, *Confronting Images*, the translator John Goodman deviates from Strachey's translation, and hence the verb 'presented'. As Botella and Botella observe, *Darstellbarkeit* was only deployed by Freud specifically in relation to dreams, further distancing it from classic understandings of mimesis.[72] To reinforce this distinction, Didi-Huberman emphasises the distance between Freud's utilisation of the term *Darstellbarkeit* and the stasis of mimesis in the original *Devant l'image*:

> La leçon freudienne du symptôme, pour l'historien de l'art que je suis, n'a donc absolument rien à faire avec une question d'origine psychologique de l'art ... Elle a, en réalité, tout à voir avec la question des conditions visuelles du rebut de la représentation, façon de parler de la 'présentation' ou de la 'présentabilité' (*Darstellbarkeit*), bref de la *figurabilité*.[73]
>
> The Freudian version of the symptom, for the art historian that I am, has absolutely nothing to do with any question of a psychological origin of art ... It has, in reality, everything to do with the question of the visual conditions of the scrap of representation, another way of saying 'presentation' or 'presentability' (*Darstellbarkeit*), in short, *figurability*.

Foucault's influence is felt through Didi-Huberman's work, especially in relation to his archaeological critique of the foundational principles organising the discipline. Art history privileges an idealism that runs from Vasari through Kant and Panofsky at the expense of other possible modes of representation. The symptom inaugurates a crisis in representation, as the image can no longer be thought of in mimetic terms. In the chapters that follow, I outline how Didi-Huberman navigates Derrida's legacy and his critique of art history's logocentrism. The symptom disrupts some of the great dualisms that have haunted the history of aesthetics and art history – the origin and copy, form and matter, representation and presentation.

Notes

1   Didi-Huberman, *Invention of Hysteria*, 138.
2   Didi-Huberman, *Confronting Images*, xx. Didi-Huberman's emphasis.
3   Didi-Huberman, 'Georges Didi-Huberman: "… Ce qui rende le temps lisible, c'est l'image"', 125. The verb *trancher* also has English-language connotations of *to settle, to decide.*
4   Georges Didi-Huberman, 'Knowing When to Cut', in François Caillat (ed.), *Foucault Against Himself* (Vancouver: Arsenal Pulp Press, 2015), 77.
5   Roy Boyne, 'Foucault and Art', in Paul Smith and Carolyn Wilde (eds), *A Companion to Art Theory* (Oxford: Blackwell, 2002), 347.
6   Geoffrey Batchen, *Burning with Desire: The Conception of Photography* (Cambridge, MA: MIT Press, 1999); Jonathan Crary, *Techniques of the Observer: On Vision and Modernity in the Nineteenth Century* (Cambridge, MA: MIT Press, 1992); John Tagg, *The Burden of Representation: Essays on Photographies and Histories* (London: Macmillan, 1988).
7   Didi-Huberman, *Invention of Hysteria*, 23.
8   Michel Foucault, *The Birth of the Clinic: An Archaeology of Medical Perception*, trans. A. M. Sheridan Smith (London and New York: Routledge, 1989), 109.
9   Svetlana Alpers, 'Interpretation without Representation, or, The Viewing of *Las Meninas*', *Representations*, 1 (1983), 31.
10 *Ibid.* See in particular 34–5.
11 Griselda Pollock, *Vision and Difference: Feminism, Femininity and Histories of Art* (London and New York: Routledge, 2003), 130.
12 Paul Veyne, 'Foucault Revolutionizes History', in Arnold I. Davidson (ed.), *Foucault and His Interlocutors* (Chicago: University of Chicago Press, 1997), 146.
13 Hubert L. Dreyfus and Paul Rabinow, *Michel Foucault: Beyond Structuralism and Hermeneutics*, 2nd edn (Chicago: University of Chicago Press 1983), xxv.
14 Gary Gutting, *Michel Foucault's Archaeology of Scientific Reason* (Cambridge: Cambridge University Press, 1989), xi.
15 Michel Foucault, *The Archaeology of Knowledge*, trans. A. M. Sheridan Smith (London and New York: Routledge, 1989), 138.
16 *Ibid.*, 192–3.
17 Didi-Huberman, *Confronting Images*, 27–8. Also see Georges Didi-Huberman, 'La couleur de chair ou le paradoxe de Tertullien', *Nouvelle Revue de Psychanalyse*, 35 (1987), 9–49.
18 Didi-Huberman, *Confronting Images*, 73.
19 *Ibid.*, 5. Didi-Huberman's emphasis.

20 Jacques Derrida, 'The Double Session', in *Dissemination*, trans. Barbara Johnson (London and New York: Bloomsbury, 1981), 204.
21 *Ibid.*, 205.
22 See, for instance, Paul Barolsky, *Why Mona Lisa Smiles and Other Tales by Vasari* (University Park: Pennsylvania State University Press, 1991); Patricia Lee Rubin, *Giorgio Vasari: Art and History* (New Haven, CT: Yale University Press, 1995).
23 Didi-Huberman, *Confronting Images*, 150.
24 Giorgio Vasari, *Lives of the Artists*, trans. George Bull, vol. 1 (London: Penguin Books, 1987), 85.
25 *Ibid.*, 61.
26 *Ibid.*, 253–4.
27 Erwin Panofsky, *Idea: A Concept in Art Theory*, trans. Joseph J. S. Peake (New York: Harper & Row, 1968), 13.
28 Didi-Huberman, *Confronting Images*, 90.
29 Immanuel Kant, *Critique of Pure Reason*, trans. Paul Guyer and Allen Wood (Cambridge: Cambridge University Press, 1998), 395–7.
30 Didi-Huberman, *Confronting Images*, 91.
31 Matthew Rampley, 'Introduction', in Matthew Rampley *et al.* (eds), *Art History and Visual Studies in Europe: Transnational Discourses and National Frameworks* (Leiden: Brill, 2012), 8. For an account of the emergence of modern art history in the German tradition, see Michael Podro, *The Critical Historians of Art* (New Haven, CT and London: Yale University Press, 1982).
32 Martin Heidegger, 'Nietzsche's Overturning of Platonism', in *Nietzsche: Volumes One and Two*, trans. David Farrell Krell and Joan Stambaugh (San Francisco: HarperSanFrancisco, 1961), 200–10.
33 *Ibid.*, 205.
34 *Ibid.*, 206.
35 Podro, *The Critical Historians of Art*, 181.
36 Didi-Huberman, *Confronting Images*, 115.
37 Here I refer to the body of literature produced by the art historians practising at EHESS including Hubert Damisch, *Fenêtre jaune cadmium, ou, les dessous de la peinture* (Paris: Seuil, 1984). Louis Marin, 'Des noms et des corps dans la peinture: marginalia au *Chef-d'œuvre inconnu*', in *Autour du 'Chef-d'œuvre inconnu' de Balzac* (Paris: École nationale supérieure des arts décoratifs, 1985), 45–60.
38 Honoré de Balzac, *The Unknown Masterpiece*, trans. Richard Howard (New York: New York Review of Books, 2001), 34.
39 *Ibid.*, 39.
40 *Ibid.*, 34.
41 *Ibid.*, 41.

42   *Ibid.*, 40.
43   Elizabeth Mansfield, *Too Beautiful to Picture: Zeuxis, Myth, and Mimesis* (Minneapolis: University of Minnesota Press, 2007), xii.
44   Hans Belting, *The Invisible Masterpiece*, trans. Helen Atkins (Chicago: University of Chicago Press, 2001), 126.
45   Balzac, *The Unknown Masterpiece*, 24.
46   *Ibid.*, 22.
47   *Ibid.*, 13.
48   *Ibid.*, 39.
49   Didi-Huberman, *Confronting Images*, 263–64.
50   Georges Didi-Huberman, 'Of Images and Ills', *Critical Inquiry*, 42:3 (2016), 465–6.
51   Georges Didi-Huberman, *La peinture incarnée* (Paris: Les Éditions de Minuit, 1985), 61.
52   Georges Didi-Huberman, 'Dialogue sur le symptôme (avec Patrick Lacoste)', *L'Inactuel*, 3 (1995), 195.
53   Sigmund Freud, 'Charcot', in James Strachey *et al.* (eds), *The Standard Edition of the Complete Psychological Works of Sigmund Freud Vol. III (1893)*, trans. James Strachey (London: The Hogarth Press, 1962), 12.
54   *Ibid.*
55   Didi-Huberman, *Invention of Hysteria*, 76.
56   Sigmund Freud, *A General Introduction to Psychoanalysis*, trans. G. Stanley Hall (New York: Horace Liveright, 1920), 221–2.
57   Didi-Huberman, *Invention of Hysteria*, 135.
58   *Ibid.*, 23. Didi-Huberman's emphasis.
59   Georges Didi-Huberman, 'Image, matière: immanence', interview by François Noudelmann, *Rue Descartes*, 38 (2002), 97–8.
60   Sigmund Freud, 'Inhibitions, Symptoms and Anxiety', in James Strachey *et al.* (eds), *The Standard Edition of the Complete Psychological Works of Sigmund Freud Vol. XX (1925–1926)*, trans. James Strachey (London: The Hogarth Press, 1959), 91.
61   Sigmund Freud, 'The Interpretation of Dreams', in James Strachey *et al.* (eds), *The Standard Edition of the Complete Psychological Works of Sigmund Freud Vol. IV (1900)*, trans. James Strachey (London: The Hogarth Press, 1953), 569. Freud's emphasis.
62   *Ibid.*
63   Sigmund Freud, 'Letter from Freud to Fliess, January 3, 1899', in *The Complete Letters of Sigmund Freud to Wilhelm Fliess, 1887–1904*, ed. and trans. Jeffrey Moussaieff Masson (Cambridge, MA: Belknap Press of Harvard University Press, 1985), 338–9.

64 Freud argues that this type of dream decryption is 'a kind of cryptography in which each sign can be translated into another sign having a known meaning, in accordance with a fixed key'. See Freud, 'The Interpretation of Dreams', 97.
65 *Ibid.*, 277.
66 *Ibid.*
67 *Ibid.*, 282. Freud's emphasis.
68 *Ibid.*, 283.
69 *Ibid.*, 284.
70 Didi-Huberman, 'Dialogue sur le symptôme', 199–200.
71 Freud, 'The Interpretation of Dreams', 277–8.
72 On the history of the French translation of *Darstellbarkeit*, see César Botella and Sárah Botella, 'Authors' Introduction to the English Edition', in *The Work of Psychic Figurability: Mental States without Representation*, trans. Andrew Weller (London and New York: Routledge with the Institute of Psychoanalysis, 2004), 1–13.
73 Didi-Huberman, 'Dialogue sur le symptôme', 201.

2

The materiality of images

With Didi-Huberman's anti-Platonism firmly established in *Confronting Images*, the following decade was dedicated to examining the image's material existence. This has been traditionally regarded as a minor concern for art historians, who have maintained a hierarchical privileging of the form over matter and signified over signifier. In this chapter I will examine Didi-Huberman's concern with matter and materiality as he participates in the broader critique of representation underway at EHESS. It is critical to recognise that Didi-Huberman is part of the younger generation of scholars who, following in the wake of Derrida, sought to work through the implications of deconstruction. This chapter will examine Didi-Huberman's retrieval of matter by way of three themes that characterised his writing through the 1990s: the *pan*, *dissemblance* and presencing.

The prioritisation of form over matter enjoys a long philosophical history reaching back to Plato and Aristotle through to Descartes and beyond. For Didi-Huberman, art history had uncritically absorbed this hierarchical binary. Extending his argument delineated in *Confronting Images*, Didi-Huberman writes:

> Sans doute Panofsky avait-il historiquement raison de souligner le caractère de *matrice d'intelligibilité* qu'a pu prendre, au long des siècles, le platonisme – '*métaphysique de la Beauté*' et '*théories des Idées*', comme il dit – dans le développement de l'"*esthétique des arts plastiques*'.[1]

> From the historical perspective, no doubt Panofsky was right in emphasising the way that platonism was able, over the centuries, to take on the character of a matrix of intelligibility – '*metaphysics of Beauty*' and '*theories of Ideas*', as he said – in the development of the 'aesthetics of the plastic arts'.

Alluding to Derrida's influence, Didi-Huberman observed that the grand binaries such as matter and form, matter and spirit had been destabilised. Despite this, matter still proved a challenge for art history: the discipline had continued to avoid, ignore and even censor matter as a scholarly concern.

With an eye to disrupting this disciplinary blind spot, the symptom returns here, this time with an emphasis on its material status as *le pan*. With no direct English-language equivalent, *le pan* has variously been translated as 'whack' or 'patch'.[2] The term first emerges in 1984 in *La peinture incarnée* and is successively reworked over the next decade. At no point does Didi-Huberman provide a precise definition of the *pan*, instead choosing to focus on the phenomenological effect on the spectator. By 1990, however, in the 'Appendix: The Detail and the *Pan*', Didi-Huberman describes the *pan* as 'a symptom of paint within the picture'.[3] Again, this statement defers the possibility of conceptual closure, his writing simulating the symptom's overdetermination. Nevertheless, it is helpful to consider the literary and psychoanalytical context of the *pan*'s development, as it tends to be omitted in Didi-Huberman's later texts.

The origin of the term is literary, borrowed from Marcel Proust's well-known passage in *À la recherche du temps perdu* where Proust's protagonist Bergotte examines a patch or *pan* of yellow in Jan Vermeer's painting *View of Delft* (1658–60) (Figure 3). In this passage, the dying Bergotte fixated his gaze on the patch of yellow and obsessively repeats the phrase '*petit pan de mur jaune*' to describe a little patch of yellow wall represented in the painting (Figure 4). Didi-Huberman observes, 'the yellow in the painting by Vermeer, as color, is a *whack*, a distressing zone of paint, of paint considered as "precious" and traumatic material cause'.[4] Didi-Huberman emphasises the *pan*'s capacity to disrupt and unsettle the spectator, drawing an analogy with Roland Barthes's punctum in *Camera Lucida*. He writes, 'Pan serait ici le mot de l'effet, structural autant que phénoménologique, par quoi l'*extensum* du tableau fait tout à coup *punctum*.'[5] ('Pan would be here the word for the effect, structural as well as phenomenological, by which the *extensum* of the painting suddenly makes a *punctum*.') Akin to the phenomenological experience of the punctum, as 'that accident which pricks me',[6] the effect is 'pour moi intensif, panique, vertigineux'[7] ('for me intense, panicky, dizzying'). Like the punctum, the *pan* is a rupture in the picture plane puncturing and piercing the spectator.

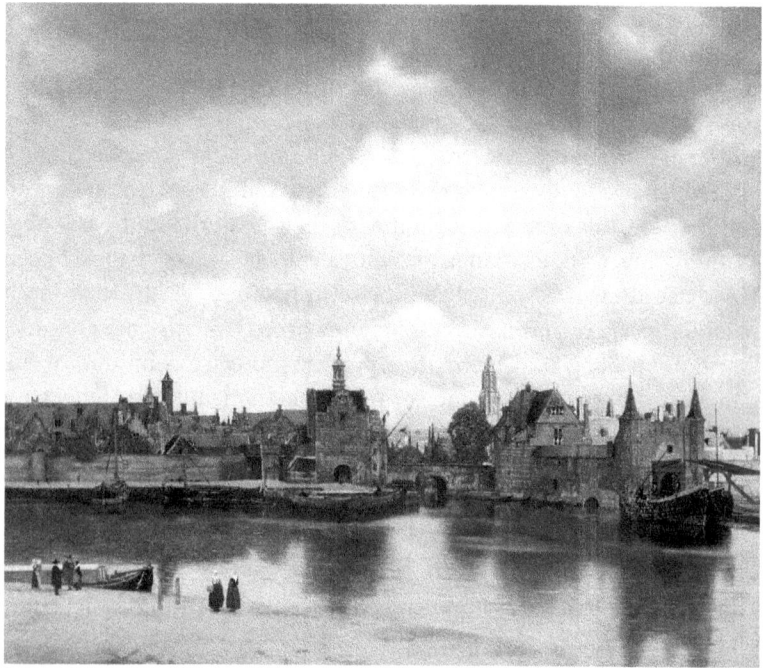

Figure 3 Jan Vermeer, *View of Delft from the Rotterdam Canal*, 1658–60

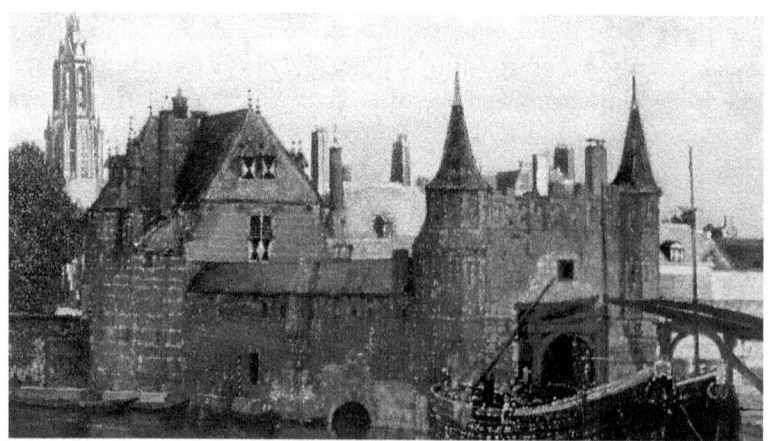

Figure 4 Jan Vermeer, *View of Delft from the Rotterdam Canal* (detail), 1658–60

If the origin of the term pan is literary, the structure is Lacanian. In *La peinture incarnée*, Didi-Huberman carefully describes the structure of the pan in relation to Jacques Lacan's *vel* of alienation outlined in *The Four Fundamental Concepts of Psychoanalysis*. Lacan's theory of alienation is predicated on a choice. It is, however, not a straightforward either–or choice. As Lacan describes it, alienation is the *impossible* choice between being and meaning. The choice is contingent on the logic that, whatever the choice, the outcome is neither one, nor the other. The subject cannot be both: 'If we choose being, the subject disappears, it eludes us, it falls into non-meaning. If we choose meaning, the meaning survives only deprived of that part of non-meaning that … constitutes in the realization of the subject, the unconscious.'[8] The 'or' is the alienated subject. In electing to choose being, the subject dissolves. Alternatively, by choosing meaning, the subject is deprived of an unconscious. Alienation is therefore an imposed choice, condemning the Lacanian subject to appearing only in division.

Lacan draws on Hegel's master–slave dialectic as an example, '*Your freedom or your life!*'[9] There can be no freedom for the slave without life, but there will be no life without freedom. Both choices are imposed, thereby becoming 'dissymmetrical'. In Hegel's *Phenomenology of Spirit*, alienation is a phase of development in the progressive freedom of self-consciousness. For Lacan, however, alienation cannot be dialecticised, the subject remaining forever split. Lacan's rent or torn model of alienation has epistemological consequences as it undermines the Kantian structure of knowledge that is transcendental, stable and centred. For Didi-Huberman, the takeaways drawn from Lacan's anecdote are clear: Didi-Huberman's subject is faced with the paradox between seeing and knowing. Akin to Lacan's *vel* of alienation, the spectator is faced with an impossible choice, a dialectical oscillation that Didi-Huberman formulates in the following terms: '*to know without seeing* or to *see without knowing*. There is loss in either case.'[10] Rather than prioritising one term over the other, or attempting to synthesise and resolve the conflict, Didi-Huberman instead elects to inhabit the ambiguity and tension between seeing and knowing.

Didi-Huberman expands the notion of the *pan* as a mode of disruption in his case study, Vermeer's *The Lacemaker* (1669–70) (Figure 5). In this painting, Didi-Huberman identifies a zone of red paint in the foreground that places the logic of the painting's mimetic representational system into crisis. At 24.5 cm × 21 cm, the painting's small scale creates

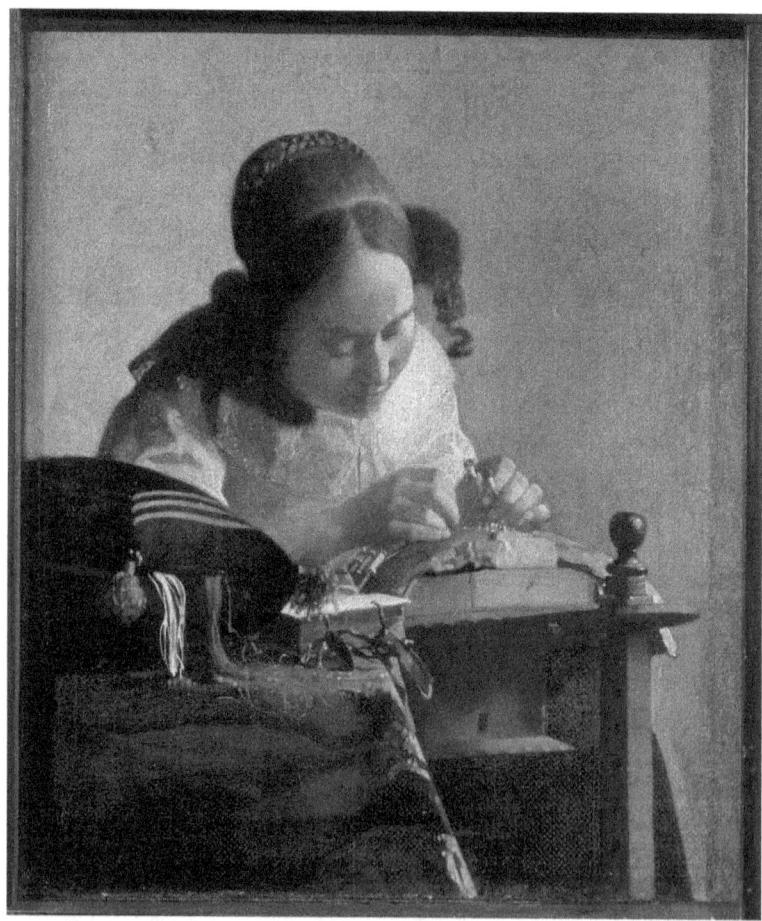

Figure 5 Jan Vermeer, *The Lacemaker, c.* 1669–70

a sense of intimacy as the spectator is lured into close physical proximity to examine Vermeer's highly realistic rendering of a domestic
interior. A young woman sits alone in a room quietly absorbed in her
work. To the left of the woman's hands lies a bundle of vermilion and
white threads that have escaped the confines of their timber box and
chaotically spill out against a mass of blue fabric. The red thread swells
forward to meet the spectator's gaze, asserting itself aggressively against
the mass of dark blue receding into the depths of the picture plane
(Figure 6).

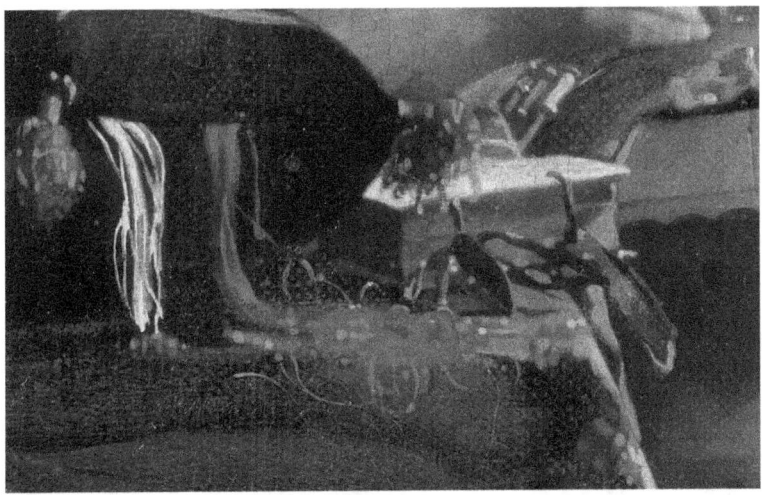

Figure 6 Jan Vermeer, *The Lacemaker* (detail), *c.* 1669–70

Didi-Huberman argues that the red skein of paint betrays its representational task and instead marks a slippage away from any verisimili-
tude or likeness to a thread. No longer charged with the role of depicting,
it is free to dissolve into chaotic loops of paint. It implodes on the surface of the canvas, an errant flow of colour undermining Vermeer's
otherwise realistic rendering of the woman tranquilly working. Didi-
Huberman muses, 'It unravels madly *before us*, like a sudden affirmation, without apparent calculation, of the picture's vertical and frontal
existence.'[11] The tension between seeing and knowing is exposed here
through the *pan* and the effect on the spectator is disconcerting. To
alternate one's gaze from the white thread rendered with linear preci-
sion to the mass of red thread erupting forth from the picture plane,
the '*pan* of red paint unsettles, even tyrannizes, the representation'[12]
For Didi-Huberman, Vermeer was certainly in possession of the technical skills to render both threads equally realistically. Despite this, he
made the choice not to. The symptom of painting is the materiality of
the paint itself. No longer repressed, it interrupts and disorders the
mimetic economy of the canvas.

Vermeer scholars have traditionally interpreted the errant red paint
in terms of the *camera obscura*. Daniel A. Fink, for instance, observed
that the details of the rough wall are exceedingly sharp and clear,

suggesting that this is where Vermeer focused the *camera obscura*. As opposed to the definition and clarity of Vermeer's rendering of the wall, the threads fall outside the depth of field and as a result are blurred and out of focus.[13] Similarly, in emphasising the descriptive function of Vermeer's paintings, Svetlana Alpers attributes Vermeer's 'circles of confusion' to the 'quirks of this device'.[14] Alpers writes:

> It would appear that those small globules of paint that we find in several works – the threads in the *Lace-maker*, the ship in the *View of Delft* – are painted equivalents of the circles of confusion, diffused circles of light, that form around unfocused specular highlights in the camera obscura image.[15]

For Didi-Huberman, the zone of red paint functions simultaneously as a theoretical and art-historical blind spot. An iconographical reading of *The Lacemaker* depends on the transparency of the mimetic sign, paradoxically blinding the spectator to the surge of painterly materiality at play in the painting. The spectator's eye tends to gloss over the *pan*, accommodating the zone of red paint and absorbing it into the overall logic of the painting. Didi-Huberman makes a simple and powerful point: the discipline omits what it cannot account for. The success of the image was to subordinate its materiality to the fidelity of the Idea. Didi-Huberman compares the *pan* to its mimetic and art-historical counterpart, the *detail*. He writes, 'So the detail is a semiotic object tending toward stability and closure, while the *pan*, by contrast, is semiotically labile and open.'[16] The detail guarantees a mimetic reading of the painting. The *pan*, however, destroys the logical coherence of the painting's mimetic function, placing it into crisis. The detail can be *read*: 'This is white thread.' The detail facilitates the categorisation of meanings and the assignment of a subject or '*istoria*'. In Panofskian terms, the detail participates in the first phase of iconological reading. It is readily identifiable. The *pan*, however, cannot be *read*. It reminds us of paint's material presence, the swirls and whorls of gesture and colour are usually subordinated to the signified.

Didi-Huberman's deconstructive analysis of the hierarchical relationship between signifier and signified confirms his participation in the intellectual concerns that were influencing the direction of research at EHESS. Responding to the broader impact of structuralism, Louis Marin, Hubert Damisch and Daniel Arasse were all participating in the general critique of representation that was well underway in other branches of the humanities. Ferdinand de Saussure's emphasis on the arbitrariness of the sign demonstrated the impossible correspondence between representation and reality, the signifier and the signified. As a logical consequence, art-historical treatment of the transparency of the representational sign and the truth claims of mimesis underwent systematic interrogation. Consider, for instance, Louis Marin's critique of Platonism, which was made explicit in the introduction, 'L'être de l'image et son efficace', to the posthumously published text *Des pouvoirs de l'image*. In this dense, evocative essay, Marin observed that the image has historically been condemned by philosophy as weaker and inferior, '*un moindre être*, un décalque, une copie, une deuxième chose en état de moindre réalité'[17] ('a lesser being, a tracing, a copy, a second thing in a state of lesser reality'). Marin argued that to submit the image to the ontological question 'what is ...?' is to negate the *force* of the image. The image's dynamism cannot be harnessed by an ontological line of questioning. The clue to the 'force' that fascinated Marin resided in the prefix 're': something that was present and not anymore is now *re*-presented. In its return, there is an intensification or magnification. Marin's thesis is an important antecedent to Didi-Huberman's own anti-Platonism and ongoing critique of mimesis.

Didi-Huberman's concern with the recovery of the matter from its subservience to form was anticipated by Hubert Damisch's 1972 *Théorie du /nuage/ (Theory of Cloud)*.[18] Damisch argued that art's history is characterised by the neutralisation of its own materiality. Damisch observed that clouds could not be accounted for in Brunelleschi's invention of single-point perspective, resulting in a signifying system based on a series of exclusions.[19] If Didi-Huberman identifies a material eruption of the *pan* in Vermeer's *The Lacemaker*, Damisch located a similar rupture of materiality in Cézanne's landscapes. Cézanne, according to Damisch, was to abandon drawing and the rules of linear perspective, replacing the drawn line with the coloured daub of paint. Of Cézanne's use of paint, Damisch writes, 'The decisive break came with the last works of Cézanne, in which, in the gaps, in what is lacking in the image, the canvas itself manifests its material nature, while the attention paid to the flat surface of the picture wins out, once and for all, over endeavours to create an illusion of depth.'[20] Like Cézanne's late landscapes, which disrupted the rules of linear perspective by abandoning drawing in favour of colour, the *pan* antagonises mimesis's repression of its own materiality.

Similarly, Daniel Arasse's work reflects the broader interest in examining painting's concern with the structure of representation itself. In his 1992 book *Le détail*, Arasse identified a dual meaning in the Italian treatment of the word 'detail': the *détail-particolare* and *detail-dettaglio*. The *détail-particolare* corresponds to our conventional understanding of a detail and represents a small part of the overall figure or object in the painting. It is iconic. The *détail-dettaglio*, however, is the result or trace of the action and, like Didi-Huberman's *pan*, performs a disruptive function in the mimetic schema of the painting. Arasse writes, 'Mais, en tant que *dettaglio*, le détail est un moment qui fait événement dans le tableau, qui tend irrésistiblement à arrêter le regard, à troubler l'économie de son parcours.'[21] ('But, as *dettaglio*, the detail is an element that marks a new phase in the painting, which tends irresistibly to interrupt the gaze, to disturb the eye's trajectory.') Arasse is adamant that the *détail-dettaglio*, 'Il ne fait pas image.'[22] ('Is not an image.') Instead he emphasises the materiality of the paint placed on the canvas. Didi-Huberman's focus on matter was part of a broader institutional discussion underway at EHESS.

In *La peinture incarnée*, Didi-Huberman draws an analogy between the *pan* and Derrida's *supplément*, writing, 'C'est quelque chose de l'ordre de l'instant, de la scansion, du supplément, du fantasme.'[23] ('It's something of the order of the moment, of the scansion, of the supplement, of the fantasy.') Didi-Huberman's analogy is worth investigating as it is omitted in later descriptions of the *pan*. Furthermore, it brings Didi-Huberman into classic Derridean territory, aligning his attack on mimesis with Derrida's critique of logocentrism and its appeal to a 'transcendental signifier'. The supplement is a key term drawn from Derrida's reading of Jean-Jacques Rousseau in *Of Grammatology*. Derrida extends Rousseau's concept of the supplement to examine the hierarchical and binary relationship between writing and speech. Rousseau condemned writing for being a representation of speech and thereby a destruction of presence. Derrida, however, demonstrated that despite Rousseau's privileging of speech as the most truthful direct expression of self, he paradoxically understood that the ability to express himself in speech was not nearly as effective as his written communication. Speech is necessarily dependent on writing and writing simultaneously undermines and supplements the presence of speech.[24]

The supplement helps us understand the pan's role as a disruption. For Didi-Huberman, the *pan* behaves like writing, marking a slippage in the order of representation and undermining the sign's assertion of presence. The *pan* reminds us that mimesis *desires* equivalence with the subject of representation. It is working to undermine the self-presence and transparency of the mimetic sign. Mimesis claims an impossible correspondence between the signifier and the signified, and despite its ambitions, will always remain condemned structurally to failure. Following the logic of the supplement, the mimetic economy of Vermeer's *The Lacemaker* becomes untenable, collapsing under the material pressure exerted from the *pan*. The pan reminds us that the painting is dependent on its materiality, despite its best attempts to repudiate it.

Fra Angelico

Didi-Huberman's focus on the image's materiality is amplified in his 1990 case study *Fra Angelico*, which emerged from a chance encounter with four *marmi finti* or fictive marble panels in the corridor of the San Marco convent in Florence (Figure 7).[25] Here, the *pan*'s materiality is put to work in an altogether different mode of address. No longer tasked with undermining the logic of mimesis, the *pan* is imagined as a pure presencing of the Divine. At first glance, the multi-coloured panels perform a purely decorative function. The panels are fictive because they have been deliberately painted to imitate marble. The paint mimics the veins and swirls which appear naturally in slabs of marble. Located directly below Fra Angelico's *Madonna delle Ombre* (*Madonna of the Shadows*) (1438–50) (Figure 8), the panels have been conspicuously absent from the existing Fra Angelico literature. In a discussion with psychoanalyst Patrick Lacoste, Didi-Huberman framed the absence in the following terms:

> Pourquoi cet aveuglement? Parce que l'histoire de l'art 'humaniste' ne voit que ce qu'elle sait à l'avance, s'inscrit dans un tableau 'clinique' à deux entrées principales, le tableau vasarien de l'*imitazione* et de l'*idea*. Les taches peintes par Fra Angelico sont donc ici comme les 'mouvements illogiques' par avance indescriptibles et même invisibles, du classique 'tableau complet et régulier' de la peinture renaissante.[26]

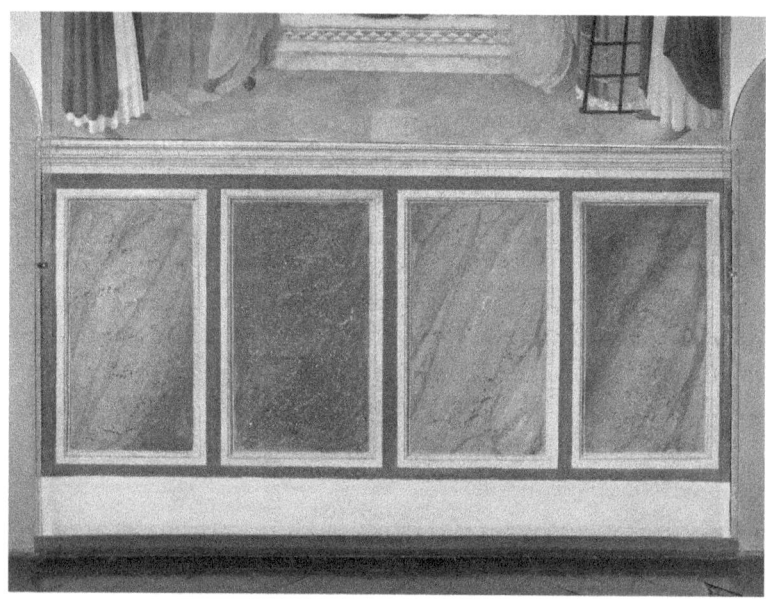

Figure 7 Fra Angelico, fake marble panels below the *Madonna delle Ombre* (*Madonna of the Shadows*), *c.* 1450

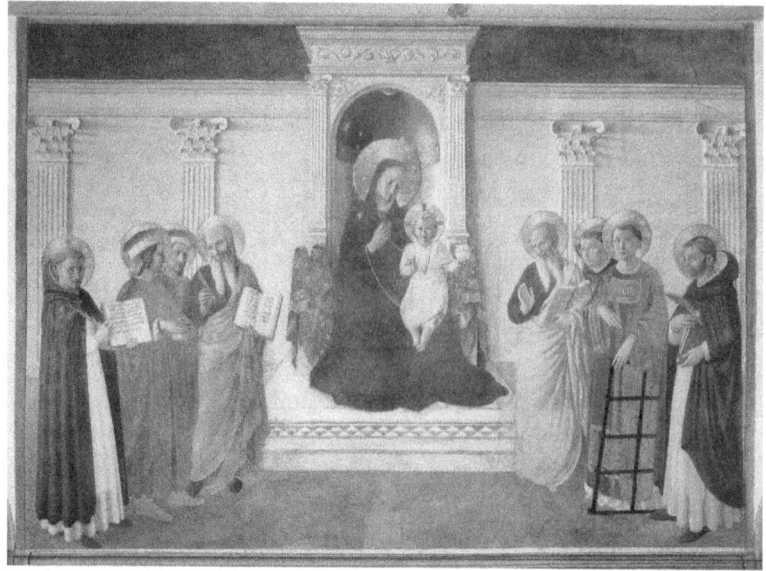

Figure 8 Fra Angelico, *Madonna delle Ombre* (*Madonna of the Shadows*)

Why this blindness? Because the history of 'humanist' art only sees what it knows in advance, it is part of a 'clinical' painting with two main entries, the Vasarian painting of *imitazione* and the *idea*. The spots painted by Fra Angelico are thus here like the 'illogical movements' which are in advance indescribable and even invisible, of the classic 'complete and regular painting' of Renaissance painting.

John Pope-Hennessy's *catalogue raisonné Fra Angelico* offered no record of the panels' existence. Pope-Hennessy's photographic reproductions are limited to displaying the top figurative half of the San Marco images.[27] The panels' decorative status has served to negate their existence in traditional art-historical analysis. Despite being a contemporary of Masaccio, Donatello and Brunelleschi and demonstrating some knowledge of Alberti's codification of perspective, Fra Angelico has not been remembered by art history in terms of the avant-garde of Renaissance perspectival painting. Emblematic of this attitude, Renaissance art historian John R. Spencer noted, 'Fra Angelico was clearly satisfied with this solution; neither he nor his closest followers, Zanobi Strozzi and Benozzo Gozzoli, depart radically from this essentially Trecento formula in their extant works.'[28]

Didi-Huberman's unique contribution to the existing body of Fra Angelico literature was to locate the artist in the tradition of medieval exegetical practice and theology. He argues: 'The eminently "medieval" character of his painting should not be envisioned as a delay, a defect, a negativity, but rather as an index of those *long Middle Ages* that Florence in the fifteenth century was far from repudiating.'[29] The original French edition *Fra Angelico: dissemblance et figuration* was published in 1990, the same year as *Devant l'image*, and delivers a practical application to the theoretical questions posed in *Devant l'image*. As we have seen in Chapter 1, at the centre of Didi-Huberman's argument is the claim that humanist art history in the tradition of Vasari, Kant and Panofsky privileged the mimetic function of the image at the expense of other possible representational strategies. Confronted with the abstract panels, he observes that the three metres of fictive marble was distinctly at odds with the technical ambitions of Renaissance painting. Departing from the disciplinary propensity to ignore the panels, Didi-Huberman argues they are integral parts of the entire work, associating the *marmi finti* along Kantian lines as parergon. He writes, 'ses parerga, ses zones marginales, les registres bien – ou bien mal – dits "inférieurs" des cycles de fresques, les registres du "décor", les simples "faux marbre" '[30] ('its parerga, its marginal zones, the appropriately – or inappropriately – named "inferior" cycles of frescoes, the registers of the "decor", the simple "false marbles" '). Acknowledging Derrida's reading of Kant's parergon, Didi-Huberman confirms that the panels are simultaneously inside and outside the work. Like the frame, the panels perform a paradoxical function – they are both subsidiary and constitutive. Following the logic of the supplement, the marginal becomes integral by virtue of its marginal status.[31]

It is Fra Angelico's rendering of panels of painted matter with no obviously discernible mimetic role that takes us right to the heart of the Christian doctrine of the Incarnation. The invisibility and unrepresentability of God has typically been understood in respect to the Hebraic ban on graven images found in Exodus.[32] Furthermore, the representation of the Divine was at odds with the Renaissance theoretical emphasis on the imitation of physical appearances: painting need only concern itself with what is visible and thereby representable. In the opening pages of his treatise *On Painting*, Leon Battista Alberti asserts, 'No one will deny that things which are not visible do not concern the painter, for he strives to represent only the things that are seen.'[33] The Incarnation therefore functions as a limit event for representation, as it cannot be rendered in visible terms.

How did Fra Angelico render the mystery of the Incarnation in visual form? This is the paradox confronting Christian artists: how to visually affirm the visibility of God, without anthropomorphising? To imagine such a paradox, Didi-Huberman argues that Fra Angelico evokes a practice of *dissemblance* that was distinctly at odds with art history's tropes of Renaissance figurative painting. Didi-Huberman asks, '[T]he mystery of the Incarnation still has to be considered as the greatest paradox of any figuration – what could the aspect congruent with a divine Word be?'[34] To answer this question, Didi-Huberman assembles the elements of early Christian theology concerning representation that were neglected by the founders of humanist art history. For Didi-Huberman, what is important here is a 'nonvisual thinking that is theological in nature'.[35] The panels do not fulfil a mimetic or decorative function. Nor are they performing illustrational and pedagogical roles for the illiterate congregation. Their function is to figure the unfigurable, the enigma of the mystery of the Incarnation. Importantly, *dissemblance* is *not* a neologism invented by Didi-Huberman to draw attention to the hegemony exercised by resemblance. Instead, *dissemblance* enjoys a long history stretching as far back as Plato, as elucidated by historians such as Étienne Gilson. It is this history that Didi-Huberman is drawing from and reactivating, after an extended period of the term falling into disuse.[36]

Didi-Huberman advances the hypothesis that Fra Angelico's panels are 'the opposite'[37] of what an art historian understands. To support his argument, Didi-Huberman retrieves a strain of negative Christian theology, specifically the texts of the mystical Christian theologian Pseudo-Dionysius the Areopagite. Writing approximately at the end of the fifth century, or the beginning of the sixth, Pseudo-Dionysius exerted a tremendous influence on the later development of thirteenth-century theology.[38] As a devout Dominican, Fra Angelico would have been familiar with his writings and the associated commentaries.[39] Pseudo-Dionysius introduced the notion of *dissimilarity* to best present the Divine. Gleaned from the Latin translation of the Greek originals, *dissimilitudo* translates as *dissemblance* in French.[40] Dionysius warned of the dangers of attempting to create a correspondence between representational forms and the Divine. Dionysius's God is unknowable and ineffable, existing beyond the limitations of human thought and representation. As such, God is formless. As nothing can appropriately resemble God, He is best addressed visually in terms of *dissemblance*. 'Images', Dionysius wrote, 'have something of the lowly and vulgar about them.'[41] As opposed to semblance, *dissemblance* is the preferred mode of presenting the Divine. The art of the four panels is the art of negative theology. As nothing can resemble God, He is defined by what he is not. Dionysius argued that even the lowliest matter can be an appropriate representational form of presenting the Divine. He claimed, 'Using matter, one may be lifted up to the immaterial archetypes ... Of course one must be careful to use the similarities as dissimilarities to avoid one-to-one correspondences.'[42]

With Dionysius's exhortation of the virtue of matter in mind, the multi-coloured panels declare their own materiality. Didi-Huberman retrieves matter from its subordination to form, arguing that 'Before representing anything, it presents matter, paint; and what it represents is also matter, a fictive multicolored marble.'[43] Paint, freed from the constraint of describing or illustrating, becomes the privileged site of spiritual exegesis, beyond the order of mimetic resemblances. Again, Didi-Huberman reminds us of his anti-idealist programme: that the 'great mimetic theme of figurative representation'[44] cannot account for the physical materiality of these images. It is important to recognise that imitation must be thought of here in terms of its limit, the Incarnation. As a result, access to God is predicated on an opening up, a rift or rent in the world of classical imitation. What is called forth is not an image of God, but a *symptom*, a material vestige, a trace of the Divine.

In underscoring the dissemblance of the panels and their material presence, Didi-Huberman argues that they are indexical:

> I have designated the specifically pictorial category of this disturbance by the (Proustian) term '*patch*' of painting. This is a way of naming those zones, those moments in the painting where the visible vacillates and spills into the visual. It is a way of naming the 'cursed part' of paintings, the indexical, nondescriptive, and dissemblant part. In fact, paintings often reserve – and this is once more their gift for disconcerting – a part of themselves for negating or clouding what they affirm in the mimetic order. Something in their aspect collapses at that point and dissemblance, a sort of disturbance, comes to reign there as the omnipotence of strangeness. There is nothing metaphysical about this strangeness in itself: it is only the power, the very symptom of painting – the materiality of painting, that is, *color* – color that no longer 'colors' objects but rather irrupts and ravages the decorum of the aspect.[45]

As we have already seen with Vermeer's *The Lacemaker*, the *pan* is characterised by its capacity to project forward, inserting itself into the spectator's space. The panels don't quietly withdraw, assuming a subordinate decorative function to the fresco above. Rather, they advance towards the spectator. Didi-Huberman writes that the panels 'burst forth selectively like extravagances in the works, almost like blotches: like *symptoms*'.[46] Akin to the errant red thread that pushes to the fore of *The Lacemaker*, the panels occupy the foreground, asserting their presence and undermining the mimeticism of Fra Angelico's fresco above.

Dissemblance and presence

Dissemblance affords Didi-Huberman the opportunity to conjure *presence* as opposed to imitation. Working at odds with conventional understandings of mimesis, the panels demonstrate a completely different understanding of the painterly sign. The iconicity of mimesis can only ever desire presence. Structurally, it is always doomed to absence. The panels are not signifiers demonstrating their own absence, but imbued with a 'quality of presence'.[47] If Didi-Huberman is to be understood as working through the implications of Derrida's project, how is his evocation of presence to be understood? At first glance it appears incompatible with Derrida's critique of the metaphysics of presence. It is worthwhile retrieving Derrida's arguments in *Of Grammatology* to demonstrate just how Didi-Huberman negotiates this. As we have seen with Derrida's reading of Rousseau, texts function in terms of binaries that contain a positive and a negative (presence versus absence, man versus woman). The positive term is complete, independent and stands in dominance to the incomplete, secondary and derisory term. In *Of Grammatology* Derrida considers the example of the speech–writing binary. He examines the privileged relationship of the signified to voice: 'The voice is *heard* (understood) – that undoubtedly is what is called conscience – closest to the self as the absolute effacement of the signifier.'[48] If speech is the privileged site of presence, immediacy and truth, writing is its secondary derivative, based not on presence, but absence as it stands in for and represents speech. Derrida demonstrates that counter to Saussure's thesis of the arbitrariness of the sign, the essence of the signified was presence. The signified is constituted in terms of presence and the signifier in terms of its absence. Derrida's insights offered important implications for mimetic representation. Just as writing never delivers full presence, mimesis was condemned only ever to express the absence of the presence it seeks to replicate.

Working against this, Didi-Huberman seeks to revive an earlier, theological understanding of representation as presentation which was ignored by the emphasis on mimesis and imitation inaugurated in the Renaissance. He returns us to a moment of the sign capable of evoking the presence of God, where 'sign and presence tend to adhere, to work in concert'.[49] Fra Angelico's panels are a different type of visual experience to that articulated by the rules of mimesis. Alberti's advice to painters was to think of the picture plane as 'transparent and like glass',[50] emphasising the transparency of the painterly material. As pure *pans* of material colour, the panels resist Alberti's metaphor of the transparent window. Didi-Huberman observes 'Here, then, was a type of painting that sought presence before representation. It was not designed to with-draw, as a classical landscape withdraws behind the "window" of its framing. On the contrary, it was designed to advance toward the eye, to disturb it, touch it.'[51] Not imitative, the panels demonstrate an alterna-tive understanding of the painterly sign. The iconicity of mimesis can only ever desire presence. Structurally, it is always doomed to absence. The panels are not signifiers demonstrating their own absence. Rather, they are 'endowed with a quality of presence'.[52]

What is at stake here is a model of representation that can no longer be thought of in figurative or mimetic terms. Like the negative theology of Pseudo-Dionysius, Didi-Huberman's God is an absent God. The Divine figure is 'a figure that moves out of itself, withdraws itself from resemblance, empties out of itself a place that could be seized upon as a univocal signification'.[53] This absence or withdrawal precludes the pos-sibility of mimetic correspondence. It is not possible to imitate God, as God has no image. Therefore, the panels are pure material *pans* of colour, a *presencing* of an absent origin.

> The dissemblance of colored blotches painted by Angelico is a way of disturbing the ordinary economy of representation in order to go beyond, that is, to endow the visible with an anagogical virtue with the aim of 'rendering a presence' – as one would say 'rendering an account' – of the mystery of the Incarnation.[54]

Interestingly, Didi-Huberman's arguments intersect with Jean-Luc Nancy's deconstruction of monotheism, particularly Christianity. Like Didi-Huberman, Nancy takes up the paradox of the Incarnation to probe the limits of imitative painting. Like Didi-Huberman's, Nancy's God is an absent one. For Nancy, Christianity is a self-deconstructive religion, characterised by the *kenosis*, or emptying out, of the Divine. The doctrine of kenosis is derived from Paul's use of the term in Philippians 2:5–9:

> Have this mind among yourselves, which is yours in Christ Jesus, who, though he was in the form of God, did not count equality with God a thing to be grasped, but emptied himself, by taking the form of a servant, being born in the likeness of men. And being found in human form, he humbled himself by becoming obedient to the point of death, even death on a cross.[55]

Nancy succinctly summarises God's unrepresentability as 'God created man in his image. But God does not have an image. So, the image of God is the image of nothing.'[56] Like Didi-Huberman, Nancy argues that Christian painting cannot be understood in imitative terms, as the Incarnation does not depend on resemblance to a pre-existing model. Rather than simply illustrating, Christian images are active and at the heart of this self-deconstructive movement.

The subject of Christian painting is taken up by Nancy in his essay 'Visitation: Of Christian Painting'. Here Nancy foregrounds his thesis that Christian painting is an ideal entry point for examining the withdrawal or absence of God with a close visual analysis of Jacopo Pontormo's *Visitation* (1528–29). In chronological terms, the Visitation occurs after the Annunciation and before the Nativity. The subject of the painting is the miracle of a Divine pregnancy as recounted in the Gospel of Luke. Mary, just pregnant herself, has learned of her cousin's pregnancy, and decides to visit. Pontormo paints the figures of Mary and Elizabeth in a warm embrace. In an entanglement of arms, robes and gazes, Mary and Elizabeth are entwined in the shape of the infinity and oblivious to the onlooking spectator. Unseen and unrepresentable are the two unborn children, Christ and St John the Baptist. Luke describes the scene: 'When Elizabeth heard Mary's greeting, the baby leaped in her womb, and Elizabeth was filled with the Holy Spirit.'[57] Akin to Fra Angelico's rendering of the Incarnation, Pontormo has painted an *event* that we cannot possibly see, the movement of a six-month-old foetus in its mother's womb. If Mary and Elizabeth are unaware of the spectator, the other two figures are certainly not. Juxtaposed against the self-enclosed unity of their embrace stand the women's servants. Both maintain a steady gaze, engaging the spectator directly. Nancy argues that it is through this complex web of gazes that the spectator is directly implicated in the intimate scene. The spectator participates in the event. Christian images cannot be reduced to the illustration of a biblical story. As Nancy writes, 'Christian painting is not a representation of a Christian subject. Rather, and conversely, Christian painting *is* Christianity – or something of Christianity in painting or as painting – caught up in the process of making painting.'[58] Representation is understood by both Didi-Huberman and Nancy not as merely illustrating, but the *presencing* of an absence.

In conclusion, by way of the *pan*, dissemblance and presencing, Didi-Huberman retrieves the materiality of the image from its subordination to the Idea or Form. In this deconstructive line of critique,

Didi-Huberman not only draws attention to the hierarchical and unequal binaries that have characterised the philosophical and historical discourses on art, he inserts new terms such as the *pan* and *dissemblance* to disrupt and unsettle the binary. Didi-Huberman's research on Fra Angelico's *marmi finti* brings his concerns into dialogue with Jean-Luc Nancy's analysis of Christianity as a self-deconstructing religion. In Didi-Huberman's retrieval of older, repressed strains of Christian theology he restores an understanding of representation that cannot be accounted for in terms inherited from the Renaissance. Furthermore, by retrieving older understandings of representation that were 'lost' or 'forgotten' in the Renaissance, Didi-Huberman introduces us to an important cornerstone of his project: images do not necessarily 'progress' or 'develop' in a linear manner. Instead, as the Fra Angelico case study demonstrates, images are the bearers of complex, anachronistic, temporalities. We will discuss this in depth in Chapter 3.

Notes

1 Georges Didi-Huberman, 'La matière inquiète (plasticité, viscosité, étrangeté)', *Lignes*, 1 (2000), 209.
2 John Goodman translates *le pan* as a 'whack' in *Confronting Images*. In *Fra Angelico*, Jane Marie Todd elects to use 'patch'.
3 See Georges Didi-Huberman, 'Appendix: The Detail and the *Pan*', in *Confronting Images: Questioning the Ends of a Certain History of Art*, trans. John Goodman (University Park: Pennsylvania State University Press, 2005), 261. The English-language translation is a reworking of an earlier article from 1986, Georges Didi-Huberman, 'L'art de ne pas décrire. Une aporie du détail chez Vermeer', *La Part de l'Œil*, 2 (1986), 102–19.
4 Didi-Huberman, *Confronting Images*, 248. Here *le pan* is translated as 'whack'.
5 Didi-Huberman, *La peinture incarnée*, 44. Didi-Huberman's emphasis.
6 Roland Barthes, *Camera Lucida*, trans. Richard Howard (London: Flamingo, 1984), 27.
7 Didi-Huberman, *La peinture incarnée*, 46.
8 Jacques Lacan, *The Four Fundamental Concepts of Psychoanalysis*, trans. Alan Sheridan (New York and London: W. W. Norton, 1998), 211.
9 *Ibid.*, 212. Lacan's emphasis.
10 Didi-Huberman, *Confronting Images*, 140.
11 *Ibid.*, 254.

12 *Ibid.*, 256. Mieke Bal extends Didi-Huberman's argument, writing, 'It is more aggressively present than it seems, so much so, in fact, that we might say it is staring the viewer in the face, thus blinding her.' See Mieke Bal, *The Mottled Screen: Reading Proust Visually*, trans. Anna-Louise Milne (Stanford: Stanford University Press, 1997), 83.

13 Daniel A. Fink, 'Vermeer's Use of the Camera Obscura: A Comparative Study', *Art Bulletin*, 53:4 (1971), 496. See also A. Hyatt Mayor, 'The Photographic Eye', *Metropolitan Museum of Art Bulletin*, 5:1 (1946), 15–26.

14 Alpers, *The Art of Describing*, 31–2.

15 *Ibid.*

16 Didi-Huberman, *Confronting Images*, 269.

17 Louis Marin, *Des pouvoirs de l'image: gloses* (Paris: Éditions du Seuil, 1993), 10.

18 Hubert Damisch, *Théorie du /nuage/: pour une histoire de la peinture* (Paris: Éditions du Seuil, 1972); Hubert Damisch, *A Theory of /Cloud/: Toward a History of Painting*, trans. Janet Lloyd (Stanford, CA: Stanford University Press, 2002).

19 Damisch, *A Theory of /Cloud/*, 121–4.

20 *Ibid.*, 226.

21 Daniel Arasse, *Le détail. Pour une histoire rapprochée de la peinture* (Paris: Flammarion, 1996), 12.

22 *Ibid.*, 268.

23 Didi-Huberman, *La peinture incarnée*, 44.

24 See Jacques Derrida, *Of Grammatology*, trans. Gayatri Spivak (Baltimore: Johns Hopkins University Press, 1976), 141–5.

25 Georges Didi-Huberman, *Fra Angelico: dissemblance et figuration* (Paris: Flammarion, 1990); Georges Didi-Huberman, *Fra Angelico: Dissemblance and Figuration*, trans. Jane Marie Todd (Chicago: University of Chicago Press, 1995).

26 Didi-Huberman, 'Dialogue sur le symptôme', 205.

27 John Pope-Hennessy, *Fra Angelico* (London: Phaidon, 1952).

28 John R. Spencer, 'Spatial Imagery of the Annunciation in Fifteenth Century Florence', *Art Bulletin*, 37:4 (1955), 274.

29 Didi-Huberman, *Fra Angelico*, 10.

30 Didi-Huberman, *Devant le temps*, 10.

31 In *The Truth in Painting*, Derrida writes: 'A parergon comes against, beside, and in addition to the *ergon*, the word done (*fait*), the fact (*le fait*), the work, but it does not fall to one side, it touches and cooperates within the operation, from a certain outside. Neither simply outside, nor simply inside.' See Jacques Derrida, *The Truth in Painting*, trans. Geoff Bennington and Ian McLeod (Chicago: University of Chicago Press, 1987), 54.

32   See Exodus 20:4–6.

33   Leon Battista Alberti, *On Painting*, trans. Cecil Grayson (London: Penguin Books, 2004), 37.

34   Didi-Huberman, *Fra Angelico*, 34.

35   *Ibid.*, 23.

36   Étienne Gilson, '*Regio Dissimilitudinis* de Platon à Saint Bernard de Clairvaux', *Medieval Studies*, 9:1 (1947), 108–30.

37   Didi-Huberman, *Fra Angelico*, 27.

38   See Eric Perl, 'Pseudo-Dionysius the Areopagite', in Lloyd P. Gerson (ed.), *The Cambridge History of Philosophy in Late Antiquity* (Cambridge: Cambridge University Press, 2010), 767–87.

39   Didi-Huberman, *Fra Angelico*, 52. Didi-Huberman notes that the library at San Marco contained at least seven copies of Dionysius's works.

40   In Colm Luibhéid's English translation, 'dissimilar' is used. Pseudo-Dionysius, *Pseudo-Dionysius: The Complete Works*, trans. C. Luibhéid and P. Rorem (New York: Paulist Press, 1987), e.g., p. 118.

41   See Pseudo-Dionysius, 'The Celestial Hierarchy', in *Pseudo-Dionysius: The Complete Works*, trans. C. Luibhéid and P. Rorem (New York: Paulist Press, 1987), 2.140A.

42   *Ibid.*, 2.144B–C.

43   Didi-Huberman, *Fra Angelico*, 55.

44   Didi-Huberman, *Confronting Images*, 186.

45   Didi-Huberman, *Fra Angelico*, 9.

46   *Ibid.*, 27.

47   *Ibid.*, 87.

48   Derrida, *Of Grammatology*, 20.

49   Didi-Huberman, *Fra Angelico*, 87.

50   Alberti, *On Painting*, 48.

51   Didi-Huberman, *Fra Angelico*, 10.

52   *Ibid.*, 87.

53   *Ibid.*, 52.

54   *Ibid.*, 87.

55   Philippians 2:5–9.

56   Jean-Luc Nancy, 'On Dis-enclosure and its Gesture, Adoration', in Alena Alexandrova *et al.* (eds), *Re-treating Religion: Deconstructing Christianity with Jean-Luc Nancy* (New York: Fordham University Press, 2012), 342.

57   Luke 1:39–56.

58   Jean-Luc Nancy, 'Visitation: Of Christian Painting', in *The Ground of the Image*, trans. Jeff Fort (New York: Fordham University Press, 2005), 122. My emphasis.

• 3 •

Timely anachronisms

In *Devant le temps*, Didi-Huberman claimed, 'Toujours, devant l'image, nous sommes devant du temps.'[1] ('Always, before the image, we are before time.') What does Didi-Huberman mean by this and how does his understanding of time depart from the conventional understandings of temporality that have sustained art's history? Didi-Huberman's long-running conversation with Freud is expanded to encompass a temporal dimension. As I discussed in Chapter 2, the symptom as the *pan* interrupts the logic of mimesis. Here, however, Didi-Huberman introduces the reader to the double paradox of the symptom: it produces both a visual and temporal disturbance. He writes, 'Mais s'arrêter *devant le pan*, ce n'est pas seulement interroger l'objet de nos regards. C'est aussi s'arrêter *devant le temps*.'[2] ('But stopping *before the pan* not only means asking questions of what we are looking at, it also means stopping *before time*.') The symptom is an anachronism, a displacement in time. An anachronistic understanding of history draws attention to the deeper, temporal assumptions about art and its history.

In *Devant le temps*, Didi-Huberman returns to the core concern of his project: to conduct an archaeological analysis of art history's foundations. Despite *Devant le temps* appearing ten years after *Confronting Images*, it is impossible to ignore the synchronicity of the two books. If the goal of *Confronting Images* was to critique the mimetic tradition underlying humanist art history, *Devant le temps* is an interrogation of the historicity of this history, of history itself. Didi-Huberman clearly states what is at stake here: 'amorcer une archéologie critique des modèles de temps, des valeurs d'usage du temps dans la discipline historique qui a voulu faire des images ses objets d'étude'[3] ('to initiate an archaeological critique of the models of times, of the values of time usage in the historical discipline whose purpose it was to make images the object of its study'). To confront the image demands a confrontation with time. If the image can no longer be imagined in purely mimetic terms, the temporal logic sustaining this history comes increasingly under pressure. For Didi-Huberman, the archaeologist's task is to interrogate the default temporal models underpinning art's history:

> Nous posons rarement un regard critique sur la façon dont nous pratiquons notre discipline; nous refusons souvent d'interroger l'histoire stratifiée, pas toujours glorieuse, des mots, des catégories ou des genres littéraires que nous employons quotidiennement pour produire notre savoir historique.[4]
>
> We rarely take a critical look at the way we practise our discipline; we often refuse to question the layers of the not always glorious history of the words, categories or literary genres that we use on a daily basis to produce our historical knowledge.

In the opening pages of *Devant le temps*, Didi-Huberman returns to one of his favourite case studies, the *marmi finti* or fictive marble panels located directly below Fra Angelico's *Madonna delle Ombre* (*Madonna of the Shadows*) in the corridor of the San Marco convent in Florence. The surfaces of the panels were sprayed by Fra Angelico with an energetic constellation of spurts and drips and resembled the natural inconsistencies of marble. The gushes of paint act as an index or trace of the event itself, leading Didi-Huberman to draw an evocative comparison with Jackson Pollock's twentieth-century drip paintings. This is not to say that Fra Angelico is the 'father' of American action painting. It is, however, impossible for the art historian to stand before the panels and successfully abandon the subjective memory and experience of previous encounters with abstract expressionism. The relationship between the image and the gaze is impure, he argues, contaminated by personal memory. As such, the image is the paradoxical site of heterogeneous and competing temporalities. Despite the age of the image, it is impossible to ignore the fact that we encounter it in our own time, bringing to bear our own subjective histories and personal memories. Despite being about objects of the past, the discipline of art history paradoxically cannot escape the present. Didi-Huberman writes: '[L]'histoire des images est une histoire d'objets temporellement impurs, complexes, surdéterminés. C'est donc une histoire d'objets polychroniques, d'objets hétérochroniques ou anachroniques.'[5] ('[T]he history of images is a history of objects that are temporally impure, complex, overdetermined. It is therefore a history of polychronistic, heterochronistic or anachronistic objects.') Art history itself is an anachronistic discipline, out of temporal step with the images and objects it studies. The collision between Jackson Pollock and Fra Angelico's panels in the San Marco chapel introduces us to one of Didi-Huberman's key ambitions: to explicate a model of temporality that disrupts formulations of history as teleological or linear. As we have seen, Fra Angelico's panels are a *symptom* in the historian's knowledge, but also present a further challenge for the history of art: *anachronism*. How to account for the subjective memory underpinning the art historian's gaze? What role does personal memory play? How is the individual art historian's own contemporaneity accounted for? An anachronistic understanding of images undermines the discipline's 'règle d'or: ne surtout pas "projeter", comme on dit, nos propres réalités – nos concepts, nos goûts, nos valeurs – sur les réalités du passé'[6] ('golden rule: you absolutely must not "project", as we say, our own realities, our concepts, our tastes, our values – on the realities of the past'). Access to the past is necessarily informed by the contemporary and, as the Pollock experience underscores, *personal memory*. Against the clear delineation of the past from the present, Didi-Huberman argues that an anachronistic understanding of images is productive, offering a rich range of possibilities for reconfiguring art's history.

My aim here is to investigate how Didi-Huberman undertakes a revision of orthodox, or conventional models of time. I will consider the philosophical and historical framework in which Didi-Huberman is operating, specifically in relation to the French reception of Hegel. I argue that Didi-Huberman goes further than any other art historian in the utilisation of anachronism as a positive disruption to chronological models of time and historical periodisation. Anachronism is no longer considered a historiographical error, but a fertile principle for understanding the complex behaviour of images. To do this, Didi-Huberman assembles a heterogeneous group of theorists and writers, including Walter Benjamin and Aby Warburg, who were exploring alternative modes of temporality in the early decades of the twentieth century. Didi-Huberman's reading of both Warburg and Benjamin is representative of a general shift in the philosophy of history from a Hegelian to a Nietzschean interpretation by Deleuze and Foucault.

The concept of historical distance was designed to safeguard against what *Annales* historian Lucien Febvre described as the 'sin of all sins', anachronism. Febvre cautioned against the dangers of contaminating the past with the present, warning:

> When dealing with sixteenth-century men and ideas, when dealing with modes of wishing, feeling, thinking, and believing that bear sixteenth-century arms, the problem is to determine what set of precautions to take and what rules to follow in order to avoid the worst of all sins, the sin that cannot be forgiven – anachronism.[7]

If anachronism is defined as the intrusion of one historical era into another,[8] art history has sought to preserve an appropriate gap from the art object to ensure the art historian's contemporaneity is kept separate and distinct. Erwin Panofsky warned, 'To grasp reality, we have to detach ourselves from the present.'[9] Panofsky's caution reflects a self-conscious historicity where the practitioner is committed to maintaining a distance with the artwork. Appropriate historical distance ensured that the threat of anachronism was minimised, a built-in safeguard designed to maintain the art historian's objectivity. Didi-Huberman's 'Pollock-like' encounter with Fra Angelico's panels is a clear rejection of Panofsky's ambitions for the art historian's scientific 'neutrality' or detachment. Didi-Huberman is seeking to restore the art historian's subjective memory that had been carefully bracketed by the positivist strain of German art history.

One of the defining principles of art history is returning the art object to its historical conditions of production. An artwork is typically understood as an expression of the historical period in which it was produced, the *Zeitgeist* or spirit of the age. This is a very Hegelian idea. One of the most compelling accounts of period specificity was articulated by Michael Baxandall. In *Painting and Experience in Fifteenth-Century Italy*, he developed his concept of the 'period eye', drawing from a range of contemporary texts, such as contracts, treatises and manuals, to examine how works of art were produced and consumed in their own historical context. Criticising Baxandall's social art history and the period eye, Didi-Huberman asks in *Devant le temps*, how is this ever truly possible, or, to extend the problematic even further, desirable?[10]

When the Hegelian narrative underpinning art's history is exhausted, what temporal models are available for art historians?

Didi-Huberman's interest in thinking through the temporal dimension of images is part of a broader conversation in France initiated
by philosopher Jacques Rancière and classicist Nicole Loraux that
has sought to recuperate anachronism from its historically pejorative
connotations. Two recent interventions have sought to examine the
stigma associated with anachronism in historical discourse. The first
was by Rancière, who coined the term 'anachronies', arguing that it was
necessary to reclaim anachronism in positive terms. Rancière argues, 'Il
n'y a pas d'anachronisme. Mais il y a des modes de connexion que nous
pouvons appeler positivement des *anachronies*: des événements, des
notions, des significations qui prennent le temps à rebours.'[11] ('There is
no anachronism. But there are modes of connection that we can posi-
tively call *anachronies*: the events, notions, meanings that reverse time.')
Building on Rancière's claims, Loraux endorsed the 'controlled use' of
anachronism, arguing that it was a 'fantasme interne'[12] (internal fantasy) for historians to continue imagining a faithful resuscitation of the
past. As opposed to a chronological or linear progression of time, Didi-
Huberman proposes to substitute a fragmented temporality where the
past, present and future are inextricably linked.

The spectre of Hegel looms large over the discipline of art history.
Like history, art history has tended to be propelled by Hegelian causal
accounts of progress.[13] Didi-Huberman directs his attention towards a
Hegelian philosophy of history that has implicitly supported art's historiography. He notes, 'There is no philosophy of art without a philosophy of history – be it merely spontaneous and not really thought
out.'[14] An archaeological reconsideration of the discipline therefore
would be incomplete without an investigation of the philosophy of
history underpinning it. At the heart of Hegel's philosophy of history
is the 'Infinite Spirit' or 'Idea' behind history that progresses dialectic-
ally through time. Hegel writes, 'The History of the World begins with
its general aim – the realization of the Idea of Spirit ... and the whole
process of History is directed to rendering this unconscious impulse a
conscious one.'[15] Hegel's history has an underlying built-in teleology,
culminating in a final stage of history as a free and rational society.

Art history as a narrative structure has been sustained by chronological time, with art historians implicitly drawing on Hegel's dialectical
progression towards Infinite Spirit. Consider, for instance, the Hegelian
impulse directing art's internal teleology in formalist accounts of twentieth century modernism. Clement Greenberg famously encapsulated

modern art's triumphant progression when he wrote, 'Modernist art develops out of the past without gap or break, and wherever it ends up it will never stop being intelligible in terms of the continuity of art.'[16] Greenberg's implicit Hegelianism was shared by Michael Fried, who argued, '[T]he fundamentally Hegelian conception of art history at work in the writings of Wölfflin and Greenberg … seems particularly well suited to the actual development of modernism in the visual arts, painting especially.'[17] Reflecting on her early career participation in the formalist criticism of high modernism, Rosalind Krauss recalled, 'I never doubted the absoluteness of that history. It was out there, manifest in a whole progression of works of art, an objective fact to be analyzed.'[18] All three examples point to a preoccupation with a Hegelian motor driving modern art's passage towards abstraction.

Didi-Huberman's commitment to an anachronistic understanding of art's history reflects broader shifts in a discipline that is increasingly questioning linear models of time and temporality. A spate of recent publications reveals a growing interest in time and temporality in what Christine Ross has described as contemporary art's 'temporal turn'.[19] Mieke Bal, Keith Moxey, Christopher Wood and Alexander Nagel have all, in their various ways, posited that images are the site of multiple temporalities.[20] Terry Smith identified one of the hallmarks of contemporaneity as the coexistence of asynchronous temporalities. Smith, however, carefully positions the contemporary from the vantage point of modernism's *aftermath*, the what-comes-next-after-modernism. He writes, 'After the era of grand narratives, they may be all that there is. Indeed – who knows? – *aftermath* may last forever.'[21] Smith's argument remains steadfastly chronological – the contemporary is still imagined in terms of modernism's internal teleology.

Didi-Huberman has criticised the temporal model proposed by the *October* group of art historians as evidence of the authors' inability to escape an implicit Hegelianism and a teleological commitment to time. The chronological year-by-year reconstruction of the development of twentieth-century art in *Art since 1900* adheres to the Hegelian dialectic. Postmodernism is presented as the logical synthesis to modernism's thesis and antimodernism's antithesis. He writes, 'Cela veut dire qu'elles se situent hors de tout sens orienté, fût-il temporalisé par dialectique chic du "modernisme", de l'"antimodernisme" et du "postmodernisme" (ici Rosalind Krauss a bien eu tort d'en appeler à des modèles temporels aussi triviaux).'[22] ('This means they lack any feeling of direction, even one that might be anchored in a time period by the chic dialectic of "modernism", "antimodernism" and "postmodernism" (here Rosalind Krauss was wrong to appeal to such trivial temporal models).') This criticism fits his general pattern of carefully distancing himself from the ready-made periodisation of art's history.

Didi-Huberman's investigation into the conditions of historicity itself signals his ongoing engagement with the arguments advanced in Michel Foucault's *The Archaeology of Knowledge*. In his opening paragraph, Foucault established archaeology's hostility towards Hegelian-inspired, progressivist views of historical continuity, the *longue durée* of the *Annales* historians:

> For many years now historians have preferred to turn their attention to long periods, as if, beneath the shifts and changes of political events, they were trying to reveal the stable, almost indestructible system of checks and balances, the irreversible processes, the constant readjustments, the underlying tendencies.[23]

Building on Gaston Bachelard's and Georges Canguilhem's preference for rupture and discontinuity, Foucault claimed that history needed to be rethought along archaeological lines, privileging disruption and disjointedness. Acknowledging historians' proclivity for linear progress, Foucault observed, 'Discontinuity was the stigma of temporal dislocation that it was the historian's task to remove from history.'[24] Unlike continuous history, an archaeological analysis embraces ruptures and displacements. Discontinuity interrupts the Hegelian progression of consciousness and the teleology of reason. Furthermore, rather than simply being removed or ignored, one of the most fertile and productive features of discontinuity is its integration into the discourse itself.

Rethinking temporality

Evidence of Didi-Huberman's anti-Hegelianism is not difficult to accrue. Didi-Huberman's commitment to a non-synthesised dialectics has remained consistent across the body of his work. In an interview with François Noudelmann, he clearly delineated his attitude towards the dialectic:

Le mot 'dialectique' a une longue histoire. Et tellement sujette aux transformations, voire aux renversements de sens … J'ai surtout été attentif à l'emploi particulier du mot 'dialectique' dans le contexte d'une constellation de penseurs grâce auxquels, dans les années vingt et trente du XXe siècle, les notions d'histoire et d'image ont été simultanément reformulées et, en un sens, refondées (bien qu'à strictement parler l'idée de fondation ne convienne pas ici). C'est à ce moment-là, en tout cas, qu'il a été véritablement possible de repenser l'histoire, l'art, et donc l'histoire de l'art.[25]

The word 'dialectic' has a long history. And as such subject to changes, even reversals of meaning … I have been especially attentive to the use of the word 'dialectic' in the context of a constellation of thinkers thanks to whom, in the twenties and thirties of the twentieth century, the notions of history and image have been simultaneously reformulated and, in a sense, refounded (although strictly speaking the idea of foundation is not suitable here). It was at that time, in any case, that it was truly possible to rethink history, art, and therefore the history of art.

What is at stake here is Didi-Huberman's place in the history of the French reception of Hegel. Didi-Huberman adds his voice to the distinctive anti-Hegelian current that has characterised French thought since the 1960s, particularly embodied in the work of Derrida, Foucault and Deleuze. Vincent Descombes described the shift in generational attitude towards the dialectic: 'Burning the idol venerated until now, this generation denounced the dialectic as the supreme illusion, from which it sought to free itself through recourse, this time, to Nietzsche.'[26] The challenge confronting these thinkers is the paradoxical impossibility of escaping Hegel's totalising schema: the negative logic of Hegelianism necessarily recuperates all that falls outside its boundaries. Recall Foucault's cautionary warning when he assumed Jean Hyppolite's chair at the Collège de France:

But to truly escape Hegel involves an exact appreciation of the price we have to pay to detach ourselves from him. It assumes that we are aware of the extent to which Hegel, insidiously perhaps, is close to us; it implies a knowledge, in that which permits us to think against Hegel, of that which remains Hegelian. We have to determine the extent to which our anti-Hegelianism is possibly one his tricks directed against us, at the end of which he stands, motionless, waiting for us.[27]

To be anti-Hegelian is to be paradoxically thoroughly Hegelian. How is it possible to be critical of a system without being recuperated by that very system? It is for this reason that Didi-Huberman's contribution to the history of the French reception of Hegel is significant: he does not attempt to disavow the negative logic of Hegelianism. Instead, he seeks to restore to the dialectic various modes of disruption, repeatedly pursuing a structure that promotes the oscillation between thesis and antithesis, without recourse to a higher synthesis. In his analysis of Hegel's reception in France, Bruce Baugh observes that dialectics requires the mediation of a third term. Otherwise, differences are left unresolved and unreconciled. Baugh writes, 'If there is no synthesis, then there can be no dialectic ... but only anti-thetics, the play of opposed terms that negate and pass into each other without ever coinciding in a meaningful whole.'[28] This is precisely the structure Didi-Huberman is intent on pursuing: a dialectics that rejects synthesis, leaving the irreconcilable reconciliation of two opposites. The symptom undermines and destabilises the opposition between terms. In *The Surviving Image*, he conjures an image of snakelike movement to emphasise the symptom's evasion of dialectical resolution: ' "Symptom" would then designate that complex serpentine movement, that nonresolved intrication, that nonsynthesis.'[29]

Didi-Huberman's emphasis on the symptom's resistance to synthesis may be traced back to Sigmund Freud's account of symptom formation. For Freud, the symptom was produced and maintained by contradictory and conflicting impulses and was therefore resistant to synthesis:

> As to the neurotic symptoms, we already know that they are the result of a conflict aroused by a new form of gratifying the libido. The two forces that have contended against each other meet once more in the symptom; they become reconciled through the compromise of a symptom development. That is why the symptom is capable of such resistance; it is sustained from both sides.[30]

Freud describes the symptom's contradictory and ambiguous nature as an 'artificially selected ambiguity – with two entirely contradictory meanings.'[31] The symptom is the product of two competing impulses, remaining resolutely impervious to an overall synthesis. Didi-Huberman accentuates this with an anti-dialectical inflection, observing 'the symptom plays with antithesis.'[32] As the symptom is overdetermined, it disrupts linear cause and effect as it contains no single point of origin: 'le symptôme comme jeu non chronologique de latences et de crises –, voilà peut-être la justification la plus simple d'une nécessaire entrée de l'anachronisme dans les modèles de temps à utiliser par l'historien'[33] ('the symptom as a non-chronological inter-play of latencies and crises – here is perhaps the simplest justification for a necessary entry of anachronism into the models of time to be used by the historian'). By eschewing the synthesis of thesis and antithesis, the symptom interferes with the behaviour of the Hegelian dialectic and its implicit teleology.

The anti-Hegelian sentiment in France is usually attributed to the generation of philosophers who came to prominence in the 1960s. Didi-Huberman, however, detects an earlier moment exhibited in the great montage projects of German avant-garde writers and theorists of the 1920s and 1930s. Like Derrida's reading of Georges Bataille before him, Didi-Huberman avoids a direct confrontation with Hegel.[34] Instead, he elects to engage Hegel through the lens of German avant-garde writers and theorists: Walter Benjamin and Aby Warburg. Both had developed a conception of historiography propelled by their theories of anachronism. Didi-Huberman argues that the group of writers and theorists perform an epistemological rupture, satisfying Foucault's demand that history is conceived in terms of discontinuity and disjuncture.

Walter Benjamin

Walter Benjamin is a critical interlocutor in Didi-Huberman's for-mulation of anachronistic models of time and temporality. Didi-Huberman privileges an anti-dialectical reading of Walter Benjamin, emphasising Benjamin's distance from the Frankfurt School's Hegelian orthodoxy. His reading of Benjamin is acute: over the body of Benjamin's writing, he returns repeatedly to several key passages to elucidate his own critique of historicism. The first is *The Origin of German Tragic Drama* of 1924, where Benjamin seeks to complicate traditional, or metaphysical, understandings of the origin. The origin is understood by Benjamin as no longer static or stable, but an unpredictable and dynamic whirlpool that can emerge at any moment during a flow. Benjamin writes:

> Origin [*Ursprung*], although an entirely historical category, has, nevertheless, nothing to do with genesis [*Entstehung*]. The term origin is not intended to describe the process by which the existent came into being, but rather to describe that which emerges from the process of becoming and disappearance. *Origin is an eddy in the stream of becoming*, and in its current it swallows the material involved in the process of genesis. That which is original is never revealed in the naked and manifest existence of the factual; its rhythm is apparent only to a dual insight. On the one hand it needs to be recognized as a process of restoration and re-establishment, but, on the other hand, and precisely because of this, as something imperfect and incomplete.[35]

In this passage, Benjamin places the principles of historical temporality under pressure. Causality and the sequencing of events are reformulated in terms of the metaphor of the *eddy* or *whirlpool*. In the French translation, the noun is *tourbillon*, or whirlpool. A whirlpool is much stronger than the gentler 'eddy'. For this reason, I will retain the French translation *tourbillon* as *whirlpool*, and depart from John Osborne's English-language translation. A *whirlpool* disrupts the notion of following a stream to its originary source. An origin understood as whirlpool is no longer associated with the ideas of genesis or birth. Nor can it be conceived as the source of a linear trajectory or flow. Didi-Huberman underscores the importance of reframing the origin in terms of a whirlpool:

> Une histoire de l'art qui, en ce sens précis, pose une question d'origine sera donc une histoire de l'art attentive aux tourbillons dans le fleuve des styles, aux fractures dans le sol des doctrines esthétiques, aux déchirures dans le tissu des représentations.[36]
> A history of art that, in this specific sense, presents a question of origin will therefore be a history of art attentive to the whirlpools in the flow of styles, to the fractures at the ground of aesthetic doctrines, to the tears in the fabric of representations.

The origin is not understood by Didi-Huberman as an originary origin. Instead, the whirlpool proposes a disturbance in the metaphysical tradition with its privileging of presence, origin and being. For this reason, Benjamin's image of the whirlpool evokes a comparison with Derrida's *différance*. In his essay 'Différance', Derrida famously established his distrust towards origins: '*Différance* is the non-full, non-simple structured and differentiating origin of differences. Thus, the name "origin" no longer suits it.'[37] Like *différance*, which for Derrida was 'neither a concept nor a word',[38] Benjamin's origin as whirlpool is neither a 'concept' nor a 'source', but a disturbance in the flow of history.

Accentuating this point, Didi-Huberman argues that the origin as whirlpool must be understood in terms of the symptom: 'l'origine surgit devant nous comme un symptôme'[39] ('the origin surges before us like a symptom'). As we have seen in Chapter 1, Freud cautions against searching for the origins of the symptom, preferring to emphasise its rhizomatic behaviour. Like Benjamin's image of the whirlpool, the symptom is overdetermined: it cannot be reduced to a single source of attribution. Didi-Huberman draws on this to further accentuate the symptom's behaviour as a temporal disturbance: 'Ce que l'image-symptôme interrompt n'est autre que le cours de la représentation ... Ce que le symptôme-temps interrompt n'est donc rien d'autre que le cours de l'histoire chronologique.'[40] ('What the symptom-image interrupts is none other than the course of representation ... What the symptom-time interrupts is none other than the course of chronological history.') Like Benjamin's whirlpool, the symptom now gives rise to new fluxes, unexpected effects and is endowed with the capacity to tamper with chronological time.

If the whirlpool is analogous to the symptom, Didi-Huberman also makes explicit the link between Benjamin and Marcel Proust. In a series of essays Benjamin attempted to account for the relationship between memory and historical time by evoking Proust's notion of *mémoire involontaire*. While commentators have discussed the convergence between Benjamin and Proust, Didi-Huberman reads Benjamin's attitude towards Proust specifically as an anachronistic understanding of time and subjective memory.[41] In his 1929 essay on Proust, Benjamin describes the *mémoire involontaire* in visual terms, as images. He observes, 'most memories that we search for come to us as visual images. Even the free-floating forms of the *mémoire involontaire* are still in large part isolated, though enigmatically present, visual images.'[42] As is well known, *mémoire involontaire* activates a previous, lost experience and is experienced as a type of jolt or shock. In *À la recherche du temps perdu*, the Narrator's taste of the madeleine spontaneously conjures up his childhood in Combray. Benjamin accentuates the disruptive power of the *mémoire involontaire*, writing, 'The true reader of Proust is constantly jarred by small shocks.'[43] The Proustian shocks, according to Benjamin, were a type of montage that could trigger a *mémoire involontaire*.

Benjamin's antagonism towards neo-Hegelian historiography and the ideology of progress is given its most complete expression in his celebrated 'Theses on the Philosophy of History'. Benjamin's enthusiasm for the Proustian *mémoire involontaire* is continued in the 'Theses'. Here, shocks, flashes and ruptures saturate his writing as he embraces the disruptive power of involuntary memory against historical models predicated on advancement and progress. For Benjamin, 'The true picture of the past flits by. The past can be seized only as an image which flashes up at the instant when it can be recognized and is never seen again.'[44] The relation between past and present is imagined not as a gentle fold in time, but as a radical collision. Evoking the Proustian shock, Benjamin urges, 'Thinking involves not only the flow of thoughts, but their arrest as well. Where thinking suddenly stops in a configuration pregnant with tensions, it gives that configuration a shock, by which it crystalizes into a monad.'[45] This collision disrupts the linearity of time, shattering history's continuum.

Writing in the earliest days of World War II, Benjamin was acutely aware that Marxism could not continue justifying the rise of National Socialism as the inevitable causal progression in the predetermined evolution of society. For Benjamin, Hegel's philosophy was incapable of adequately accounting for the acute levels of human suffering. Benjamin sought to articulate a new understanding of history that could properly account for the neglected and overlooked. History, he argued, occurred not in the smooth 'progression through a homogeneous, empty time',[46] but in the fissures and cracks. For history to escape a linear or teleological trajectory it was necessary to rethink its very linearity as an artificial construction and identify a temporal model that could account for contradiction and discontinuity. In Benjamin's 'fight for the oppressed past'[47] it was therefore essential to disrupt the flow of linear time.

The unsolicited shock of the *mémoire involontaire* is evoked by Didi-Huberman to convey the force of the anachronism triggered by the '*ressemblance déplacée*'[48] (displaced resemblance) in the San Marco chapel. Didi-Huberman described the experience in terms of the shock of *mémoire involontaire*. He writes, 'un choc, une déchirure de voile, une irruption ou apparition du temps, tout ce dont Proust et Benjamin ont si bien parlé sous l'espèce de la "mémoire involontaire"'[49] ('a shock, a tear in the veil, an interruption or appearance in time, all that Proust and Benjamin have described so well under the heading of the "involuntary memory"'). The force of the involuntary memory triggered by Fra Angelico's panels is analogous to the Narrator's madeleine experience. For Didi-Huberman, the memory experience standing before the *marmi finti* provokes an entirely new constellation of associations. The art historian's own contemporaneity is evoked here as an anachronism, serving to undermine the disciplinary claim to objectivity and the careful cultivation of appropriate historical distance.

Benjamin's debt to Proust highlights the fact that Didi-Huberman's utilisation of anachronism is much broader and more ambitious than simply a dislocation in time. Didi-Huberman is pursuing a model of temporality capable of accounting for the events of memory. This has two characteristics. The first, as we have seen, is the subjective memory of the art historian. The second recognises that the image is endowed with its own memory. Didi-Huberman maintains, 'Bien avant que l'art n'ait une histoire –, les images ont eu, ont porté, ont produit de la mémoire.'[50] ('Long before art had a history –, images had, carried, produced memory.') With its capacity to create its own memories, the image Didi-Huberman describes now exhibits agency. To understand this claim further, it is necessary to turn now to Didi-Huberman's reading of Aby Warburg.

Aby Warburg

The second critical interlocutor in Didi-Huberman's retrieval of anachronism from its pejorative connotations is German art historian Aby Warburg. Traditionally, Warburg has been remembered for his influence on other art historians such as Ernst Gombrich and Erwin Panofsky. The past two decades, however, have witnessed a surge of scholarly interest in Warburg's legacy.[51] One of the most influential accounts is Didi-Huberman's *L'image survivante* (*The Surviving Image*) of 2002. Ten years in development, it is the longest and most extensive monograph on an art historian's body of work ever to be completed. In his book on Warburg, two terms, *Nachleben* and *Pathosformel*, are crucial for Didi-Huberman to formulate an anachronistic history that is made up of ghosts, survivals and phantoms. From the German *nach*, meaning 'after', and *Leben*, 'life', a direct translation into English of the first term as 'survival' belies the complexity of the term. It is not simply a matter of conjuring another life, beyond this one. Instead, *Nachleben* is better understood in terms of a continuum, where a plurality of pasts coexist. Didi-Huberman underscores the sensation of this temporal intermingling: *'the present is woven from multiple pasts'.*[52] Against formulations of Renaissance 'rebirth' and 'renewal', *Nachleben* lends itself to a ghostlike mode of temporality, capable of haunting the present. Images 'survive' as anachronisms, reappearing after long periods of absence. I argue that Warburg's model of *Nachleben* is recast by Didi-Huberman along a Nietzschean–Deleuzian axis as part of his broader project of rethinking the philosophical framework underpinning the discipline. By discarding Hegel for Nietzsche, Warburg puts into play a model of imitation not predicated on technical improvement, but an *intensification* in its return.

Didi-Huberman's key contribution to the recent body of Warburg literature is his restoration of *Nachleben* to its English-language origins. Didi-Huberman attributes the source of Warburg's elusive concept of *Nachleben* to English anthropologist Edward Burnett Tylor and his concept of 'survival', drawn from Tylor's *Primitive Culture* of 1871. Didi-Huberman argues that Tylor's theory of cultural evolutionism clearly impacted on the development of Warburg's own project. Tylor described 'survivals' in the following terms:

> These are processes, customs, opinions, and so forth, which have been carried on by force of habit into a new state of society different from that in which they had their original home, and they thus remain as proofs and examples of an older condition of culture out of which a newer has been evolved.[53]

Tylor's theories of cultural evolutionism described a model of temporality not based on linear causality, but connections between ancient and primitive customs with contemporary superstitions, games and folklore. Didi-Huberman demonstrates that Tylor's concept of survival is crucial in understanding the temporal dimension of Warburg's project, arguing that Warburg, following Tyler, established a clear connection between history, anthropology and time. Underscoring the importance of Tylor's theorisation of time to Warburg's project, Didi-Huberman argues: 'Warburg *opened up the field* of art history to anthropology, not only in order to discover in it new objects for study, but in order to *open up time* to a new approach, as well.'[54]

The second important term in Warburg's vocabulary is *Pathosformel*, or *pathos formulas*, which is understood as emotive formulas. Warburg observed certain emotional gestures migrate and return, after long periods of dormancy. These gestures are endowed with a heightened degree of intensity. The twin concepts of *Nachleben* and *Pathosformel* are introduced by Warburg in a small essay of 1905, 'Dürer and Italian Antiquity'.[55] Warburg commences with an analysis of a woodprint created by Albrecht Dürer (Figures 9–10) and works backwards in time to ancient Greek vases to demonstrate his thesis that heightened emotional gestures migrate across geographies and temporalities (Figures 11–12). In Dürer's print, Orpheus is shown kneeling with his hand raised in a defensive gesture protecting his head from the oncoming blows of the Thracian women. Warburg argues that Dürer's protective gesture is 'directly informed by the emotive gestural language defined by Greece for this same tragic scene'.[56] The repetition of postures and expressions was considered by Warburg as evidence of the ancient world's re-entry into Renaissance art and formed one of the cornerstones of his historiographical programme. The 1497 Venetian edition of Ovid (Figure 11) was proof, according to Warburg, than an antique emotive formula (*Pathosformel*) had clearly established itself in Renaissance artistic circles. Throughout his writing, the motif of *survival* reoccurs, as Warburg sought to articulate a mode of image transmission that was not necessarily linear or sequential.

Displacing Winckelmann's temporal models of 'greatness and decline', Didi-Huberman argues that Warburg introduced a mode of temporality akin to the symptom. Like the symptom, a 'surviving' image is highly overdetermined, displaced from its original meaning and context. Nevertheless, it returns, like a ghost, to re-emerge in the future. For Didi-Huberman, Warburg opened the discipline up to the broader life sciences of philosophy, psychology, anthropology and history. Warburg's goals were to rebuild the history of art as *Kulturwissenschaft*, born from a general dissatisfaction with the formalism of his immediate predecessors Heinrich Wölfflin and Aloïs

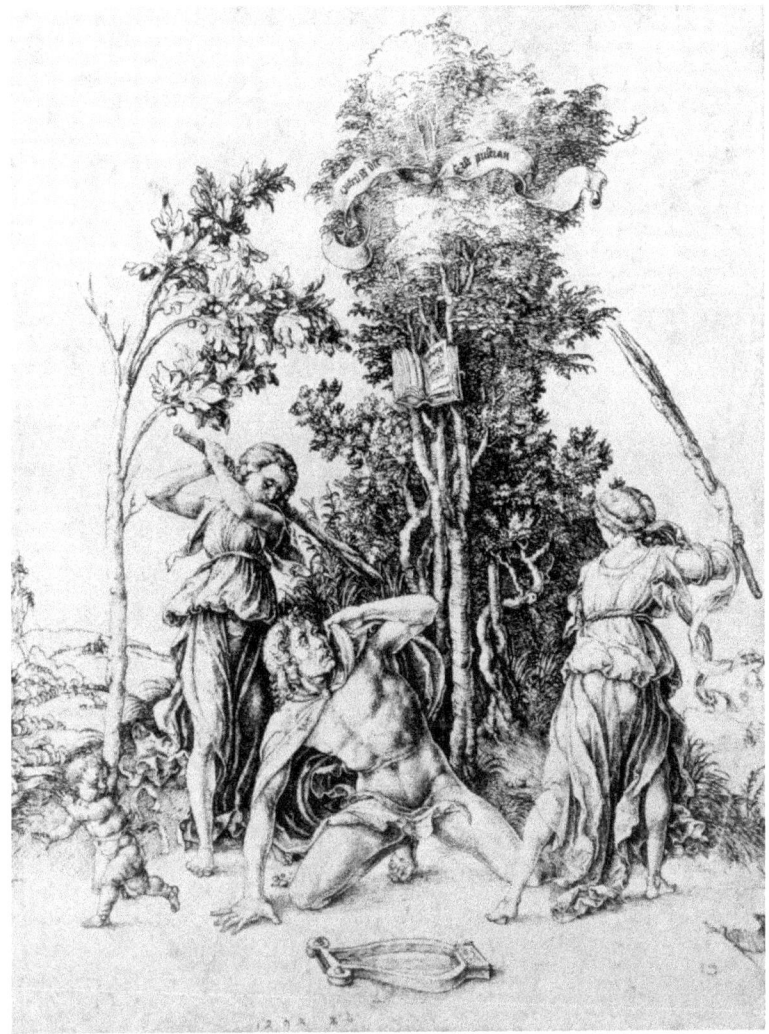

Figure 9 Albrecht Dürer, *Death of Orpheus*, 1494

Riegl. By disrupting art-historical periodisation, *Nachleben* displaces the arbitrary constraints imposed by a strict linear chronology. Furthermore, what is at stake here in *Nachleben* brings Warburg into direct dialogue with Hegel: 'The concept of *Nachleben*, as Warburg understands it, therefore, is linked to a whole theory of history; it is

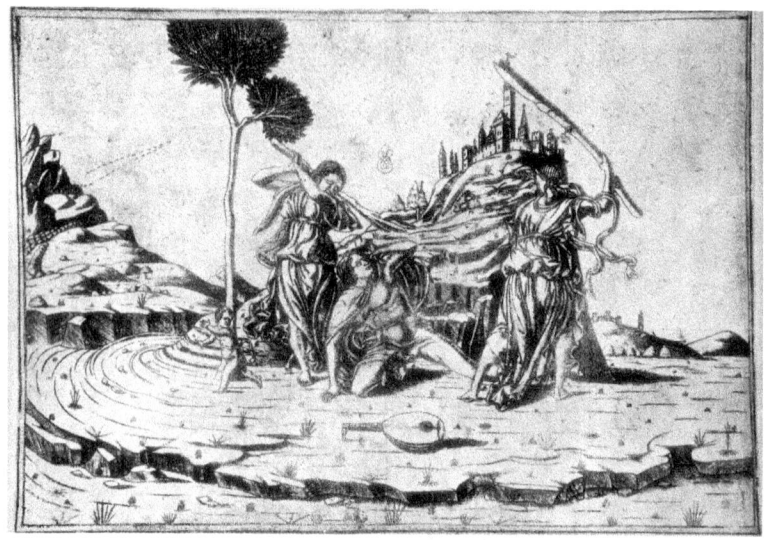

Figure 10   Anonymous, Northern Italian, *Death of Orpheus, c.* 1470–80

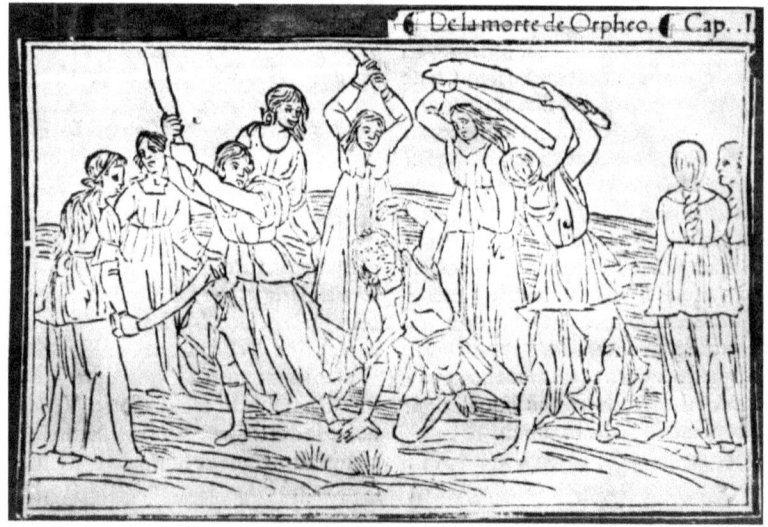

Figure 11   Anonymous, Venice, *Death of Orpheus*, 1497. Woodcut from Ovid, *Metamorphoses*

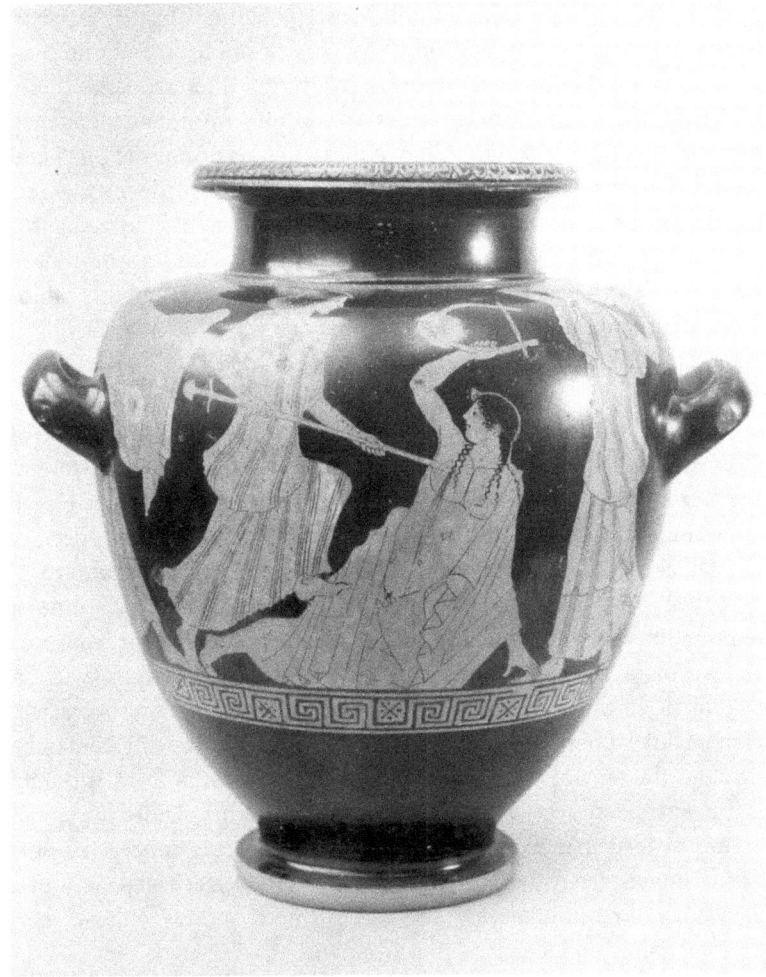

Figure 12 Anonymous, *Death of Orpheus*, detail of vase from Nola, *c.* 475–50 BC

with respect to Hegelianism that we must ultimately take the measure of such a concept and judge it.'[57]

Nachleben and *Pathosformel* have relevance in every sphere of Didi-Huberman's thought. Didi-Huberman argues that Warburg 'decomposed, surreptitiously deconstructs all the epistemological models employed in Vasarian and Winckelmannian history of art'.[58] Images no longer can be accounted for in terms of technical improvement, but 'survive' as anachronisms. Warburg's interest in the transhistorical behaviour of images frees art's history from its dependency on Vasari's cyclical metaphors and Winckelmann's notions of birth and rebirth. Furthermore, *Nachleben* and *Pathosformel* provide the theoretical departure points for exhibitions Didi-Huberman has curated, most notably *Atlas: How to Carry the World on One's Back?* at the Museo Nacional Centro de Arte Reina Sofía in Madrid in 2011.[59] In this exhibition, Didi-Huberman examined the various ways the atlas has been taken up as an ongoing concern in contemporary art.

It is my assertion that Didi-Huberman accentuates certain strains in Warburg's thinking that are complementary to his own critique of German art history and its commitment to idealism, positivism and the Hegelian dialectic. Underscoring Warburg's departure from Hegel, Didi-Huberman draws him in the direction of Nietzsche, specifically Gilles Deleuze's reading of the eternal return first introduced in *Nietzsche and Philosophy*. At stake for Didi-Huberman is a mode of temporality that is not linear or constant. The resurgence or reappearance of ancient gestures cannot be explained as a form of appropriation or rebirth. In the resurgence of the gesture, something *new* is created. Here, Didi-Huberman reads Warburg's relationship with Nietzsche through the lens of Deleuze. The migration of motifs from antiquity is not considered by Warburg in imitative terms. Didi-Huberman argues instead that 'Warburg developed all his ideas concerning surviving images from the perspective – again a Nietzschean one – of a genealogy of resemblances.'[60] This was distinctly at odds with a disciplinary emphasis on technical improvement.

To understand my claim further, it is necessary to quickly recap key operative terms in Deleuze's vocabulary: difference and repetition. Importantly, Deleuze does not approach the terms as they have traditionally been understood. The question that Deleuze asks throughout his 1968 text *Difference and Repetition* is what makes difference possible? How can difference be grasped other than subordination to the same? If difference has typically been defined as difference to and from the same, it has therefore been subordinated to identity, recognition, analogy and imitation. How, then, can difference be imagined not as the other to or opposed to? Repetition is important here for unlocking Deleuze's reformulation of difference, as it does not equate to equivalence or sameness. Instead, repetition is best appreciated in terms of the production of something new. Repetition is therefore not produced through identity and recognition, but difference. This is Deleuze's departure from conventional understandings of representation. Repetition does not seek to emulate original Platonic forms, or engage in the endless production of copies. No longer imitative, repetition becomes generative.

The notion of repetition as generative and affirmative is drawn from Deleuze's reading of Nietzsche's doctrine of eternal return with its emphasis on movement, change and alteration. As Deleuze observes in *Nietzsche and Philosophy*, the eternal return for Nietzsche was not linked to the repetition of the same, but on the contrary, marked a slippage or even a mutation. Contra Hegel, difference, in Nietzsche's hands, is affirming, and is 'opposed to the dialectical "no"; affirmation to dialectical negation'.[61] In other words, the eternal return is the recurrence of difference, of difference in itself. Once repetition is freed from the strictures of imitation, it becomes productive. Accentuating Warburg's proximity to Nietzsche, the resurgence or reappearance of *Pathosformel* is more than a straightforward imitation or appropriation: in the repetition of the gesture, something new and powerful is created. Moreover, there is a certain 'selective character' that Deleuze detects in the behaviour of Nietzsche's eternal return: 'Only the extreme forms return – those which, large or small, are deployed within the limit and extend to the limit of their power'.[62] The eternal return signals not simply a return of the same, but an amplification and affirmation. The intensification of the return is something Warburg himself commented on in his discussion of emotive gestural forms. In a 1914 text he described the influence of antiquity on Renaissance art that 'led to an idealized style of *intensified* mobility'.[63]

Montage

Critical to Didi-Huberman's critique of linear time is montage. Didi-Huberman's utilisation of montage is extremely broad. More than a cinematic editing technique, montage is understood as a mode of epistemological disturbance. With its capacity to disrupt chronological narrative, montage serves to disperse and fragment, only to be reassembled in an infinitely varied number of ways. To develop this line of thought, Didi-Huberman turns to some of the great avant-garde montage projects of the early twentieth century: Walter Benjamin's *The Arcades Project* (1927–40) and Aby Warburg's *Mnemosyne Atlas* (1925–29). For Benjamin, montage was conceived as a means of disrupting a totalising and idealist understanding of history. Warburg's *Mnemosyne Atlas* gave physical form to *Nachleben* and the survival of images through the ages. Both projects remained incomplete at the time of the authors' deaths.

Didi-Huberman's retrieval of these montage projects is deeply indebted to cinema, specifically Deleuze's account of time in *The Time-Image*. Deleuze famously argued that time is freed from its subordination to movement in post-war European cinema. In a footnote in the opening pages of *Devant le temps*, Didi-Huberman declares his debt to Deleuze, arguing that it is necessary to understand the text as 'd'un hommage rendu à l'image-temps deleuzienne'[64] ('a tribute paid to the Deleuzian time-image'). Deleuze examines temporal structures that do not conform to linear past-present-future configurations. The movement-image is akin to a Hegelian logic and a chronological formulation of history. The time-image, however, is Nietzschean. In the transition from movement-image to time-image, Deleuze describes the pivotal role assigned to the cinematic technique of aberrant movement. The linear narrative maintained by the movement image was gradually replaced by the disjointed and discontinuous temporality of the 'aberrant movement'. Deleuze writes, 'What aberrant movement reveals is time as everything, as "infinite opening", as anteriority over all normal movement defined by motivity.'[65] Akin to historians' treatment of anachronism, aberrant movements 'were recognized, but warded off'.[66] The aberrant movement allowed time to decouple itself from movement. Drawing on Shakespeare's celebrated anachronism in *Hamlet*, Deleuze underscored aberrant movement's anachronistic behaviour, observing, ' "Time is out of joint": it is off the hinges assigned to it by behaviour in the world, but also by movements of the world. It is no longer time that depends on movement; it is aberrant movement that depends on time.'[67] Time is now anterior, preceding movement. Unimpeded from its chronological dependency on movement, the image is now anachronistic, discontinuous and a rupture in the temporal order. Didi-Huberman draws an analogy between the symptom and 'aberrant movement':

C'est ce que Gilles Deleuze, sur le plan philosophique, a fortement indiqué lorsqu'il a introduit la notion d'image-temps dans la double référence au montage et au 'mouvements aberrants' (que je nommerai, pour ma part, le symptôme).[68] This is what Gilles Deleuze, on the philosophical level, strongly indicated when he introduced the notion of time-image in the double reference to montage and to the 'aberrant movements' (which I will call, for my part, the symptom).

With this declaration in mind, Didi-Huberman's decoupling of time and temporality from its subordination to chronological history is a distinctly Deleuzian gesture. Didi-Huberman makes a clear distinction: '*the time of the image is not the time of history*.'[69] Returning to his experience before Fra Angelico's panels, Didi-Huberman argues that the panels are not simply a collision of the contemporary and the past, but a montage of heterogeneous temporalities. Standing before the panels is not simply looking forward to Jackson Pollock, but simultaneously a retrieval of Pseudo-Dionysius's negative theology stemming from the late fifth and early sixth centuries. This is what Didi-Huberman means when he writes, 'Nous voici bien *devant le pan* comme devant un objet de temps complexe, de temps impur: un extraordinaire *montage de temps hétérogènes formant anachronismes*.'[70] ('Here we are before the *pan* as before an object of complex, impure time: an extraordinary *montage of heterogeneous times forming anachronisms*.') In a similar vein, Deleuze described the plurality of temporalities in his theorisation of time, claiming that 'there is no present which is not haunted by a past and a future, by a past which is not reducible to a former present, by a future which does not consist of a present to come.'[71]

Benjamin's utilisation of montage is given its most complete expression in his monumental *The Arcades Project*. Consisting of more than 900 pages, *The Arcades Project* is a collection of fragmentary aphorisms, historical quotations and Benjamin's own commentary. Built in the early nineteenth century, Paris's arcades were a symbol of modernity and the birth of the bourgeois. Constructed from iron and glass, the arcades were a visible representation of the industrial revolution and were considered the pinnacle of Parisian luxury and culture. Despite this, the arcades had long been in physical decline. By the time of Benjamin's permanent relocation and exile to Paris in 1933, the arcades had become fusty nineteenth-century relics. Benjamin's sources are many and varied as he assembles a dizzying array of diverse fragments stretching from nineteenth-century tourist guides, extracts from Baudelaire's poetry and Haussmann's memoirs. The montage format of *The Arcades Project* provides the reader with an inexhaustible series of combinations and opportunities for potential assembly. As a result, the experience of reading the text is a restless, fragmentary and incomplete one. By rejecting the form of chronological narrative, Benjamin reminds us of the power of montage to reconfigure and reassemble material anew. He described his method as a form of 'literary montage' and elaborated: 'I needn't say anything. Merely show.'[72]

It is from Benjamin's *The Arcades Project* that Didi-Huberman extracts the celebrated passage concerning the 'dialectical image'. Benjamin does not clearly define the term dialectical image and it remains endlessly open to interpretation.[73] Benjamin writes:

> [I]mage is that wherein what has been comes together in a flash with the now to form a constellation. In other words: image is dialectics at a standstill. For while the relation of the present to the past is purely temporal, the relation of what-has-been to the now is dialectical: not temporal in nature but figural <*bildlich*>. Only dialectical images are genuinely historical – that is, not archaic – images.[74]

Importantly, for Benjamin, the past is not inert or immobile, existing independently of the present. Instead, the past constantly reasserts itself in the present. In this passage Benjamin argues that history's 'legibility' should be linked to its concrete, immanent readability. Therefore, the task for the historian was to 'carry over the principle of montage into history'.[75] The past becomes readable and therefore knowable when singularities appear, not engulfed in the homogenising structures of the vast universalism of orthodox materialism.

Didi-Huberman divides the term into two: 'Dialectical' because Benjamin searched for a temporal model that could take contradictions into account, never to appease or tame them, but to 'retenir de Hegel la puissance prodigieuse du négative, et rejeter de Hegel la synthèse réconciliatrice de l'Esprit'[76] ('retain from Hegel the prodigious power of the negative and to reject from Hegel the reconciling synthesis of the Spirit'). Benjamin proposed a flexible and open, non-axiomatic use of the dialectic. 'Image' because the image is different from a picture or a figurative illustration. The image is a crystal of time, a collision between the 'Now' and that 'what-has-been'. The temporal relationship here is not linear or causally implicit in the continuum between the present and the past, but a collision, 'an image that emerges suddenly, in a flash'.[77] The dialectical image disrupts the progression of the dialectic. It is the site of collision, an interruption in the predetermination of history's teleology.

In sum, Didi-Huberman's symptomatic negotiation of time and history reflects an ongoing engagement with the epistemological foundations of the discipline. His theorisation of the symptom illustrates a deep commitment to proposing new and alternative models of temporality for a discipline that can no longer be justified by a Hegelian teleology. Furthermore, the symptom reflects his ongoing commitment to the dominant strains of recent French intellectual history. In line with the previous generation, Didi-Huberman responds to the general rejection of Hegel and the totalising tendencies attributed to the dialectic. To do this, he carefully draws on Walter Benjamin's and Aby Warburg's 'theoretical tools'[78] to develop a critique of art history's historicity. This understanding of anachronism is sustained by a dual mode of temporality. The first is the utilisation of montage and its capacity to cut and reconfigure history. The second is a Deleuzian reading of Warburg's *Nachleben* as a ghostlike temporality of eternal return. Both contribute to an understanding of art's history that is necessarily impure and traversed by a multiplicity of possible histories. Just as the symptom problematises representation, it also serves to disrupt chronological history, rendering it impossible to think of history without its anachronistic counter rhythm. The symptom demands that history is reconsidered from the angle of its own unconscious: as a series of repressed delays, disruptions and anachronisms.

Notes

1 Didi-Huberman, *Devant le temps*, 9.
2 *Ibid.*, 13.
3 *Ibid.*
4 *Ibid.*, 23.
5 *Ibid.*, 22.
6 *Ibid.*, 13.
7 Lucien Febvre, *The Problem of Unbelief in the Sixteenth Century: The Religion of Rabelais*, trans. Beatrice Gottlieb (Cambridge, MA: Harvard University Press, 1985), 5.

8   O. Dumoulin, 'Anachronisme', in A. Burguière (ed.), *Dictionnaire des sciences historiques* (Paris: Presses Universitaires de France, 1986), 34.

9   Erwin Panofsky, 'The History of Art as a Humanistic Discipline', in *Meaning in the Visual Arts* (Harmondsworth: Penguin Books, 1970), 48.

10   Didi-Huberman, *Devant le temps*, 17. Later, Didi-Huberman reinforced this point: 'L'histoire n'est pas exactement la science du passé parce que le "passé exact" n'existe pas.' 36. ('History is not exactly the science of the past, because the "exact past" does not exist.')

11   Jacques Rancière, 'Le concept d'anachronisme et la vérité de l'historien', *L'Inactuel*, 6 (1996), 67.

12   Nicole Loraux, 'Éloge de l'anachronisme en histoire', *Le Genre Humain*, 27 (1993), 27.

13   On Hegel's persuasive influence on the discipline of art history, see E. H. Gombrich, 'The Father of Art History', in *Tributes: Interpreters of Our Cultural Tradition* (Oxford: Phaidon, 1984), 51–69; Holly, *Panofsky and the Foundations of Art History*, 27–30; Keith Moxey, 'Art History's Hegelian Unconscious', in Mark A. Cheetham, Michael Ann Holly and Keith P. F. Moxey (eds), *The Subjects of Art History: Historical Objects in Contemporary Perspectives* (Cambridge: Cambridge University Press, 1998), 25–51.

14   Didi-Huberman, *The Surviving Image*, 4.

15   G. W. F. Hegel, *Lectures on the Philosophy of History*, trans. J. Sibree (London: Bell, 1878), 26.

16   Clement Greenberg, 'Modernist Painting', in Gregory Battcock (ed.), *The New Art: A Critical Anthology* (New York: Dutton, 1973), 75.

17   Michael Fried, *Art and Objecthood: Essays and Reviews* (Chicago: University of Chicago Press, 1998), 217.

18   Rosalind Krauss, 'A View on Modernism', in *Perpetual Inventory* (Cambridge, MA: MIT Press, 2013), 122.

19   Christine Ross, *The Past is the Present, It's the Future Too: The Temporal Turn in Contemporary Art* (New York: Bloomsbury, 2012).

20   Mieke Bal, *Quoting Caravaggio: Contemporary Art, Preposterous History* (Chicago: University of Chicago Press, 1999); Moxey, *Visual Time*; Nagel and Wood, *Anachronic Renaissance*.

21   Terry Smith, *What is Contemporary Art?* (Chicago: University of Chicago Press, 2012), 6. My emphasis.

22   Georges Didi-Huberman, *Sur le fil* (Paris: Les Éditions de Minuit, 2013), 13. Didi-Huberman is referring to Hal Foster, Yve-Alain Bois, Rosalind Krauss, Benjamin H. D. Buchloh and David Joselit, *Art since 1900: Modernism, Antimodernism, Postmodernism* (London and New York: Thames and Hudson, 2004).

23   Foucault, *The Archaeology of Knowledge*, 4.

24 *Ibid.*, 8.
25 Didi-Huberman, 'Image, matière: immanence', 96–7.
26 Vincent Descombes, *Modern French Philosophy*, trans. L. Scott-Fox and J. M. Harding (Cambridge: Cambridge University Press, 1980), 10.
27 Michel Foucault, *The Archaeology of Knowledge; and The Discourse on Language*, trans. A. M. Sheridan Smith (New York: Pantheon Books, 1972), 235.
28 Bruce Baugh, *French Hegel: From Surrealism to Postmodernism* (New York: Routledge, 2003), 5–6.
29 Didi-Huberman, *The Surviving Image*, 175.
30 Sigmund Freud, 'The Development of Symptoms', in *A General Introduction to Psychoanalysis*, trans. G. Stanley Hall (New York: Horace Liveright, 1920), 311–12.
31 *Ibid.*, 313.
32 Didi-Huberman, *The Surviving Image*, 192.
33 Didi-Huberman, *Devant le temps*, 43.
34 Jacques Derrida, 'From Restricted to General Economy: A Hegelianism without Reserve', in *Writing and Difference*, trans. Alan Bass (London and New York: Routledge, 1978), 317–50.
35 Walter Benjamin, *The Origin of German Tragic Drama*, trans. John Osborne (London: Verso, 1998), 45. My emphasis.
36 Didi-Huberman, *Devant le temps*, 83.
37 Jacques Derrida, 'Différance', in *Margins of Philosophy*, trans. Alan Bass (Chicago: University of Chicago Press, 1982), 11.
38 *Ibid.*
39 Didi-Huberman, *Ce que nous voyons*, 127.
40 Didi-Huberman, *Devant le temps*, 40.
41 The literature discussing the relationship between Benjamin and Proust is vast. See, for example, Krista R. Greffrath, 'Proust et Benjamin', in Heinz Wismann (ed.), *Walter Benjamin et Paris* (Paris: Les Éditions du Cerf 1986), 113–31; Matthew Rampley, *The Remembrance of Things Past: On Aby M. Warburg and Walter Benjamin* (Wiesbaden: Otto Harrassowitz, 2000); Rainer Rochlitz, 'Walter Benjamin: une dialectique de l'image', *Critique*, 431 (1983), 287–319.
42 Walter Benjamin, 'The Image of Proust', in Hannah Arendt (ed.), *Illuminations*, trans. Harry Zohn (New York: Schocken Books, 2007), 214.
43 *Ibid.*, 208.
44 Walter Benjamin, 'Theses on the Philosophy of History', in Hannah Arendt (ed.), *Illuminations*, trans. Harry Zohn (New York: Schocken Books, 2007), 255.
45 *Ibid.*, 262–3.

46   *Ibid.*, 261.
47   *Ibid.*, 263.
48   Didi-Huberman, *Devant le temps*, 20.
49   *Ibid.*
50   *Ibid.*, 19.
51   See, for example, Rampley, *The Remembrance of Things Past*; Michaud, *Aby Warburg and the Image in Motion*; Christopher D. Johnson, *Memory, Metaphor, and Aby Warburg's Atlas of Images* (Ithaca, NY: Cornell University Press, 2012).
52   Didi-Huberman, *The Surviving Image*, 30. Didi-Huberman's emphasis.
53   Edward B. Tylor, *Primitive Culture: Researches into the Development of Mythology, Philosophy, Religion, Language, Art and Custom*, vol. 1, 3rd US from 2nd UK edn (New York: Henry Holt and Company, 1889), 16.
54   Didi-Huberman, *The Surviving Image*, 27. Didi-Huberman's emphasis.
55   See Aby Warburg, 'Dürer and Italian Antiquity (1905)', in *The Renewal of Pagan Antiquity: Contributions to the Cultural History of the European Renaissance* (Los Angeles: Getty Research Institute for the History of Art and the Humanities, 1999), 553–8.
56   *Ibid.*, 553.
57   Didi-Huberman, *The Surviving Image*, 46.
58   *Ibid.*, 12.
59   Georges Didi-Huberman, *Atlas: How to Carry the World on One's Back?* (Madrid: Museo Nacional Centro de Arte Reina Sofía, 2011).
60   Didi-Huberman, *The Surviving Image*, 106.
61   Gilles Deleuze, *Nietzsche and Philosophy*, trans. Hugh Tomlinson (New York: Bloomsbury, 2006), 9.
62   *Ibid.*, 41.
63   Aby Warburg, 'The Emergence of the Antique as a Stylistic Ideal in Early Renaissance Painting (1914)', in *The Renewal of Pagan Antiquity: Contributions to the Cultural History of the European Renaissance* (Los Angeles: Getty Research Institute for the History of Art and the Humanities, 1999), 271. My emphasis.
64   Didi-Huberman, *Devant le temps*, 25–6, n. 31.
65   Gilles Deleuze, *Cinema 2: The Time-Image*, trans. Hugh Tomlinson and Robert Galeta (London and New York: Continuum, 1989), 36.
66   *Ibid.*, 38.
67   *Ibid.*, 39.
68   Didi-Huberman, *Devant le temps*, 25.
69   Didi-Huberman, *The Surviving Image*, 19. Didi-Huberman's emphasis.
70   Didi-Huberman, *Devant le temps*, 16.
71   Deleuze, *The Time-Image*, 36.

72 Walter Benjamin, *The Arcades Project*, trans. Howard Eiland and Kevin McLaughlin (Cambridge, MA: Belknap Press of Harvard University Press, 1999), 460.

73 In his essay accompanying *The Arcades Project*, Rolf Tiedemann stresses the opacity of the terms *dialectic* and *dialectical image*. He notes, 'Dialectical image and dialectic at the standstill are, without a doubt, the central categories of the *Passagen-Werk*. Their meaning, however, remained iridescent; it never achieved any terminological consistency.' Rolf Tiedemann, 'Dialectics at a Standstill', in Walter Benjamin, *The Arcades Project*, trans. Howard Eiland and Kevin McLaughlin (Cambridge, MA: Belknap Press of Harvard University Press, 1999), 942.

74 Benjamin, *The Arcades Project*, 463.

75 *Ibid.*, 461.

76 Didi-Huberman, *Devant le temps*, 241.

77 Benjamin, *The Arcades Project*, 473.

78 Didi-Huberman, *Devant le temps*, 85.

4

The empreinte

The dual strains of materiality and temporality I have been investigating come to the fore in the exhibition *L'empreinte* (*The Imprint*) held at the Centre Pompidou in 1997. Co-curated with Didier Semin, the exhibition signalled the culmination of ten years of Didi-Huberman's research into the shadowy and neglected status of the *empreinte* in art's history. Challenging its apparent simplicity, Didi-Huberman argued that the *empreinte* performs a '*contre-modèle de la notion d'art*'[1] ('counter model to the idea of art'). The exhibition assembled a diverse assortment of moulds, casts, traces and imprints ranging from Duchamp's *Female Fig Leaf* (1950–51) to Giuseppe Penone's frottages and Rachel Whiteread's negative spaces. The exhibition gave visual form to Didi-Huberman's transhistorical thesis: the practice of imprinting spans both modern and contemporary art. Paradoxically, the *empreinte* is also age-old. Stoically defiant of historical, geographical and cultural categorisations, imprinting reaches back to the ancient memorial practices of death masks, effigies and votive offerings.

The implications of Didi-Huberman's treatment of the *empreinte* have yet to be fully realised in English-language communities due to translation delays.[2] Firstly, let's establish some definitions. What does it mean to make an *empreinte*? Didi-Huberman defines the task of the *empreinte* as to 'produire une marque par la pression d'un corps sur une surface'[3] ('produce a mark by pressing an object onto a surface'). The result is a recessed or embossed mark. It is difficult to gain a direct translation of the French term, *empreinte*, as it is much broader than the English-language equivalent, imprint. Its connotations can incorporate print, impression and trace. Importantly, the *empreinte* suggests both a process and an object. To make an *empreinte*, therefore, is both the mechanical process of imprinting, and the final object, the imprinted image. For this reason, I will retain the original French. Didi-Huberman argues that it is difficult to speak of the *empreinte* in general terms: it spans an array of heterogeneous mediums, from clay, plaster, wax and photography. The *empreinte* is both singular and multiple, origin and its copy, present and absent. Imprinting is both a critical component in the sculptural process, however, and also invisible and disposable. For Didi-Huberman, the *empreinte* is heuristic: unpredictable and unstable, it can yield unexpected results. Finally, the *empreinte* contains a temporal complexity that belies its apparent simplicity. The *empreinte* is anachronistic: as a cast or mould, it simultaneously points towards the past and to a future that is yet to come.

The *empreinte* is indexical because it is the result of a material contact on a surface. It is my contention that Didi-Huberman pulls the *empreinte* in the direction of the Derridean trace, as opposed to the index. This is a deliberate strategy to create distance from Rosalind Krauss's famous two-part article 'Notes on the Index'.[4] Writing from the vantage point of the late 1970s, Krauss was retrospectively activating an alternative to Greenbergian modernism. Marcel Duchamp was credited as the historical point of origin for American artists such as Dennis Oppenheim, Vito Acconci and Gordon Matta-Clark. Didi-Huberman acknowledges Krauss's influence over the field:

> Tressant avec promptitude la notion linguistique d'embrayeur et la catégorie peircienne de l'indice, Rosalind Krauss ouvrait là une perspective remarquable, presque une façon de voir.[5]
> Swiftly weaving together the linguistic notion of the shifter and the Peircian category of the index, Rosalind Krauss opened this remarkable perspective, almost a way of seeing.

For Didi-Huberman, Krauss's reading of Duchamp has placed the index 'sous l'autorité du *paradigme photographique*'[6] ('under the authority of the *photographic paradigm*'). Here, he identifies a latent idealism lurking at the heart of Krauss's evocation of the index. In language strongly reminiscent of his argument advanced in *Confronting Images*, Didi-Huberman maintains that the photographic

> sauvegardait un *sens idéal de l'art*, vu comme la production 'purifiée' d'une sorte de *disegno* lumineux, hors de toute 'cuisine' matérielle, de tout archaïsme technique, de toute désorientation anachronique.[7]

preserved an *ideal sense of art*, seen as the 'purified' production of a kind of luminous *disegno*, distinct from any material 'cooking', of any technical archaism, of any anachronistic disorientation.

By reducing the complexity of the index to something created by light, the material, temporal and transhistorical characteristics are repressed. As I will argue in this chapter, the *empreinte*, understood as a trace, allows Didi-Huberman to tease out the phenomenological, ductile and anachronistic dimensions that the index does not permit. Didi-Huberman seeks to destabilise some of the discipline's governing terms, such as authorship and originality. The *empreinte* must therefore be conceived in terms of his general revision of representation, and is structured along two distinct lines: the first is epistemological, an examination of the discipline's unconscious biases. The second is temporal, allowing Didi-Huberman to develop and explore anachronistic modes of temporality. The *empreinte* is formulated by Didi-Huberman as 'un *malaise dans la représentation*: une "ressemblance-symptôme" … un *malaise dans l'histoire*: un "symptôme-temps" '[8] ('an *uneasiness in representation*: a "resemblance-symptom" … an *uneasiness in history*: a "time-symptom" '). The *empreinte* as a *symptom* is a disturbance to notions of both representation and time.

Simon Hantaï

One possible entry point for teasing out the salient characteristics of the *empreinte* is via Simon Hantaï's practice of *pliage* and its obsessive, repetitive steps of folding, unfolding, refolding and painting. Hungarian-born French painter Hantaï was the subject of Didi-Huberman's 1998 text *L'étoilement: conversation avec Hantaï*, and three of his works were curated in the 1997 exhibition *L'empreinte*. Between 1960 and 1982, Hantaï pursued *pliage*, a technique where he would fold and paint the canvas. The *pli*, or fold, became known as Hantaï's signature method. Hantaï first discovered *pliage* in 1960, after a decade of intense experimentation that included an initial affiliation with the Surrealist circle around André Breton and an early encounter with Jackson Pollock's all-over dripping technique on exhibit in Paris. Over the decades Hantaï experimented with various types of *pliage*, achieving a range of variable results.[9] Starting with an unstretched canvas, Hantaï would crumple, knot, roll or tie the canvas. He would then paint the still-folded canvas, allow it to dry and subsequently unfold. Sometimes, he would repeat the process, refolding to build up the density of the overlapping painterly areas. Hantaï's method was extraordinarily straightforward, almost automatic, and signalled an evacuation of subjectivity. As Didi-Huberman emphasises, 'la patience mécanique, sans affect'[10] ('mechanical patience, without affect'). The subject of Hantaï's *pliage* is the mechanical, repetitive nature of the imprinting process itself.

Hantaï's practice is a powerful example of how versatile the *empreinte* is, and of its ability to cut across genres and mediums. In Hantaï's case, the canvas itself is a mould, an active agent in the imprinting process. Didi-Huberman makes the point that Hantaï's canvas can no longer be thought of in Albertian terms, as a window to the world, but as a *matrice* or mould. Importantly, Hantaï's process of imprinting through folding is wildly erratic. Far from producing predictable results, the procedural, motorised, repetitive aspect of *pliage* paradoxically gives rise to the accidental and the irregular. Didi-Huberman creates an opposition here: against an *axiomatic* or rule-based approach, to make an *empreinte* is a *heuristic* gesture. It is experimental and open. For the artist, it is akin to testing a hypothesis, *to see what happens*. There is always an element of chance and risk, as the outcome is uncertain. Accentuating the heuristic nature of the printing process, the final form is 'invisible' – the work is always the result of the unexpected, unstable and irregular that takes place in the *pliage* process. Consider, for instance, the '*étoilement*' or 'star spray-effect' in Hantaï's *Tabula* series (1973–82).[11] Hantaï created the stars by tying knots at regular intervals along the surface of the canvas. When the canvas was unfolded, a grid was revealed. Each star separating the solid areas of colour was singular and unique, depending on the way the canvas was knotted, and the individual tension of each knot. *Pliage* is necessarily blind, open to random moments of chance that will invariably impact the result. Emphasising this procedural 'blindness', Didi-Huberman writes:

> Hantaï a connu l'expérience de l'aveuglement et il expérimente avec le pliage une sorte d'aveuglement processuel: dès lors que la toile est pliée, ce qui se passe dans le pli échappe au regard du peintre.[12]
>
> Hantaï has known the experience of blindness and with pliage he experiments with a kind of procedural blindness: as soon as the canvas is folded, what happens in the fold escapes the painter's gaze.

The painterly effects created in the fold escaped or even exceeded the gaze of the artist. Hantaï applied the paint to the parts of the canvas that could be seen. The invisible or interior sections remained unpainted. The technique creates an interweaving of positive and negative, visible and invisible, form and *informe*. In this way, Didi-Huberman draws Hantaï close to Derrida and, ultimately, Merleau-Ponty. In *Memoirs of the Blind*, Derrida stressed the interrelation between the visible and the invisible, writing, 'this invisibility would still inhabit the visible, or rather, it would come to haunt it to the point of being confused with it'.[13] No longer binary and oppositional, the link between the visible and invisible becomes an interlacing (*l'entrelac*), a chiasmus. In Didi-Huberman's view, the invisible leaves its trace on the unfolded canvas in a chiasmic intertwining between the seen and the unseen.

Empreinte *as trace, trace as* empreinte

Didi-Huberman's investigation into the *empreinte* returns him to a classic deconstructivist position. The *empreinte* is a test of oppositional logic and puts binaries under pressure: contact with or loss of origin? Authenticity of presence or the loss in its reproducibility? Original or copy? Resemblance or dissemblance? Form or *l'informe*? Artistic decision or chance and accident? Same or other? The *empreinte* is part of Didi-Huberman's broader strategy of displacing the metaphysical foundations of a discipline that remains beholden to a privileging of idealism, presence and origin. He clearly signals his proximity to Derrida when he writes, 'Le vocabulaire de l'empreinte recouvre en grande partie celui de la *trace*'.[14] ('The vocabulary of the *empreinte* covers largely that of the *trace*.') Didi-Huberman does not seek to restore the sensible over the intelligible. He is careful not to consign the *empreinte* to the *other* of the idea and imitation. Instead, he understands the difference between the two terms as chiasmic, an interlacing:

> La *partie* se joue surtout au grand jour, et la *contrepartie* se joue partout aux marges ou dans les interstices: dans les ombres ou dans les contre-jours, dans une visibilité trop offusquée ou trop crue, moins apte au discernement, moins lisible. L'empreinte est la contrepartie nécessaire de l'imitation, comme le contact – le *haptisch*

dont parlait Aloïs Riegl – est la contrepartie nécessaire de toute dimension optique.[15]

The *game* is played mostly in broad daylight, and the *counterpart* is played everywhere at the margins or in the interstices: in the shadows or in the backlit areas, in a visibility too obscured or too raw, less suitable for discernment, less readable. The *empreinte* is the necessary counterpart of imitation, as the contact – the *haptisch* of which Aloïs Riegl spoke – is the necessary counterpart of any optical dimension.

By choosing not to overturn an existing binary with a subordinated term, Didi-Huberman allows for an entwining or cohabitation between the terms. Elsewhere, Didi-Huberman has described this strategy as the 'dual system' (*double regime*) of images: the visible and the *visuel*, the detail and the *pan*, resemblance and dissemblance, form and *informe* and so on.[16] The trace exceeds the metaphysical commitment to the idea and presence. It is neither present nor absent, inside nor outside, before nor after, there nor not there. By emphasising this dual interconnected system, Didi-Huberman resists the temptation simply to reverse the hierarchical binary.

According to Didi-Huberman, the *empreinte*'s marginalisation, with its attendant issues of physical materiality and contact, is the result of a metaphysical idealism underwriting the discipline of art history. As Derrida writes in *Of Grammatology*:

> What the thought of the trace has already taught us is that it could not be simply submitted to the onto-phenomenological question of essence. The trace is *nothing*, it is not an entity, it exceeds the question *What is?* and contingently makes it possible.[17]

Three aspects of Derrida's thinking on the trace are crucial for Didi-Huberman's enquiry into the *empreinte*. Firstly, the trace exists outside the history of metaphysics and is crucial in his reformulation of origins at the heart of this tradition. Derrida writes, 'But a meditation upon the trace should undoubtedly teach us that there is no origin, that is to say simple origin; that the questions of origin carry with them a metaphysics of presence.'[18]

Akin to the trace, the *empreinte* is simultaneously 'there' and not 'there'. The *empreinte* is not absent or present, origin or copy. This ambiguity disrupts a metaphysical understanding of the image that is still assuming unity with its referent. Secondly, echoing the behaviour of Derrida's *supplement*, the trace is not part of Saussure's sign system, but paradoxically the system is dependent on it. Recall Saussure's key insight that signs are not independent entities, but can be understood only by their differences – signs signify via their differences from other signs. Derrida describes this co-dependency of signs on other signs: 'no element can function as a sign without referring to another element which itself is not simply present.'[19] Nothing in this signifying system is entirely absent or present. 'There are only, everywhere, differences and traces of traces.'[20] The trace is a necessary part of the signifying process, but it is a sign system that can no longer claim self-contained unity. The result, or final image, is dependent on the process of printing, casting and moulding. Nevertheless, this process of imprinting remains indiscernible as the trace ensures its own disappearance and invisibility. The trace itself is self-effacing. Derrida describes this hiddenness: 'But the movement of the trace is necessarily occulted, it produces itself as self-occultation.'[21] The process of imprinting thereby ensures its own invisibility. In presenting itself, it becomes effaced. It can never be entirely absent or entirely present.

Finally, like most of Derrida's key terms, there is a temporal aspect at play. The trace exists *before* the sign: 'The trace must be thought before the entity.'[22] This suggests that, for Didi-Huberman, the *empreinte* signals a shift to an anterior, or pre-understanding of the origin. Didi-Huberman turns to classic Derrida and *différance* to emphasise the temporal discontinuity of the *empreinte*, observing: 'La trace comme "devenir-temps de l'espace" s'éclaire dans la notion de *différance*, qui peut être lue elle-même comme une formulation originale de l'anachronisme.'[23] ('The trace as 'becoming-time of space' becomes clear in the notion of *différance*, which can itself be read as an original formulation of anachronism.') The *empreinte* as trace points to anteriority: the cast exists *before* the sculpture, the sculpture is produced *after* the cast has been cast. It is the movement of differance – of differing and deferring – that allows the *empreinte* (Didi-Huberman) or sign (Derrida) to exist. Derrida explicitly links differance and the imprint, writing 'Differance is therefore the formation of form. But it is *on the other hand* the being-imprinted of the imprint.'[24] The *empreinte* is differance. It puts into play an anachronistic understanding of temporality as both differing and deferring.

Against Vasari

As I have discussed in Chapter 1, one of Didi-Huberman's primary ongoing concerns is interrogating the epistemological foundations and the philosophical biases of the discipline. The role of the *empreinte* is a curious blind spot in art's history. This liminal existence provides a fertile case study for investigating what has been concealed and repressed, the 'not-said'[25] that runs counter to the discourse itself. To do this, Didi-Huberman revisits Vasari's *Lives* to examine how a humanist art history developed and maintained its structures of exclusion. Two distinct themes emerge in Didi-Huberman's re-engagement with Vasari's *Lives* through the lens of the *empreinte*. Firstly, we can recognise an ongoing critique of the idealism Didi-Huberman argues continues to underwrite the discipline. Vasari's aesthetic theory was outlined in the opening lines of the 'Life of Giotto'. Vasari observed that all representation is imitative and draws its inspiration from nature, 'whose finest and most beautiful aspects painters are always striving to imitate and reproduce'.[26] Vaguely Platonic, nature provided the model and ideal form for artists to copy, thereby entrenching a model of representation that implicitly informed the discipline well into the twentieth century. Didi-Huberman has consistently maintained that the long-term consequence of Vasari's legacy was the subordination and repression of the image's materiality.

The clue to this idealism is detected in Vasari's use of the word *disegno*. Didi-Huberman argues that Vasari appropriates the term from Cennino Cennini's early fifteenth-century text *The Craftsman's Handbook* and distorts it, severing it from Cennini's intended practical treatment of the term.[27] For Vasari, the idea originated in the artist's mind, and was subsequently executed by the hand. This creates a hierarchical binary, with the idea assuming primacy over the materiality of the actual art work. Vasari's privileging of the intellectual idea can be seen in his descriptive anecdote of Leonardo da Vinci being called to account by the Duke of Milan to explain his slow progress on the *Last Supper* (1495–98). Vasari writes that da Vinci

> explained that men of genius sometimes accomplish most when they work the least; for, he added, they are thinking out inventions and forming in their minds the perfect ideas which they subsequently express and reproduce with their hands.[28]

Furthermore, Vasari could not account for the *empreinte* as it did not fit into his hierarchical schema that separated the liberal from the mechanical arts. Unlike the clearly defined mediums of painting, sculpture and architecture, the *empreinte* spanned a range of diverse and heterogeneous mediums such as death masks, votive offerings, wax portraits, medal making and printmaking practices that defied Vasari's taxonomy. As a result, the *empreinte* was at best paired with the less prestigious mechanical arts. At worst, it was ignored. The *empreinte* did not accord with the idealism privileged by Vasari's humanism. Against the lofty idealism of painting, for instance, casting was relegated to a preparatory stage in the sculptural process. We can detect this sentiment in da Vinci's preference for painting:

> Sculpture is not a science but a very mechanical art, because it causes its executant sweat and bodily fatigue … The sculptor undertakes his work with greater bodily exertion than the painting, and the painter undertakes his work with the greater mental exertion.[29]

The physical exertion of sculpting was no match for the cool intellectualism of painting.

According to Didi-Huberman, the implications for the discipline are long lasting, 'une sorte de refoulement du paradigme de l'empreinte'[30] ('a sort of repression of the paradigm of the *empreinte*'). The mechanical process of imprinting is neglected in favour of the final product. Consider Vasari's opening remarks in the 'Preface' to the *Lives*:

> Now the material in which God worked to fashion the first man was a lump of clay. And this was not without reason; for the Divine Architect of time and of nature, being wholly perfect, wanted to show how to create by a process of removing from and adding to material that was imperfect in the same way that good sculptors and painters do when, by adding and taking away, they bring their rough models and sketches to the final perfection for which they are striving.[31]

As Vasari reminds us, modelling in clay and wax was a preparatory step in the sculptural process, however, this step was never valued in its own right. Vasari's concern with printmaking was limited to print's status as a reproductive medium and recording the *disegno* and *invenzione* of the great painters. For Vasari, it was not possible for a print to be recognised as a work of art in its own right.[32]

Didi-Huberman problematises art history's genealogical origins by turning from Vasari to the *other* 'origin' of the discipline, Pliny the Elder's *Natural History*. Didi-Huberman rereads Pliny against Vasari, teasing out key concepts that he argues Vasari suppressed fifteen centuries later. At the crux of Didi-Huberman's argument is the claim that Vasari remade Pliny in the humanist image of himself. To develop this line of thought, Didi-Huberman performs a close reading of the first fifteen paragraphs of Book 35, paying close attention to some of the more ambiguous strains in Pliny's writing. Pliny's notion of history is not understood in chronological terms. On the topic of the prehistory of art, for example, Pliny himself complicates notions of origins, refusing to nominate an exact geographical origin for painting. Pliny writes, 'The question as to the origin of the art of painting is uncertain and it does not belong to the plan of this work.'[33] Pliny's art had no origin, because resemblance was already *dead*. In paragraph four Pliny writes, 'The painting of portraits, used to transmit through the ages extremely correct likenesses of persons, has entirely gone out.'[34] The history of art begins with its own death-of-art-thesis. This inserts a fertile anachronism into Pliny's account, with Didi-Huberman declaring, 'Le "début de l'histoire de l'art" est donc bien *l'originaire fin*.'[35] ('The "start of the history of art" is the original ending.') This stands at odds with Vasari's theorisation of history, which is triumphant and teleological, culminating in Michelangelo's glory.

Having established Pliny's distance from Vasari's linear formulation of history, Didi-Huberman turns to his other ongoing thematic concern: Vasari's idealism. Against this, he teases out Pliny's materialism. Art was conceptualised by Pliny in accordance with an order of materials. Book 35 is dedicated to an extensive discussion of matter including metals, rocks and gold as 'processes of carving and modelling and dyeing'.[36] Pliny's *Natural History* was encyclopaedic and anthropological, with the aesthetic notion of *artes* being one form of expression amongst many. Finally, in the fourth paragraph of Book 35, Pliny speaks of the *imaginum pictura*, which in English is translated as 'painting of portraits'. Didi-Huberman argues that this translation from the Latin is misleading and the term is better understood as the painting of the *wax moulds* of the faces of deceased family members, or 'ancestors'.[37] In paragraph six Pliny creates a broader context:

In the halls of our ancestors it was otherwise; portraits were the objects displayed to be looked at, not statues by foreign artists, nor bronzes nor marbles, but wax models of faces were set out each on a separate side-board, to furnish likenesses to be carried in procession at a funeral in the clan, and always when some member of it passed away the entire company of the house that existed was present.[38]

The *imago* is formulated by Pliny as an *empreinte*. It is a moulded image produced by direct contact of the face with wax. The *imago* is presented by Pliny as legitimate resemblance. Against this technique of moulding likenesses, Pliny opposed the *luxuria* of the artifice of painted portraits. As a result, Pliny writes: 'nobody's likeness lives and they leave behind them portraits that represent their money, not themselves'.[39] The *empreinte* is understood by Pliny in juridical and genealogical terms and as either just or unjust, legal or illegal. This is distinctly at odds with Vasari's aesthetic judgements of good and bad painting.[40]

On the liminal status of wax

Vasari elevated his concepts of the *idea* and *disegno* as artistically superior to the mechanical reproductive techniques of casting and imprinting. This is not to say Vasari was entirely quiet on the subject of the *empreinte*. On the topic of wax votives, for instance, Vasari discussed the Florentine practice of votive offerings that were 'crudely fashioned in wax'.[41] In a passage in the *Lives* Vasari described in some detail Andrea del Verrocchio's study of wax under the expert tutelage of master craftsman Orsino. Together, they were responsible for the three life-size wax figures of Lorenzo de Medici. Vasari described the result as 'wonderfully attractive and lifelike', remarking that the figures 'seemed real and alive'.[42] Nevertheless, Vasari maintains a clear and hierarchical distinction between Orsino as *fallimagini* or 'image maker' and the preeminence of Verrocchio's *disegno*.

Didi-Huberman identifies a deeply ambivalent attitude towards the *empreinte*. On one hand, he argues that it drove many of the extraordinary technical achievements of the Renaissance: the *empreinte* propelled new print media techniques of engraving and woodcut printing practices, the refinement of sculpture and the revival of commemorative medal-making by practitioners such as Pisanello. Despite this, the *empreinte* was beleaguered by its materiality. Didi-Huberman writes:

> La forme obtenue par empreinte fait obstacle à la notion, à l'idéal de l'art, en ce qu'elle procède trop directement d'une matière déjà existante, et pas assez de cette *idea* si chère à la théorie classique de l'art. À la fois 'empruntée' (prélevée) et 'empreintée' (physiquement marquée), *elle passe directement de matière à matière.* Pour exister, elle n'a nul besoin de se 'former' dans l'esprit de l'artiste.[43]

The shape obtained by an imprint interferes with the notion, with the ideal of art, by proceeding too directly from something that already exists, and not enough from the *idea* that was so dear to the classical theory of art. Both 'borrowed' (sampled) and 'imprinted' (physically marked), form was transferred directly from matter to matter. To exist, it did not have to be 'formed' in the artist's mind.

This ambivalence is continued well into the twentieth century as art historians have remained mute on the *empreinte* as a *procedure*. The process of casting was viewed a by-product of artistic production, an invisible intermediate series of steps before the final work was produced. The use of wax, for instance, was considered a preliminary, investigative stage before the sculptor took to carving from marble. Rudolf Wittkower, for instance, described Michelangelo's use of wax in the following terms: 'Such models had, as a rule, a dual function: first, they helped to solidify his ideas, and secondly, they could be used for consultation while work on the marble was in progress.'[44]

The materiality of wax provides a fertile case study for investigating art history's general aversion to matter. Despite Vasari's brief comments in the *Lives*, the discipline was silent on the medium of wax until Aby Warburg's extraordinary 1902 essay on fifteenth-century Florentine portraiture.[45] Here, Warburg described the Florentine tradition of placing life-sized wax effigies or votive offerings in the church of Santissima Annunziata. In his essay, Warburg investigated the growing secularisation of the Church by way of a comparison between Giotto's mural in *The Confirmation of the Franciscan Rule* in the Bardi chapel and Domenico Ghirlandaio's treatment of the same subject 160 years later in the Sassetti chapel. Warburg argued that Ghirlandaio's highly realistic inclusion of the patron Francesco Sassetti and his family into the scene must be understood as an effigy and was motivated by the desire to offer a votive gift to the Divine by way of extreme realism. Warburg maintains that Ghirlandaio expands the conventionally modest understanding of the status of the patron's portrait and instead Sassetti 'coolly assume[s] the privilege of free access to the sacred narrative, as onlookers or even as participants in the action'.[46] Extraordinarily, Warburg observed that the pagan practice of offering wax effigies (*voti*) was endorsed by the Church and continued until the seventeenth century at Santissima Annunziata.

The essay is a poignant reminder of Warburg's interest in a broader, anthropological understanding of images. Importantly, for Didi-Huberman, Warburg introduces a temporal impurity that undermines the teleological development of Renaissance portraiture. Didi-Huberman contends that Warburg's account introduces 'une impureté justement liée aux procédures de l'empreinte'[47] ('an impurity rightly linked to the procedures of the *empreinte*'). As we have seen in Chapter 3, Warburg proposed a modality of temporality where the past is in a constant process of re-insertion into the present. The survival of the past is understood as an anachronistic disruption to the discourse emphasising Renaissance purity. Wax does not readily fit into available art-historical categories and is therefore omitted from a history of style. As devotional expressions of thanks or prayer, wax votive offerings or ex-votos are anachronistic, 'traversent le temps'[48] ('traverse times'). *Ex-votos* do not 'evolve' or improve. An *ex-voto* of a human ear today is the same as one fashioned 2,000 years ago. Wax necessarily upsets notions of linear progress, putting Hegelian models of temporality under pressure.

The first systematic treatise dedicated to wax was Austrian art historian Julius von Schlosser's *History of Portraiture in Wax* of 1910. In the text, Schlosser distanced itself from Vasari's chronological understanding of time. As he summarises in his conclusion:

> We now take a sceptical attitude toward all teleological inspired assertions and value judgements, whether under the guise of progress in the absolute sense or not, and exclude them from our methodology. Adoption of the primitive notions of 'youth', 'maturity', and 'decay' in relation to art would merely put us back in the days of Vasari, the true propagator of classicist, normative historiography of art.[49]

Schlosser argued that it was impossible to consider wax through the existing aesthetic categories of art and beauty. Schlosser attributes this primarily to wax's *magical* qualities, which immediately puts him at odds with the positivist ambitions of his contemporaries. In his obituary for Schlosser, Ernst Gombrich mentioned his doctoral supervisor's interest in the medium, but dismissed Schlosser's choice of subject as evidence of his quirky research tendencies: 'It is characteristic of his method, that he chose such an odd and out of the way subject as portraiture in wax for one of his profoundest investigations into the questions of naturalism.'[50]

The wax imprint has a long association with an extreme realism. As Pliny the Elder discussed in Book 35 of *Natural History*, wax was used to mould likenesses that were used to line the corridors of the family home. Wax is also iconic, hyperreal even. Like a photograph, it can straddle the components of Peirce's triad – it is both an index and an icon. Wax is the most malleable, but also unstable, of all materials. Wax can be moulded, sculpted and chiselled. Wax can change states, moving between solid and liquid. Wax responds to heat. It moves. It can also be melted down into liquid. Against marble's and bronze's claims to a temporal perpetuity, wax can disappear and deteriorate. Wax is the most ancient of all materials, but simultaneously the most ephemeral, transient and entropic. Wax, more than any other medium, is distinguished by its proximity to human flesh. Wax is incarnational, endowed with a *plasticity* than enables it to change and alter its material state. The 'magic' of contact and resemblance is intertwined in the wax votive as both imprint and image. Beyond iconic and indexical resemblances, Didi-Huberman makes the point that wax resembles via a quality internal to the material itself ('*la ressemblance une qualité interne au matériau*').[51]

Wax's materiality has long engendered suspicion. In a memorable passage towards the end of *Being and Nothingness*, Jean-Paul Sartre described 'A slimy substance like pitch is an aberrant fluid … This fixed instability in the slimy discourages possession.'[52] Ernst Gombrich exhibited a similar distaste directed towards wax: 'The proverbial wax image … often causes us uneasiness because it oversteps the boundary of symbolism.'[53] David Freedberg has observed that the realism of wax stages a confrontation with our fear of the lifelike.[54] More than any other artistic medium, wax is capable of exceeding the constraints of mimesis. The success of mimesis is predicated on the spectator's suspension of disbelief. The spectator is secure knowing that what they are looking at is indeed an artwork, despite how realistic it may indeed be. Wax, however, surpasses this, marking a deep disturbance in the subject–object relationship. This relationship is no longer hierarchical, but threatening, the source of anxiety and perhaps even terror in the spectator. Sartre writes: 'Actually we have here the image of destruction-creation ... Only at the very moment when I believe that I possess it, behold by a curious reversal, it possesses me.'[55]

The excessive materiality of wax is comparable with the *pan* as a material disturbance in the mimetic economy of painting. To return to the case study of Jan Vermeer's *Lacemaker* (1669–70), the red thread swells forward to meet the spectator's gaze, asserting itself aggressively against the mass of dark blue quietly receding into the depths of the picture plane (Figure 6). No longer charged with the role of imitating, the thread dissolved into chaotic loops of paint. Wax goes even further in declaring its own materiality: the materiality of the work *is* the work. The logic of mimesis is predicated on the successful subordination of the material being to the ideal form. Here, however, the materiality of matter is extreme and the source of anxiety.

The material-to-material contact of the *empreinte* follows the structure of Lacan's description of the *point de capiton*, or quilting point. This is the point where the signifier adheres to the signified. Lacan's analogy is drawn from the upholstery practice of keeping the stuffing in place by way of a button. The *point de capiton* is both a prick in the surface of the material, where the needle is inserted, as well as the point where the material adheres and joins. Lacan's metaphor is interesting from a representational perspective: classical mimesis is predicated on the structural impossibility of the sign achieving parity with its referent. The *point de capiton*, however, demands adherence between signifier and signified. This notion of contact is particularly potent for thinking through the realism of the wax *ex-voto*. The signifier is no longer pointing to a signified. Instead, the wax imprint is simultaneously both signifier and signified, the point of contact where body parts, flesh and wax adhere. Moreover, there is a temporal dimension, conjuring the anachronistic capacity of the *empreinte*, as it exists both before and possibly long after the subject. As Lacan writes: 'It's the point of convergence that enables everything that happens in the discourse to be situated retroactively and retrospectively.'[56]

The index as vestige

A distinguishing aspect of the *empreinte* is its indexical nature. The process of imprinting creates a mark or impression on a surface. The index, as defined by Charles Sanders Peirce, stands in contrast to the icon's resemblance and the symbol's conventionality. Didi-Huberman is deliberately seeking to complicate the disciplinary reliance on the Peircean index. What's at stake here is an entire line of thought that has laid claim to the authority of the index and its privileged relationship to the referent. This includes theorists as diverse as André Bazin, Susan Sontag, Roland Barthes and Rosalind Krauss, who each, in their various ways, have sought to examine the causal materiality between an object and its image. Krauss observed that the index is established via its physical relationship to its referent, writing that indexes 'are the marks or traces of a particular cause, and that cause is the thing to which they refer, the object they signify'.[57] Krauss theorises a privileged relationship between index and referent. By drawing an analogy between Duchamp and photography, Krauss evokes the authority of the photograph with its claims to authenticity and truth. Ironically, Krauss's treatment of the index enacts a faith in its authority as an evidential sign. In Derridean terms, we might say that Krauss maintains a commitment to a privileging of presence, truth and origin.

Didi-Huberman's relationship with the index, however, is not as straightforward and he seeks to distance himself from this line of thought and its adherence to the authority of a referent. Didi-Huberman's interest in displacing a Peircean or semiotic formulation of the index may be detected as early as 1984 in his essay 'The Index of the Absent Wound'.[58] Didi-Huberman discusses photographer Secondo Pia's extraordinary 1894 image of the Shroud of Turin and his subsequent revelation that Christ's face was unveiled during the photographic process. Didi-Huberman works to decouple the index's relationship with an origin. What Pia saw in the darkroom was a double displacement, the index of another index. The negative imprint on the photographic plate revealed the previously undetected imprint of Christ in the positive. Pia's photographs are both necessary and constituent of the authorial chain. Didi-Huberman is working here in explicitly Derridean terms, simultaneously evoking the behaviour of the *supplement* and the trace. The supplement *supplements*. It is both essential and indispensable in the logic of the chain of authenticity stretching from image to shroud. Paradoxically, the authenticity of the stain is verified by its lack of mimetic resemblance to Christ's face. It was the authority of the photographic image that verified Christ's body. Without Pia's image, Christ's face would have remained a stain. The objectivity of the photograph, therefore, is both necessary and constitutive in the granting of the authority and status of the shroud as a sacred relic, the cloth that covered the body of Christ.

Pia's photograph is 'proof' of the presence of the originary trace, imprinted by the body of Christ. We also know from Derrida that the trace exceeds a metaphysics of presence. As we have already seen, for Derrida, the trace was decidedly anti-originary.[59] The Derridean trace complicates origins and the physical link back to Christ's body. This is accentuated by Didi-Huberman, who, at the end of the essay, with tongue firmly in cheek, turns to Thomas Aquinas, who, on the subject of Christ's Resurrection, had much to say about His blood being kept on earth as relics:

> All the blood which flowed from Christ's body, belonging as it does to the integrity of human nature, rose again with His body ... but the blood preserved as relics in some churches did not flow from Christ's side, but is said to have flowed from some maltreated image of Christ.[60]

The blood, according to Aquinas, is not from the actual body of Christ, but an *image*, thereby further displacing the imprint's claim to indexical truth. The *empreinte* as index is typically related to touch and contact. Following on from Aquinas, it may also be understood as a form of withdrawal and loss.

Didi-Huberman's discussion of the Shroud of Turin reminds us that the Christian mystery of the Incarnation underpins much of his inquiry into representation. Didi-Huberman works to reinscribe the index from semiotics (Peirce) to the theological-philosophical tradition of Thomas Aquinas. To do this, he reaches back to key passages in Thomas Aquinas's *Summa Theologica*, with particular emphasis on the Latin *vestigum* or vestige. Against the image, which he understood in imitative terms, Aquinas deployed the *vestige*, with all its connotations of the trace and the imprint. Aquinas writes:

> Even though there is some degrees of resemblance to God in all creatures, it is only within the creature endowed with reason that the

resemblance to God is in the form of an image; in all other creatures, it is in the form of a vestige ... the reason for this can be clearly understood if we observe the respective means through which the image and the vestige constitute a representation. For the image, as we have said, represents according to a specific resemblance, whereas the vestige represents in the way an effect represents its cause without attaining a specific resemblance, just as we call the prints left by animals' movements vestiges, or as ashes are called vestiges of the fire, or the desolation of a country is called the vestiges of the enemy army.[61]

Following Aquinas, Didi-Huberman draws two important conclusions: firstly, he makes a distinction between the image and a vestige or trace. Didi-Huberman dialecticises this relationship, creating an oppositional pairing between image and vestige, resemblance and *dissemblance*. If the image is formulated in terms of likeness and resemblance, the vestige is understood as a material cause and effect. The vestige is an effect that reveals the causality of the cause. It does not, however, reveal the form of the cause itself. The vestige instead points to the most Divine aspect, the presence of a hidden God. This remains non-figural as the Divine has no image. Didi-Huberman's recovery of the Thomist vestige signals a clear shift from the semiotic dominance of the Peircian index formulated by Krauss. Didi-Huberman shares with Krauss the notion that the index is a trace record of a material cause. Importantly, however, the vestige signals both the disappearance and the trace of its disappearance.

The index as vestige is understood by Didi-Huberman as a withdrawal. Didi-Huberman's preference for the theological vestige over the semiotic index may be detected in his reading of Fra Angelico's *Noli me tangere* (1438–50) in the San Marco convent. Here, he argues that the small red flowers are unable to maintain their iconicity. Instead, they belong to the order of the vestige. Didi-Huberman describes this slippage: '[W]e had to borrow the category of the index from Peirce's semiotics: the term should be understood here not only as the material remains of a past enigma, its trace, obvious or invisible, but also as the vestige of a *contact*, a blow, a material imprint.'[62] Didi-Huberman goes even further to decouple the vestige from an originary source: 'The word should be understood in the sense of a *symptom*.'[63] From Freud, we know that the symptom is overdetermined, with no single point of origin. By reconceptualising the index in terms of the *vestigum*, the point of origin is displaced. Rather than the presence of an originary object, it is the absence of the Divine, an unknowable and unrepresentable God.

Didi-Huberman's recovery of a strain of medieval theology that has emphasised the formlessness of a God who cannot be represented anticipates an important current in French philosophy: Jean-Luc Nancy's deconstruction of monotheism, with a particular focus on Christianity. As we have seen in Chapter 2, for Nancy, Christianity is a self-evacuating religion, a religion that turns away from itself: God is not present, but absent, having retreated from the world. Unlike the Greek and Roman gods who busied themselves participating in human affairs, the monotheistic gods withdrew. Nancy's thesis is clearly stated in his essay 'The Deconstruction of Monotheism', where God is no longer understood in the world, but has withdrawn. Therefore, God's Divinity is absent. Nancy writes, 'He is a god whose absence in itself creates divinity.'[64] In representational terms, God's kenotic withdrawal reminds us that there is no original model or source of imitation. At the heart of Christianity resides a Divine absence. This is precisely the point of intersection between Didi-Huberman's and Nancy's respective projects. What is at stake here is a retrieval of a strain of medieval theology specifically at odds with Vasari's idealism. To return to the opening lines of Vasari's *Lives*, Vasari writes that God is the 'Divine Architect of time and nature'.[65] By emulating God, human beings strive to attain perfection. Against Vasari and the entire humanist tradition, the image is formulated by Didi-Huberman in negative terms: God is understood by what he is *not*. The *empreinte* as vestige emphasises the effect without assuming a resemblance. As opposed to imitating God, God is understood in terms of his *dissemblance*.

In conclusion, this chapter has traced the dual concerns that have determined Didi-Huberman's writing on the *empreinte*. The first is epistemological, an investigation into what the founding texts of the discipline have omitted and repressed. Didi-Huberman's attentiveness to the material, sensible and sensual aspects of the image is foregrounded against the intellectual idealism inherited from Vasari. A kenotic understanding of images displaces the disciplinary preoccupation with idealism in its humanist and linguistic forms. Didi-Huberman's reactivation of a medieval understanding of images, especially in the work of Thomas Aquinas, is a powerful anachronistic mechanism for displacing period categorisation – the Renaissance, twentieth-century modernism and its postmodern successor are all problematised by the *empreinte* that cuts across such artificial categorisation. Didi-Huberman's proximity to Derrida is given its fullest expression; by undermining notions pertaining to origin, authenticity and truth, the *empreinte* allows Didi-Huberman to critique a discipline implicitly entangled in a metaphysics of presence. Finally, the stage is set for Didi-Huberman's ultimate assault on representation's idealism: to develop an immanent theorisation of the image that exists anterior to thinking and thought itself. In Chapter 6, we will take up Didi-Huberman's treatment of montage as a form of representation that 'thinks', further disrupting the subject–object relationship.

Notes

1 Georges Didi-Huberman, *La ressemblance par contact: archéologie, anachronisme et modernité de l'empreinte* (Paris: Les Éditions de Minuit, 2008), 102. Didi-Huberman's emphasis.

2 At the time of writing, both the exhibition catalogue *L'empreinte* and Éditions de Minuit's 2008 reprint of Didi-Huberman's catalogue essay, *La ressemblance par contact*, remain untranslated. A limited translation of Didi-Huberman's 'Ouverture' in *La ressemblance par contact* is available: see Georges Didi-Huberman, 'Opening Up an Anachronistic Point of View', in Ruth Pelzer-Montada (ed.), *Perspectives on Contemporary Printmaking: Critical Writing Since 1986* (Manchester: Manchester University Press, 2018), 184–95.

3 Didi-Huberman, *La ressemblance par contact*, 27.

4 Rosalind Krauss, 'Notes on the Index', in *The Originality of the Avant-Garde and Other Modernist Myths* (Cambridge, MA: MIT Press, 1985), 196–210.

5 Didi-Huberman, *La ressemblance par contact*, 190. For an analysis of the historical reception of Krauss's treatment of the index in France, see Katia Schneller, 'Sur les traces de Rosalind Krauss: la réception française de la notion d'index, 1977–1990', *Études Photographiques*, 21 (2007), 123–43.

6 Didi-Huberman, *La ressemblance par contact*, 187. Didi-Huberman's emphasis.

7 *Ibid.*, 192.

8 *Ibid.*, 310.

9   For an overview of each of Hantaï's *pliage* periods and styles between 1960 and 1982 see Dominique Fourcade, 'Hantaï, an Exhibition', in *Simon Hantaï* (Paris: Éditions du Centre Pompidou 2013), 19–186.

10   Georges Didi-Huberman, *Létoilement: conversation avec Hantaï* (Paris: Les Éditions de Minuit, 1998), 45.

11   *Étoilement*, or 'starring', is Didi-Huberman's neologism.

12   Didi-Huberman, *Létoilement*, 15.

13   Jacques Derrida, *Memoirs of the Blind: The Self-Portrait and Other Ruins*, trans. Pascale-Anne Brault and Michael Naas (Chicago: University of Chicago Press, 1993), 51.

14   Didi-Huberman, *La ressemblance par contact*, 314.

15   *Ibid.*, 61.

16   Didi-Huberman, *Images in Spite of All*, 79.

17   Derrida, *Of Grammatology*, 75.

18   *Ibid.*, 74.

19   Jacques Derrida, *Positions*, trans. Alan Bass (London: Athlone Press, 1987), 26.

20   *Ibid.*

21   *Ibid.*, 47.

22   *Ibid.*

23   Didi-Huberman, *La ressemblance par contact*, 314.

24   Derrida, *Of Grammatology*, 63. Derrida's emphasis.

25   The term is Michel Foucault's. Foucault writes, 'this "not-said" is a hollow that undermines from within all that is said'. Foucault, *The Archaeology of Knowledge*, 25.

26   Vasari, *Lives*, vol. 1, 57.

27   See Didi-Huberman, *La ressemblance par contact*, 97–8; Cennino d'Andrea Cennini, *The Craftsman's Handbook*, trans. Daniel V. Thompson (New York: Dover Publications, 1954).

28   Vasari, *Lives*, vol. 1, 262–3.

29   Leonardo da Vinci, *Leonardo on Painting: An Anthology of Writings by Leonardo da Vinci, with a Selection of Documents Relating to His Career as an Artist* (New Haven, CT and London: Yale University Press, 1989), 38.

30   Didi-Huberman, *La ressemblance par contact*, 94.

31   Vasari, *Lives*, vol. 1, 25.

32   David Landau and Peter Parshall, *The Renaissance Print: 1470–1550* (New Haven, CT and London: Yale University Press, 1994), 103. Also see David Landau, 'Vasari, Prints and Prejudice', *Oxford Art Journal*, 6:1 (1983), 3–10.

33   Pliny the Elder, *Natural History*, trans. H. Rackham, vol. 35 (Cambridge, MA: Harvard University Press, 1952), 15.

34   *Ibid.*, 4.

35 Didi-Huberman, *La ressemblance par contact*, 65.
36 Pliny the Elder, *Natural History*, vol. 35, 1.
37 Georges Didi-Huberman, '"Imaginum pictura ... in totum exoleuit": début de l'histoire de l'art et fin de l'époque de l'image', *Critique* 52:586 (1996), 138–50. On the political function of the Roman ancestor masks, see Harriet I. Flower, *Ancestor Masks and Aristocratic Power in Roman Culture* (Oxford: Clarendon Press, 1996).
38 Pliny the Elder, *Natural History*, vol. 35, 6.
39 *Ibid.*, 5.
40 On the juridical and genealogical role of the *imago* in Pliny's *Natural History*, see Georges Didi-Huberman, 'The Molding Image: Genealogy and the Truth of Resemblance in Pliny's *Natural History*, Book 35, 1-7', in Costas Douzinas and Lynda Nead (eds), *Law and the Image: The Authority of Art and the Aesthetics of Law* (Chicago: University of Chicago Press, 1999), 71–88.
41 Vasari, *Lives*, vol. 1, 239.
42 *Ibid.*, 239–40.
43 Didi-Huberman, *La ressemblance par contact*, 121.
44 Rudolf Wittkower, *The Sculptor's Workshop: Tradition and Theory from the Renaissance to the Present* (Glasgow: University of Glasgow Press, 1974), 8.
45 See Aby Warburg, 'The Art of Portraiture and the Florentine Bourgeoisie (1902)', in *The Renewal of Pagan Antiquity: Contributions to the Cultural History of the European Renaissance* (Los Angeles: Getty Research Institute for the History of Art and the Humanities, 1999), 185–221.
46 *Ibid.*, 188.
47 Didi-Huberman, *La ressemblance par contact*, 13.
48 Georges Didi-Huberman, *Ex-voto: image, organe, temps* (Paris: Bayard, 2006), 7; Georges Didi-Huberman, 'Ex-Voto: Image, Organ, Time', *L'Esprit Créateur*, 47:3 (2007), 7–16.
49 Julius von Schlosser, 'History of Portraiture in Wax', in *Ephemeral Bodies: Wax Sculpture and the Human Figure* (Los Angeles: Getty Research Institute, 2008), 302.
50 E. H. Gombrich, 'Julius von Schlosser', *Burlington Magazine for Connoisseurs*, 74:431 (1939), 98–9.
51 Didi-Huberman, *Ex-voto: image, organe, temps*, 75.
52 Jean-Paul Sartre, *Being and Nothingness: An Essay on Phenomenological Ontology*, trans. Hazel E. Barnes (London: Methuen, 1957), 607.
53 E. H. Gombrich, *Art and Illusion: A Study in the Psychology of Pictorial Representation* (London: Phaidon Press, 1960), 60.
54 David Freedberg, *The Power of Images: Studies in the History and Theory of Response* (Chicago: University of Chicago Press, 1989), 221.

55 Sartre, *Being and Nothingness*, 608.
56 Jacques Lacan, *The Seminar of Jacques Lacan, Book III: The Psychoses (1955–1956)*, trans. Russell Grigg, ed. Jacques-Alain Miller (New York: W. W. Norton, 1997), 268.
57 Krauss, 'Notes on the Index', 198.
58 Didi-Huberman, 'The Index of the Absent Wound (Monograph on a Stain)'.
59 Derrida, *Of Grammatology*, 74.
60 Thomas Aquinas, *Summa Theologica*, trans. Fathers of the English Dominican Province (London: Burns & Oates, 1947), III, Q. 54. Art. 3.
61 *Ibid.*, I, Q. 93, Art. 6.
62 Didi-Huberman, *Fra Angelico*, 7.
63 *Ibid.*
64 Jean-Luc Nancy, 'The Deconstruction of Monotheism', in *Dis-Enclosure: The Deconstruction of Christianity*, trans. Bettina Bergo, Gabriel Malenfant and Michael B. Smith (New York: Fordham University Press, 2008), 36.
65 Vasari, *Lives*, vol. 1, 25.

5

Making monsters

In the preface to the 2018 English-language translation of *The Eye of History*, Didi-Huberman recounts how his 2001 analysis of four photographs snatched by an inmate at Auschwitz-Birkenau marked an enormous shift in his own intellectual development. He writes:

> If I have taken the liberty to return, in these introductory words, to an almost twenty-year-old study, it is because the photographs by the *Sonderkommando* of Auschwitz-Birkenau represent an extreme example for any notion of visual testimony and its political impact. It is also because it was, for me, a crucial opportunity to examine more explicitly the position that the eyes of an ethical subject (even in the depths of sadness) and then the images themselves (even in their most improbably viability) are capable of adopting, in spite of everything, *in front of history*.[1]

Didi-Huberman was reflecting on a catalogue essay, 'Images malgré tout', that he wrote in 2001 to accompany a photographic exhibition, *Mémoire des camps*, held at the Hôtel de Sully in Paris. In the essay, Didi-Huberman phenomenologically reconstructed the movements of a Greek Jew called 'Alex', as he surreptitiously photographed the open pyres where the bodies burned.[2] The first two photographs were taken inside the gas chambers of members of the *Sonderkommando* managing the task of burning the bodies in outdoor funeral pyres. The first is taken hiding inside the gas chamber in Crematorium V and is blurry, slightly out of focus (Figure 13). The second image is clearer, as if the photographer momentarily forgot the extreme danger he had placed himself in (Figure 14).

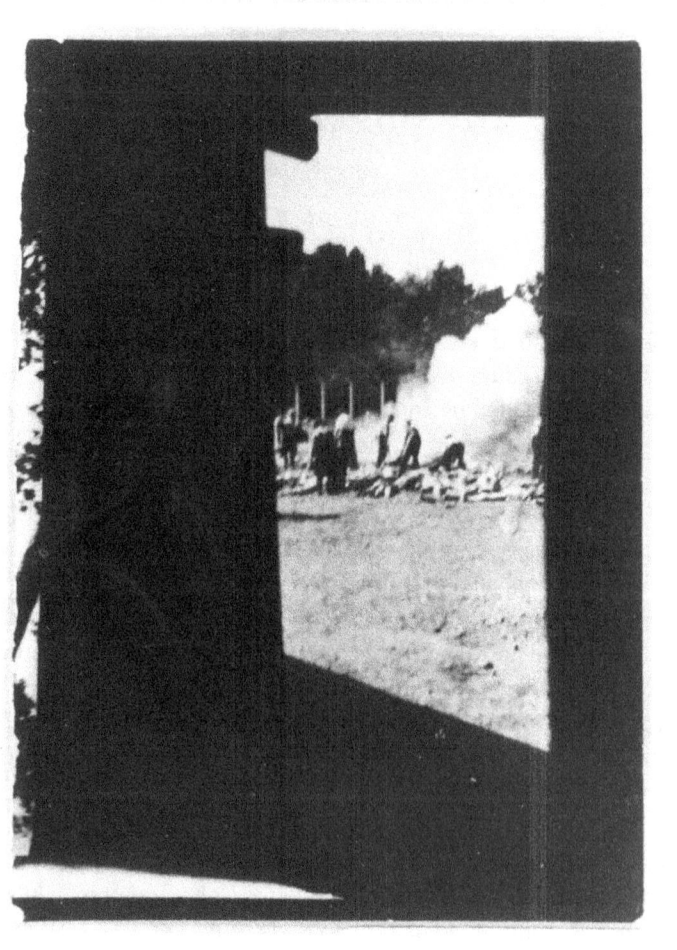

Figure 13 Anonymous (member of the *Sonderkommando* of Auschwitz), *Cremation of Gassed Bodies in Open-Air Incineration Pits, in Front of the Gas Chamber of Crematorium V in Auschwitz,* August 1944

The next two images proved increasingly difficult to take. Having left the relative safety of the gas chambers, the photographer 'snatches' the images, without having the time to focus the camera's lens. In the third

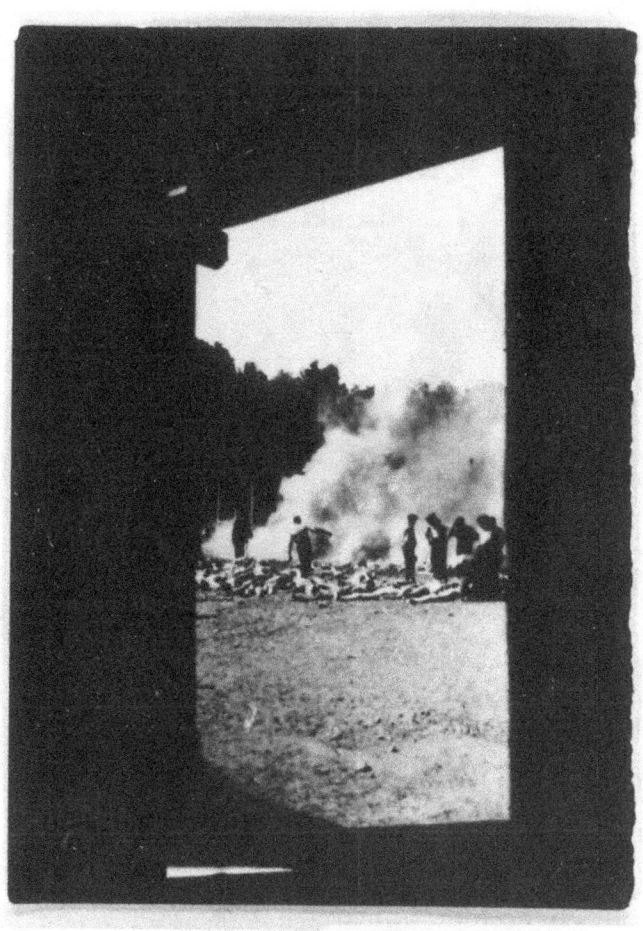

Figure 14 Anonymous (member of the *Sonderkommando* of Auschwitz), *Cremation of Gassed Bodies in Open-Air Incineration Pits, in Front of the Gas Chamber of Crematorium V in Auschwitz*, August 1944

image in the sequence, it is possible to detect a group of women walking, truncated by the birch trees (Figure 15). The final image is completely abstract (Figure 16). These are the only existing photographs taken

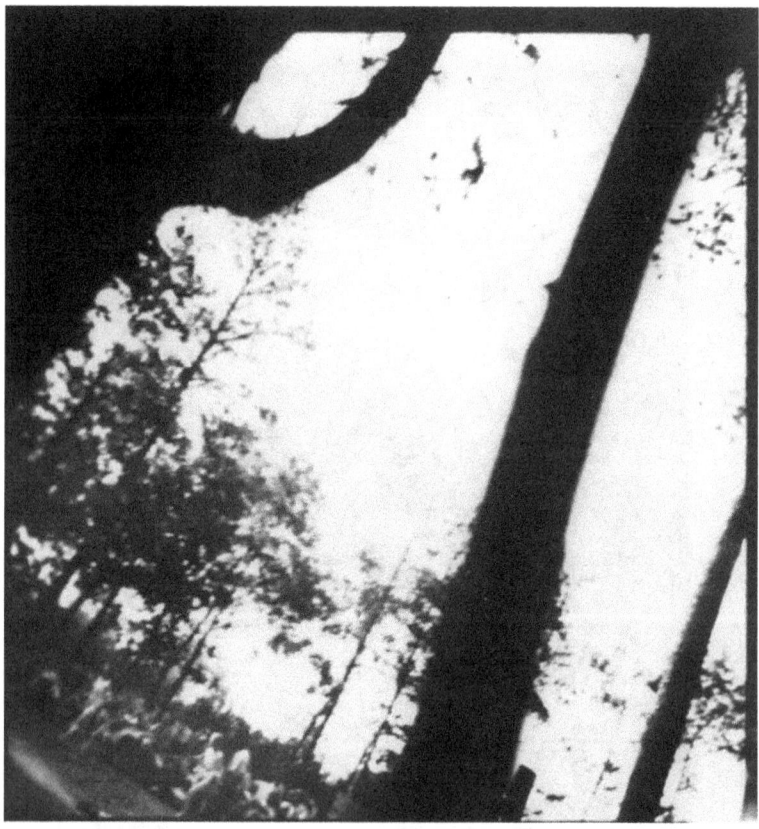

Figure 15 Anonymous (member of the *Sonderkommando* of Auschwitz), *Women Pushed towards the Gas Chamber of Crematorium V in Auschwitz*, August 1944

from inside the gas chambers documenting the procedure of mass extermination. The images exist, in spite of all attempts by the SS to eliminate all records.

There is a vast corpus of archival Holocaust photographs available. What makes these photographs unique, however, is they are the only ones that document the mechanics of mass extermination inside the concentration camp Auschwitz-Birkenau. The film was smuggled out of the camps in a tube of toothpaste, and eventually reached the Polish resistance. Despite operating in an impossible situation, the inmate maintained the belief that these images could provide visual proof of the existence of

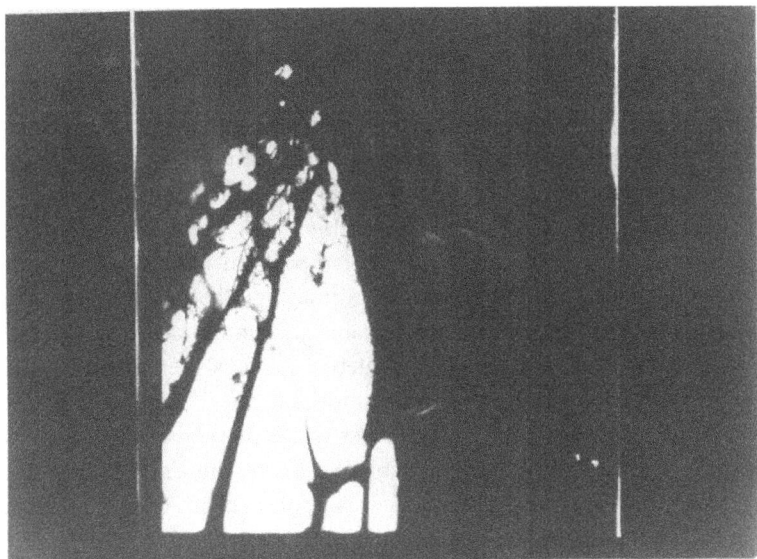

Figure 16 Anonymous (member of the *Sonderkommando* of Auschwitz), August 1944

the gas chambers. Awkwardly framed, blurry and out of focus, the four photographs are testimony produced within the event itself.

They were secretly shot by shadowy figures in the history of Auschwitz-Birkenau, the euphemistically named 'Special Squads' or *Sonderkommando*, groups of mainly Jewish prisoners charged with the day-to-day running of the crematoria. Their task was to maintain order amongst new arrivals, usher the prisoners into the changing rooms and gas chambers and deliver the bodies to the crematoria or the open cremating pyres. Later, they were to sort through their possessions, including separating the prisoners' valuables, gold teeth and jewellery. They also disposed of the human ashes as landfill or into the river, before the process was repeated.[3] For Auschwitz survivor Primo Levi, when writing on the subject of the *Sonderkommando*, the task assigned to history was therefore ethical: 'One is tempted to turn away with a grimace and close one's mind: this is a temptation one must resist.'[4]

Didi-Huberman's *Images malgré tout* was significant for several reasons. The text reflected a shift in the discourse of Holocaust unrepresentability that has dominated French intellectual thought since the 1980s. This is a line of thought that can be traced from Theodor Adorno's oft-cited warning not to write lyric poetry after Auschwitz, through to Jean-François Lyotard's reading of the Kantian sublime. Lyotard famously compared the attempt to exterminate the Jews to an earthquake that exceeds the tools used to measure its impact.[5] More recently, philosophers such as Giorgio Agamben, Jean-Luc Nancy and Jacques Rancière have all, in various and interconnected ways, questioned the prohibition of representation.[6] Didi-Huberman's polemical essay questioned the philosophical tradition that has rendered the Holocaust as 'unimaginable', 'unknowable' and 'unthinkable'. Denigrated and derided, images have been treated suspiciously, emphasising the irretrievable gap between representation and the Holocaust. Against this, Didi-Huberman sought to interrogate the claim that there is such a thing as the 'unrepresentable'. Secondly, the English-language translation, *Images in Spite of All*, was published in 2008, expanding Didi-Huberman's reach to a broader, interdisciplinary audience. His arguments have been taken up by Holocaust scholars, photographic historians, film and trauma theorists, subsequently becoming an indispensable touchstone in recent Holocaust research.[7] Finally, the project signalled a significant change of focus, as Didi-Huberman's attention shifted from issues pertaining to Renaissance representation to examining the relationship between images and history that forms the core of the book series 'L'œil de l'histoire'.

The ensuing controversy that played out in the French press and academic journals has been well documented.[8] Didi-Huberman responded to the fierce criticism with the subsequent publication of the text *Images malgré tout* (2003), which included the original catalogue essay, as well as a series of rebuttals to his fiercest critics, Elizabeth Pagnoux and Gérard Wajcman. By choosing to discuss the images, Didi-Huberman was subjected to accusations of fetishism, voyeurism, Holocaust denial and idolatry. Writing for *Les Temps Modernes*, a journal edited by filmmaker Claude Lanzmann, both Pagnoux and Wajcman emphasised the unspeakable, representational nature of the Shoah. Pagnoux accused Didi-Huberman of a certain 'jouissance par l'horreur'.[9] ('pleasure through horror'). Pagnoux argued that the camps demanded an ineffability, or silence: 'L'horreur génère le silence: elle ne le dit pas, elle l'impose. Il n'y a rien à dire, on ne peut rien dire.'[10] ('The horror generates silence: it does not express it, it imposes it. There is nothing to say, nothing we can say.') The second essay by Gérard Wajcman went further, asserting: 'Il n'y a pas d'images de la shoah. C'est-à-dire qu'on ne connaît à ce jour ni photographie ni film montrant la destruction des juifs dans les chambres à gaz.'[11] ('There are no images of the Shoah. That is to say, to date there is no known photograph or film showing the extermination of the Jews in the gas chambers.') As no images of the Holocaust exist, specifically images inside the gas chambers, representation creates a false *idol*, a misrepresentation of the event. There is, therefore, no way to represent the *truth* of the Holocaust. The passionate disputes demonstrated the high degree of sensitivity the Holocaust continues to hold in contemporary French thought and the challenges the camps pose for archival photography, memory and ultimately representation itself.

The furore that followed in the wake of the *Mémoire des camps* exhibition has a historical echo here, and it is worth pausing to recall the 1930s Realism–Modernism debates between members of the Frankfurt School. Here, Theodor Adorno and Georg Lukács endorsed an autonomous aesthetic, which was based on withdrawal. Against this, Bertolt Brecht and Walter Benjamin advocated for the disruptive potential of direct artistic engagement.[12] Old arguments are rekindled with the controversy born from the exhibition. The discourse of Holocaust unrepresentability demanded, not unlike Adorno's and Lukács's ambitions for modern art, a complete aesthetic withdrawal. Emblematic of this mode of address was Claude Lanzmann's *Shoah* (1985). In his ground-breaking nine-and-a half-hour film, Lanzmann famously eschewed all available archival material in favour of the verbal testimony of survivors, perpetrators and witnesses who participated in the Holocaust. Lanzmann summarised the challenge the Holocaust poses to representation: 'C'est tout le problème de l'image, et tout le problème de la représentation. Rien de ce qui s'est passé ne ressemblait à ça, même si tout paraît authentique.'[13] ('That's the whole problem of the image, and the whole problem of representation. Nothing that happened was like that, even though everything seems authentic.') For Lanzmann, any attempt to represent the Holocaust will inevitably fail, by misrepresenting it. It was therefore necessary to privilege the spoken word, or testimony, over images to take us closer to the 'truth' of the Holocaust.

Against this, Didi-Huberman's essay provocatively commenced with Lanzmann clearly in his sights. Didi-Huberman writes, 'In order to know, we must *imagine* for ourselves.'[14] Lanzmann had famously declared that archival images are images 'without imagination':

J'ai toujours dit que les images d'archive sont des images sans imagination. Elles pétrifient la pensée et tuent toute puissance d'évocation. Il
vaut bien mieux faire ce que j'ai fait, un immense travail d'élaboration,
de création de la mémoire de l'événement.[15]
I have always said that archival images are images without imagination. They petrify thought and kill all power of evocation. It is much
better to do what I did, an immense work of development, a creation
of the memory of the event.

For Didi-Huberman, the terms of Lanzmann's arguments had been
largely left unexamined, helping explain the mystical reverence that
accompanies the film. Didi-Huberman cautions against the impulse
of speaking in absolute terms: 'generally well intentioned, apparently
philosophical, and actually lazy – "unsayable" and "unimaginable"'.[16]
This amounts to a pointed and emphatic rejection of Lanzmann's thesis
that the Holocaust is unimaginable, therefore unpresentable.

After a generation of postmodernist scepticism and 'a consequent
weakening of historicity' famously described by Fredric Jameson,[17]
Didi-Huberman's position must be understood as a resolute counter-
manoeuvre, aimed at restoring the image's critical capacity to inter-
vene. The image, he writes, 'is *the eye of history*: its tenacious function of
making visible'.[18] The photographs snatched by the desperate member
of the *Sonderkommando* cannot tell the *whole* truth of Auschwitz-
Birkenau. This would be to demand too much of them. Alternatively,
to consign as simulacrum is to negate the lived experience of 'Alex' and
the risk he undertook to take the photographs. It is to abdicate our ethical responsibility to look, and to imagine. 'An image without imagination', Didi-Huberman claims, 'is quite simply an image we have not
taken the time to work on.'[19]

Didi-Huberman's arguments have had enormous implications for
a younger generation of scholars and filmmakers. Libby Saxton has
observed that questions pertaining to an ethics of representation have
gained increasing momentum in recent years, as a diverse range of aesthetic responses have begun to emerge in Holocaust cinema.[20] I contend
this is most evident in Hungarian director László Nemes's debut feature
film, *Saul Fia* (*Son of Saul*) (2015). Winner of the 2015 Grand Prix at
Cannes and Best Foreign Film at the 2016 Academy Awards, Nemes
delivered an important update to the history of Holocaust film and the
question that now resides at the core of Didi-Huberman's project: how

can images make history visible? The complexity of Nemes's response has developed, I argue, in direct dialogue with Didi-Huberman's arguments advanced in *Images in Spite of All*.

Son of Saul

Fast forward to August 2015, and Didi-Huberman wrote an open letter to Nemes. It commenced with a dramatic mode of address:

> Cher László Nemes,
> Votre film, *Le Fils de Saul*, est un monstre. Un monstre nécessaire, cohérent, bénéfique, innocent.[21]
> Dear László Nemes,
> Your film, *Son of Saul*, is a monster. A necessary, coherent, beneficial, innocent monster.

What are we to make of Didi-Huberman's opening lines? How does one create monsters? Written in the immediate aftermath of Didi-Huberman's viewing of the film, the letter is an intimate and emotional tribute to Nemes's harrowing portrayal of misery and attempted escape set inside the gas chambers at Auschwitz-Birkenau concentration camp in 1944. The letter was quickly published by Les Éditions de Minuit in late 2015. Didi-Huberman provides a critical reading of the film, locating it in a literary and philosophical framework wholly committed to a broader rethinking of the visual legacy of the Holocaust. *Son of Saul* was developed explicitly in dialogue with Didi-Huberman and Nemes has taken up many of Didi-Huberman's arguments concerning the ethical responsibility of representation in *Images in Spite of All*.

Like all filmmakers who have responded to the subject of the Holocaust, Nemes was confronted with the question of how cinema may best represent the enormity of the event, and film's highly contested role as a witness to history. Cinematic responses have ranged from Alain Resnais's *Nuit et Brouillard* (1956), to Claude Lanzmann's *Shoah* (1985) and Steven Spielberg's *Schindler's List* (1993). This has been accentuated by fierce debates between Jean-Luc Godard and Claude Lanzmann about whether the gas chambers should be represented. In 1998, Godard described the issue confronting filmmakers and the prohibition of representation, particularly Lanzmann's emphatic rejection of images in favour of testimony:

> Je n'ai aucune preuve de ce que j'avance, mais je pense que si je m'y mettais avec un bon journaliste d'investigation, je trouverais les images des chambres à gaz au bout de vingt ans. On verrait entrer les déportés et on verrait dans quel état ils ressortent. Il ne s'agit pas de prononcer des interdictions comme le font Lanzmann ou Adorno, qui exagèrent parce qu'on se retrouve alors à discuter à l'infini sur des formules du style 'c'est infilmable' – il ne faut pas empêcher les gens de filmer, il ne faut pas brûler les livres, sinon on ne peut plus les critiquer.[22]

Although I have no proof of this, but I think that if I got to work with a good investigative journalist, I would find images of the gas chambers after twenty years. We would see the prisoners coming in and what state they were in when they came out. There is no room for issuing prohibitions like Lanzmann or Adorno, who exaggerate because otherwise we end up arguing ad infinitum about ways of expressing it, such as 'it's unfilmable'. We must not stop people filming, we must not burn books. Otherwise we will no longer be able to critique them.

Unlike Resnais's retrieval of archival film footage, or Lanzmann's extraordinary commitment to testimony, *Son of Saul* delivers an altogether different set of aesthetic decisions. Nemes combines actual historical events with a fictional narrative, exploiting the tension between fiction and a Bazinian confidence in film's indexicality. As such, Nemes adds his voice to a long and contested history of philosophical debates concerning the relationship between the Holocaust and the status of the image. As Didi-Huberman puts it in his letter to Nemes: 'Vous avez pris le risque de construire un certain réalisme face à une réalité historique souvent qualifié d'inimaginable.'[23] ('Faced with a historic reality often called unimaginable, you have taken the risk of constructing a certain realism.')

Saul Ausländer (Géza Röhrig) is a Hungarian prisoner and member of the *Sonderkommando*. One day, while clearing the bodies from the gas chambers, Saul discovers a young boy, who somehow managed to survive, only to be suffocated by an SS doctor. The child's body, a curiosity, is sent away for an autopsy. In the face of such horror, Saul claims the boy as his son and plans a single act of redemption: to find a rabbi and give the boy a proper burial. The film follows Saul's frenetic search for a rabbi over the course of one and a half days. Whether the child is indeed Saul's is beside the point, as we will never know. If this is the main story line, there are other subnarratives that Saul encounters in his frantic search around the camp. The first shows Saul and a fellow *Sonderkommando* member furtively taking photographs from inside the crematoria of the burning bodies outside in the pits. The gas chambers provided relative shelter from the unyielding surveillance exerted by the SS. The second was the planning and subsequent uprising against the guards. Nemes blends fact and fiction, folding both historical incidents into the storyline.

Saul's search for a rabbi is an astonishing act of resistance, based on a powerful paradox: the already dead are trying to save the already dead. In order to maintain absolute secrecy, the *Sonderkommando* were routinely liquidated. In the film, as desperate plans are formulated for an armed insurrection, lists are simultaneously being drawn up, nominating the 'expendables'. When Abraham (Levente Molnár) bitterly accuses Saul of betraying the *Sonderkommando* by hiding the boy's body in the sleeping barracks and placing the group at risk, Saul affectlessly responds: 'We are already dead.' To accentuate this point, Saul is rendered corpse-like, his gaunt face, affectless (Figure 17). It is this non-space between life and death, human and inhuman that Saul inhabits. Despite this, Saul is motivated by the very human desire to save the boy's soul, and, perhaps, even his own.

In an interview with French film critic Antoine de Baecque, Nemes declared his debt to Didi-Huberman's analysis of the photographs:

> These four photographs deeply affected me. They attest to the extermination, they constitute evidence, and ask essential questions. What should be done with an image? What can it represent? What viewpoint should we have when faced with death and barbarity?[24]

If Lanzmann's *Shoah* is the cinematographic reference point for the extermination of European Jews, *Son of Saul* signals a distinct update, with a younger generation of scholars and filmmakers increasingly questioning the injunction against representation. Against Lanzmann's privileging of the truth value assigned to testimony, *Son of Saul* is a hybrid cinematic form, blending fiction with real historical events. As

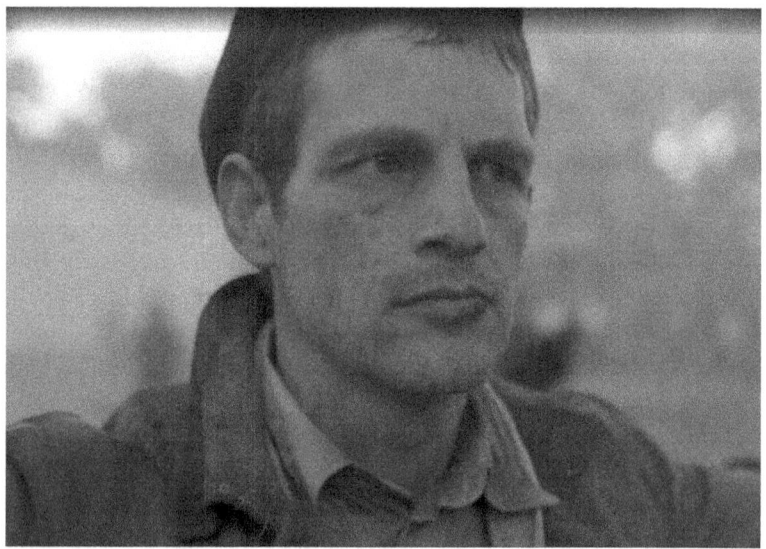

Figure 17 László Nemes, *Son of Saul*, 2015

Didi-Huberman argues in *Images in Spite of All*, the four photographs snatched by 'Alex' in August 1944 cannot tell us the 'entire' or absolute truth of the Holocaust. This is to ask too much from the image. Nevertheless, as Didi-Huberman claims, there is a truth value ascribed to the photographs. 'But they *are* for us – for our eyes today – truth itself, meaning its vestige, its meagre shreds: what remains, visually, of Auschwitz.'[25] An image may be incapable of telling the whole and absolute truth of the gas chambers. It can, however, reveal a partial truth, a fragmented truth, but a truth, nevertheless.

In *Son of Saul*, Nemes recreates the actual historical event of 'Alex' taking the photographs. Saul and another inmate, posing as locksmiths, sought to photograph the pits of burning bodies from the shelter of an adjacent shed (Figure 18). Nemes recalled:

> We integrated this moment into the heart of the film, as it corresponds to a segment of Saul's journey through the camp when suddenly, just for a moment, he participates in the construction of our view of the extermination. And also, because of the representation of the image within itself, we are, at that point and only then, questioning the very status of representation.[26]

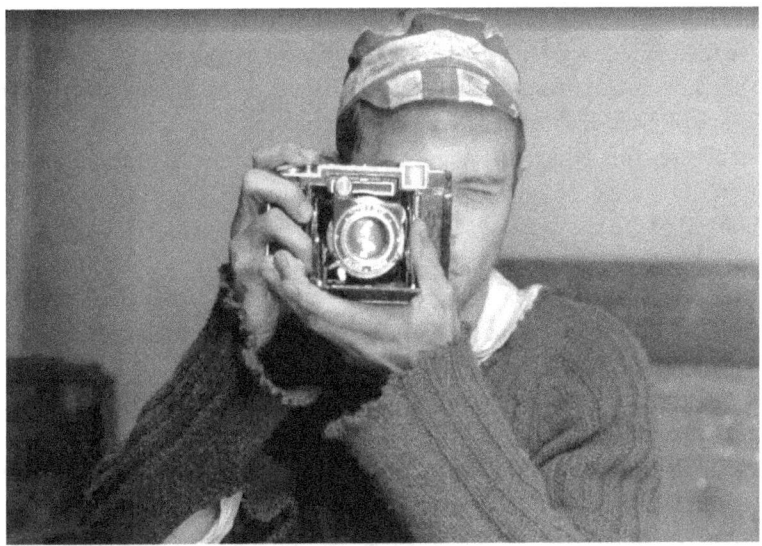

Figure 18 László Nemes, *Son of Saul*, 2015

As we have seen, Didi-Huberman's essay recreated the phenomenological experience of Alex, seeking to restore agency to the inmate who
risked his life to take the photographs. The photographer's clandestine movement past the crematorium pits that resulted in the blurred,
out-of-focus shots, is a visual record of the inherent difficulty of capturing an image without detection from the guards. In *Images in Spite
of All*, Didi-Huberman argued, 'It is simply not possible to take out
the camera, even less possible to aim it. The "unknown photographer"
takes two snapshots, furtively, without looking, perhaps even while
walking.'[27] Nemes has integrated this turbulent and frenetic camerawork into the logic of the film. The indistinct blur leads Didi-Huberman
to describe the image as a 'panic image'. Didi-Huberman writes, 'c'est un
véhicule visuel de la peur'[28] ('it is a visual vehicle of fear'). The camera's
movements, as we closely follow Saul, follow the fear. This is not the
panopticon gaze of Jeremy Bentham's all-seeing, all-pervasive surveillance of the SS from their watchtowers. Instead, it is the panicked and
clandestine gaze of a prisoner, furtively searching for a rabbi in amongst
the chaos of the camps. As a result, *Son of Saul* is physically difficult
to watch. This is Nemes's point: it is our ethical responsibility not to
avert our gaze from the unfolding horror. Furthermore, it reminds us

of Didi-Huberman's earlier plea not to look away: 'It is a response that we must offer, as a debt to the words and images that certain prisoners snatched, for us, from the harrowing Real of their experience.'[29] At the heart of Didi-Huberman's text is an ethics of spectatorship. Nemes structures this ethics into the logic of the camerawork itself. The lack of respite is agonising, with Nemes never relinquishing his tightly held control of the spectator's gaze.

Following cinematic convention, the opening sequence of *Son of Saul* begins with a long shot. It is a long shot, however, with a crucial difference: rather than setting the scene and orientating the spectator, the image does exactly the opposite. The image is completely blurred, out of focus, and refuses to coherently resolve. Birds tweet and the wash of green cues the spectator that the scene is set in a countryside. Gradually, out of the blur, appears a human silhouette, followed by three others. The figure slowly comes into focus, and we are introduced to Saul Ausländer. Acutely rendered in the camera's close-up, Saul stands in stark contrast to the blurred green backdrop. We are left to study the details of his face: his stubble, a lesion on his bottom lip, flecks of grey in his dark hair. Saul's face remains expressionless. Again, the background sound functions to provide vital cues: new prisoners have arrived. A cacophony of voices, noises, whistles, languages and the ominous barking of guard dogs. The camera remains tightly focused on Saul's face, which is impassively neutral and gives the prisoners no clue as to their fate. His eyes remain averted, and his actual physical contact with the prisoners is minimal. Saul and the other *Sonderkommando* members usher the prisoners into the changing rooms and finally into the gas chambers, where they are promised a shower, followed by warm soup. Occasionally, a face will come into perspective, but it is only ever momentarily, and it quickly disappears, falling away from the camera's relentless focus on Saul.

Son of Saul is organised in long sequence shots, combined with Nemes's persistent use of the close-up. We are left to concentrate on the subtlest of Saul's facial expressions. Tiny, virtually imperceptible movements become events in the landscape of Saul's face. Frequently, the hand-held camera is located behind Saul's head as he navigates the labyrinthine of corridors and chambers. The effect is disquieting, as the extreme proximity places the spectator into the scene itself. We go where Saul goes. The camera's tight framing, combined with the agonising length between cuts, provides the spectator with no visual respite. There are no horizons here to seek solace and rest one's gaze.

The extremely shallow depth of field positions Saul at the centre of this chaotic universe. As Saul moves through the gas chambers, the spectator is aware that piles of dead bodies lie on the boundaries of the camera's frame. Nemes solicits our voyeuristic desire to look, only to frustrate it, by leaving the bodies abstracted, blurred and out of focus. The spectator's desire to assume mastery of the scene is denied by the blurring effect. Thwarted, the spectator's gaze is returned to the figure of Saul, whose face remains startlingly clear in the close-up. Didi-Huberman measures this shallow depth of field in tactile terms. 'The image that leaves the dark', he writes,

> se caractérise donc par ses propres limites tactiles: là où elle survient nettement, l'épaisseur – la profondeur de champ – est infime. La zone de netteté est comme une lame: elle est une coupe dans l'espace visible, mais son intervalle d'efficacité, son lieu de coupe, est extrêmement mince. L'horreur est *tranchante*, en effet.[30]
> is characterised by its own tactile limits: where it appears clearly, the thickness – the depth of field – is tiny. The area of sharpness is like a blade: it is cut into visible space, but its effective space, the space of the cut, is extremely thin. Indeed, the horror *cuts* sharply.

The visual instability created between the detail of the close-up and the indistinct blur on the periphery of the shot is deployed constantly throughout the film. In this way, Nemes carefully navigates within the camera's frame a tension between realism and abstraction. The spectator knows that the people, bodies and fellow inmates are there, but is unable to properly visually grasp, leaving the scopic field as incoherent and indistinct. As a result, our imagination must fill the gaps. Unlike Lanzmann's criticism of an 'image without imagination', imagination is not understood here as reproductive, or an inferior copy. Instead, imagination is productive. It is in these blurs and absences that something new is created.

It is worth pausing to consider the title of Didi-Huberman's text, *Sortir du noir*, which translates into English as 'leave the dark'. In the interview with Antoine de Baecque, Nemes described Auschwitz as a type of 'black hole' in his family's history:

> A part of my family was assassinated in Auschwitz. It was something we talked about every day. When I was little, I had the impression

that 'evil had been done'. I imagined it like a black hole burrowed within us; something had broken, and my inability to grasp exactly what it was kept me isolated.[31]

Didi-Huberman argues that Nemes has done the very opposite. The 'black hole' becomes a key operative metaphor in Didi-Huberman's letter to Nemes, as images of dark and light pervade the *Sortir du noir*. The shed where Saul tries to take the photographs is reimagined as a type of darkroom, or *camera obscura*. The inmate hides inside the darkness and cover offered by the gas chambers, and takes pictures of the burning bodies in a pit outside. Importantly, Didi-Huberman builds a bridge back to Adorno's image of darkness as a necessary precondition for contemporary art. Adorno famously expressed his preference for aesthetic disengagement and withdrawal. Didi-Huberman draws on a passage from *Aesthetic Theory*, where Adorno described an aesthetic of darkness as a necessary response to the aftermath of the horrors of World War II. Adorno writes:

> To survive reality at its most extreme and grim, artworks that do not want to sell themselves as consolation must equate themselves with that reality. Radical art today is synonymous with dark art; its primary color is black ... The ideal of blackness with regard to content is one of the deepest impulses of abstraction.[32]

Against an aesthetic of darkness, Didi-Huberman argues that the film has *left the dark*. Didi-Huberman notes:

> Or vous, cher László Nemes, vous n'avez choisi ni le noir radical ni le silence radical. Votre film est terriblement impur, sonore et coloré ... Vous n'avez donc pas oublié le noir. Mais vous l'avez sorti de son abstraction.[33]
> But you, dear László Nemes, you have chosen neither radical black nor radical silence. Your film is terribly impure, sonorous and expressive ... So you have therefore not forgotten the dark. But instead you have taken it out of its abstraction.

The hell Nemes has created is a noisy, coloured hell. Splashes of colour explode from the indistinct blur: the red cross on the back of Saul's jacket, marking his status as a *Sonderkommando* member; the victim's blood after the gassing, the grey of the smoke emerging from the human ashes; and the film's opening and closing scenes that are bathed in the vibrant green of the birch forest. The extraordinary soundscape is a richly layered mêlée of languages, screams for help and the ever-present rumbling of the crematoria.

Like Nemes, Didi-Huberman lost members of his family in the Holocaust, and he has returned to the question of Holocaust representation in an ongoing series of articles and essays since the 2001 exhibition. *Bark*, for instance, is a highly personal photo-essay documenting a trip Didi-Huberman made to Auschwitz-Birkenau in June 2011.[34] The title of the small text is derived from three fragments of bark taken by Didi-Huberman from the distinctive birch trees that surround the camps, the same trees that bore witness to the camp's atrocities sixty years earlier. Nineteen photographs are reproduced in the book, each accompanied with Didi-Huberman's observations. The notion of imagination returns here, as Didi-Huberman continues an ongoing dialogue with Lanzmann. This time, it is Didi-Huberman's own imagination that comes to the fore, as he records his observations during his stroll (*déambulation*) around the camps. One of Didi-Huberman's photographs is an image of the birch trees that create a limit of the horizon. It is distinguished by strong horizontals, and heavy clouds intersect with the distant birch forest. Quietly sitting to the right is a single watchtower. Didi-Huberman asks, 'But what is a horizon at Birkenau? What is a horizon in this place conceived to shatter all hope?'[35] The trees that form the horizon at Birkenau reappear in the film, reinforcing the prisoner's sense of confinement. In *Son of Saul*, the birch forest is both a natural barrier as well as camouflage, and Nemes exploits the lack of horizon to reinforce the film's intense sense of claustrophobia.

In *Sortir du noir*, Didi-Huberman suggests that the film inaugurates a new genre of 'documentary fable' (*conte documentaire*). To do this, Didi-Huberman draws on two interconnected strains in Walter Benjamin's writing in the 1930s. The first strain positions *Son of Saul* as a literary montage. Benjamin was deeply interested in the radical possibilities of montage for literature. For Benjamin, the montage technique derived from Dada artistic practices signalled the invention of a new 'epic' form of literature. In his 1930 essay, 'The Crisis of the Novel', Benjamin enthusiastically wrote, 'The montage explodes the framework of the novel, bursts its limits both stylistically and structurally, and clears the way for new, epic possibilities.'[36]

Didi-Huberman observes that in *Son of Saul,* fragments of ancient fables are woven together, creating a new documentary genre of storytelling. The film is a cinematic fable, drawing on ancient literary traditions and deeply engrained in mythology and oral legends. Take, for example, Saul's travels through the camp's hell, the labyrinth of changing rooms, gas chambers, barracks and crematoriums. Saul becomes an Orpheus-like figure, voyaging through the underworld to save Eurydice. Akin to Orpheus's journey to the underworld to meet Hades, Saul confronts the space of death that is Auschwitz-Birkenau. Like Orpheus, Saul seeks to *exit the dark* with his beloved. Like Orpheus, his journey is condemned from the outset ('*we are already dead*').

Or else consider the final escape sequence, where the boy's body slips from Saul's grasp during the river crossing in the flight from the SS troops. We are presented with a cruel inversion of one of the foundational stories in the history of Judaism, the story of Moses. Recall from the Book of Exodus, the pharaoh's decree that all male Hebrew children should be drowned. Moses was set adrift on the Nile, to be rescued by the pharaoh's daughter and raised as an Egyptian prince. Unlike the boy, Moses survives, to eventually lead the Israelites in the flight from slavery. Didi-Huberman detects a montage impulse in the collision of Greek myths and stories from the Hebrew Bible. Didi-Huberman's letter to Nemes concludes with the observation that the film is 'tirant sa logique de traditions littéraires à la fois très anciennes et très modernes'[37] ('drawing its logic from literary traditions very old and very modern'). Ancient fables and stories survive, juxtaposed to create new narrative forms.

The second strain is Benjamin's lament for the dying tradition of storytelling. In his 1936 essay, 'The Storyteller: Observations on the Works of Nikolai Leskov', Benjamin argued that crucial to the art of storytelling was the communication of shared experience. Benjamin recognised that soldiers returning from World War I struggled to find appropriate language and audiences to communicate their experiences. Arriving home from the battlefields, they found a new, modern world of mass media and information that placed no value on older, oral forms of communication passed down by storytellers. Against the isolation of the novelist, and the ephemeral, limited value of news information, the storyteller takes his material from experience, and shares this with his listeners. The story is in turn internalised by the audience, becoming a collective, shared experience. Benjamin writes, 'The storyteller takes what he tells from experience – his own or that reported by others.

And he in turn makes it the experience of those who are listening to his tale.[38] Storytelling, for Benjamin, is the craft of imparting knowledge and wisdom, and passing this on through the generations. It would be a mistake to measure *Son of Saul* in terms of its documentary accuracy. It is, as Didi-Huberman suggests, a documentary fable, as ancient as the stories of Orpheus and Moses. Nemes is our storyteller, a chronicler of experiences. He passes these experiences to us, and Nemes's narrative becomes our narrative, our own shared experience.

The relationship between cinema and the Holocaust has a long and vexed history. By making the *Sonderkommando* and gas chambers the subject of *Son of Saul*, Nemes delivers a significant update to this history. *Son of Saul* firmly eschews the notion of aesthetic withdrawal as an appropriate response to the Holocaust. Against Lanzmann's prioritisation of testimony over images, Nemes reverses this, firmly placing the image, and its claims to historical truth and veracity, at the centre of his enquiry. The dialogue that has developed between Didi-Huberman and Nemes reminds us that the four photographs snatched by 'Alex' in August 1944 present an ongoing, living legacy. Nemes is thinking through arguments presented by Didi-Huberman in cinema itself. This is not a mere illustration, but an integration of an ethics of spectatorship into the film's form. Nemes's demands on the spectator are high: do not avert your gaze; to look away is to surrender your ethical responsibility to look, and to *imagine*.

Notes

1 Georges Didi-Huberman, *The Eye of History: When Images Take Positions*, trans. Shane B. Lillis (Cambridge, MA: MIT Press, 2018), xxiii–xxiv.

2 Didi-Huberman's original essay 'Images malgré tout' was first published in Chéroux, *Mémoire des camps*. The essay was republished in Didi-Huberman's book of the same name, *Images malgré tout*; Didi-Huberman, *Images in Spite of All*.

3 On this emerging area of Holocaust scholarship, see Adam Brown, *Judging 'Privileged' Jews: Holocaust Ethics, Representation, and the 'Grey Zone'* (New York and Oxford: Berghahn Books, 2013); Nicholas Chare and Dominic Williams (eds), *Testimonies of Resistance: Representations of the Auschwitz-Birkenau Sonderkommando* (New York and Oxford: Berghahn Books, 2019); Isabel Wollaston, 'Emerging from the Shadows? The Auschwitz Sonderkommando and the "Four Women"

in History and Memory', *Holocaust Studies: A Journal of Culture and History*, 20:3 (2014), 137–70.

4   Primo Levi, *The Drowned and the Saved*, trans. Raymond Rosenthal (London: Penguin Books, 1988), 37.

5   Theodor Adorno, *Prisms*, trans. Samuel and Shierry Weber (Cambridge, MA: MIT Press, 1981); Jean-François Lyotard, *The Differend: Phrases in Dispute* (Minneapolis: University of Minnesota Press, 1988).

6   Nancy, 'Forbidden Representation'; Jacques Rancière, 'Are Some Things Unrepresentable?', in *The Future of the Image*, trans. Gregory Elliot (London: Verso, 2007), 109–38; Giorgio Agamben, *Remnants of Auschwitz: The Witness and the Archive*, trans. Daniel Heller-Roazen (New York: Zone Books, 1999).

7   On the ongoing reception of Didi-Huberman's essay see, for instance, Marianne Hirsch, 'The Generation of Postmemory', *Poetics Today*, 29:1 (2008), 103–28; R. E. Kelsey and B. Stimson, *The Meaning of Photography* (Williamstown, MA: Sterling and Francine Clark Art Institute, 2008); Judith Keilbach, 'Photographs, Symbolic Images, and the Holocaust: On the (Im)possibility of Depicting Historical Truth', *History and Theory*, 48:2 (2009), 54–76.

8   Bruno Chaouat, 'In the Image of Auschwitz', *Diacritics*, 36:1 (2007), 86–96; Sven-Erik Rose, 'Auschwitz as Hermeneutic Rupture, Differend, and Image *malgré tout*: Jameson, Lyotard, Didi-Huberman', in David Bathrick, Prager Brad and Richardson Michael D. (eds), *Visualizing the Holocaust* (Rochester, NY: Camden House, 2008), 114–37; Emmanuel Alloa, 'The Most Sublime of All Laws: The Strange Resurgence of a Kantian Motif in Contemporary Image Politics', *Critical Inquiry*, 41:2 (2015), 367–89.

9   Elizabeth Pagnoux, 'Reporter photographe à Auschwitz', *Les Temps Modernes*, 56:613 (2001), 94.

10   *Ibid.*, 93.

11   Gérard Wajcman, 'De la croyance photographique', *Les Temps Modernes*, 56:613 (2001), 47.

12   See Ernst Bloch, *Aesthetics and Politics* (London: NLB, 1977). For a historical analysis, see Eugene Lunn, *Marxism and Modernism: An Historical Study of Lukács, Brecht, Benjamin, and Adorno* (Berkeley: University of California Press, 1984).

13   Claude Lanzmann, 'Holocauste, la répresentation impossible', *Le Monde*, 3 March 1994, 7.

14   Didi-Huberman, *Images in Spite of All*, 3.

15   Claude Lanzmann, 'Le monument contre l'archive?', interview by Régis Debray, Daniel Bougnoux, Claude Mollard *et al.*, *Les Cahiers de Médiologie*, 11 (2001), 274.

16   Didi-Huberman, *Images in Spite of All*, 25.
17   Fredric Jameson, *Postmodernism, or, The Cultural Logic of Late Capitalism* (Durham, NC: Duke University Press, 1991), 6.
18   Didi-Huberman, *Images in Spite of All*, 39.
19   *Ibid.*, 116.
20   Libby Saxton, *Haunted Images: Film, Ethics, Testimony and the Holocaust* (London and New York: Wallflower Press, 2008).
21   Georges Didi-Huberman, *Sortir du noir* (Paris: Les Éditions de Minuit, 2015), 7.
22   Jean-Luc Godard, 'La légende du siècle', *Les Inrockuptibles*, 170 (1998), 170.
23   Didi-Huberman, *Sortir du noir*, 25.
24   Antoine de Baecque, 'Interview with László Nemes, *Son of Saul*', *Rendez Vous* (2015).
25   Didi-Huberman, *Images in Spite of All*, 38.
26   de Baecque, 'Interview with László Nemes'.
27   Didi-Huberman, *Images in Spite of All*, 16.
28   Didi-Huberman, *Sortir du noir*, 30.
29   Didi-Huberman, *Images in Spite of All*, 3.
30   Didi-Huberman, *Sortir du noir*, 29–30.
31   de Baecque, 'Interview with László Nemes'.
32   Theodor Adorno, *Aesthetic Theory*, trans. Robert Hullot-Kentor (London and New York: Continuum, 2002), 39–40.
33   Didi-Huberman, *Sortir du noir*, 15–16.
34   See, for example, Georges Didi-Huberman, 'Ouvrir les camps, fermer les yeux', *Annales. Histoire, Sciences Sociales* 61:5 (2006/5), 1011–49; Georges Didi-Huberman, *Écorces* (Paris: Les Éditions de Minuit 2011); Georges Didi-Huberman, *Bark*, trans. Samuel E. Martin (Cambridge, MA: MIT Press, 2017).
35   Didi-Huberman, *Bark*, 53.
36   Walter Benjamin, 'The Crisis of the Novel', in Michael W. Jennings, Howard Eiland and Gary Smith (eds), *Walter Benjamin: Selected Writings*, vol. 2: *1927–1934*, trans. Rodney Livingstone *et al.* (Cambridge, MA: Belknap Press of Harvard University Press, 1999), 301.
37   Didi-Huberman, *Sortir du noir*, 49.
38   Walter Benjamin, 'The Storyteller: Observations on the Works of Nikolai Leskov', in Howard Eiland and Michael W. Jennings (eds), *Walter Benjamin: Selected Writings*, vol. 3: *1935–1938*, trans. Edmund Jephcott, Howard Eiland *et al.* (Cambridge, MA: Belknap Press of Harvard University Press, 2002), 146.

• 6 •

Thinking images

The final chapter takes its departure point from Didi-Huberman's enigmatic proposal in *Images in Spite of All* that 'Montage is the art of producing this form that thinks.'[1] Didi-Huberman's passing observation was made in respect to the series of four photographs taken by 'Alex', the member of the *Sonderkommando* in the Auschwitz-Birkenau concentration camp. The sentence is slight, and he does not elaborate, leaving us to question what it means for an image to think. If montage and images can generate thought, what state is the subject left in? In this chapter I contend that Didi-Huberman advances a slippage in the subject–object relationship, with the image being understood as capable of engineering its own forms of knowledge. What is at stake here is a model of representation that is no longer imitative, but capable of generating its own theoretical and intellectual undertaking. By emphasising montage's capacity to create new meaning and generate alternative lines of thought, the image becomes a theoretical object, a thing that 'thinks'.

The idea that images contain a life of their own, contain memory and even agency has gathered increasing momentum amongst art historians and visual and literary theorists in recent years. Loosely aggregated under the rubric of object-orientated ontology and new materialism, theories as diverse as anthropologist Alfred Gell's consideration of agency, Bill Brown's 'Thing Theory' and W. J. T. Mitchell's 'pictorial turn' reflect broader shifts in the humanities' growing preoccupation with the material reality of objects and things. Exhausted with the 'linguistic turn' and the notion that images are a language that can be 'read' and 'interpreted', Keith Moxey has observed that works of art are best encountered, rather than deciphered.[2] One of the threads unifying this cross-disciplinary impulse is a reconsideration of the subject–object relationship. The subject is bracketed and the object becomes the focus of the enquiry. In *Camera Lucida*, Roland Barthes made this curious and elusive observation: 'Ultimately, Photography is subversive not when it frightens, repels, or even stigmatizes, but when it is *pensive*, when it thinks.'[3] Although Barthes does not elaborate further, Hanneke Grootenboer has argued that pensive images occupy a privileged position in French thought, extending from artists, philosophers and art historians as diverse as Nicholas Poussin, Jacques Derrida and Hubert Damisch.[4]

The repositioning of the object enjoys a long history in French psychoanalytical and literary traditions. Recall Jacques Lacan's anecdote concerning the glimmering sardine can he saw floating on the water as a young man on a fishing trip. In his theorisation of the gaze in *Seminar XI*, Lacan reversed the dominant theory of vision, asserting 'things look at me'.[5] The subject, no longer the originating point of vision, was ensnared in the object's gaze. Alternatively, consider the tactile power assigned to objects in Jean-Paul Sartre's 1937 novel, *Nausea*. The main protagonist, Antoine Roquentin, suffered from acute bouts of nausea as a response to the sudden awareness of being touched by objects. Akin to Lacan's horror of being looked at, Roquentin described his dismay:

Objects ought not to touch, since they are not alive. You use them, you put them back in place, you live among them: they are useful, nothing more. But they touch me, it's unbearable. I am afraid of entering in contact with them, just as if they were living animals.[6]

The tactile experience of holding a pebble on the beach generates 'sweet disgust. How unpleasant it was!'[7] If Lacan's sardine has the capacity to look, and contact with objects can trigger nausea, we are not so far away from Didi-Huberman's proposition that images can think.

In this final chapter I argue that Didi-Huberman is responding to the various genealogical strains of the 'posthuman turn' and French antihumanism initiated by Foucault and Deleuze in the 1960s. As is well known, Foucault inaugurated his death-of-man thesis with the sentence: 'As the archaeology of our thought easily shows, man is an invention of a recent date. And one perhaps nearing its end.'[8] This particular configuration of knowledge is a product of what Foucault calls the 'modern episteme'. For Foucault, the modern episteme was approaching its end. Foucault's announcement ushered in a general questioning of received humanist values and ideals. Less well known is

Foucault's critique of humanism and anthropomorphism in the opening pages of *The Archaeology of Knowledge*, published three years afterwards. In Foucault's sights was history, which had stubbornly refused to shift from a subject-orientated position and remained committed to its anthropological and humanist foundations. Foucault was calling into question the ongoing positioning of Man at the centre of world history, underpinned by the telos of reason and rationality.[9]

Foucault's death-of-man thesis pointed to a shift or reorientation from the subject to the object and contained significant repercussions for younger scholars such as Didi-Huberman. The critique of human-centred humanism has resided at the centre of Didi-Huberman's project since its inception. Didi-Huberman recognised that art history, practised in the humanist tradition, was no longer viable or desirable. The notion that art history could continue promoting a rational, all-knowing mode of knowledge and authorial dominance over the image was a form of power that could no longer be comfortably maintained. This is most explicit in *Confronting Images*, where Didi-Huberman took careful aim at Erwin Panofsky's dictum that art history is a humanist discipline.[10] Following Foucault, Didi-Huberman called into question the humanist tendency of placing Man at the centre of the discourse, and more specifically, the authorial voice of the art historian.

The second posthumanist strain that is important to Didi-Huberman is located in Gilles Deleuze's *Cinema* books. Deleuze famously argued that he was not 'applying' philosophy to cinema, but instead cinema generated its own philosophical project. Cinema is understood here less as a visual spectacle, but as a form of thought. Cinema thinks in images, but these images are not imitative or derivative. Instead, cinema is self-generative, capable of creating its own concepts, not merely illustrating a pre-existing argument or giving visual form to a philosophical precept. If we were to reach back further, the origins of Deleuze's claims may be identified as early as 1964 in his book on Marcel Proust. For Deleuze, Proust's writing 'vies with philosophy. Proust sets up an image of thought in opposition to that of philosophy.'[11] In this early text, Deleuze signals his interest in departing from philosophy's pre-existing normative frameworks, or thought based on resemblance, recognition and identity.

Deleuze's 'image of thought' that is opposed to philosophy is given its fullest and most complete expression in the third chapter of *Difference and Repetition*. Before we begin thinking, our thought is already predetermined by a series of pre-existing postulates or assumptions. In an interview, Deleuze formulated the problem of the image of thought in the following terms: 'We live with a particular image of thought, that is to say, before we begin to think, we have a vague idea of what it means to think, its means and its ends.'[12] The Cartesian method of doubt was designed to ensure there were no presuppositions left. Descartes's cogito, 'I think', is preceded by assumptions of 'I', 'think', and 'am', or self, subjectivity and being. These assumptions are predicated on the notion that the human subject is universal (everybody knows what it means to think), stable and centred. Deleuze's point is that whilst philosophy has taken care to eliminate preceding suppositions, it has never been entirely successful in eliminating them completely. The 'I' of the humanist subject can no longer be identified as the foundational source of all knowledge. Following Nietzsche, Deleuze argues that it is futile to continue equating thought with truth. The challenge, therefore, for modern philosophy, is to free itself from the image preceding thought.

Deleuze's attack on the subject as the origin of knowledge points to a decentring of subjectivity that corresponds with his contemporaries. In a similar vein, Foucault recognised that the Cartesian 'I think' no longer equates to the 'I am'. In the closing pages of *The Order of Things*, Foucault signalled that the 'modern *cogito*' would not necessarily be human:

> In this form, the *cogito* will not therefore be the sudden and illuminating discovery that all thought is thought, but the constantly renewed interrogation as to how thought can reside elsewhere than here, and yet so very close to itself; how it can *be* in the forms of non-thinking.[13]

Foucault's comments point to the possibility of a shift or reorientation from the subject to the object.

For Deleuze, it is an image that lingers at the heart of representation's residual subjectivity: 'Image in general which constitutes the subjective presupposition of philosophy as a whole'.[14] The image is understood by Deleuze in Platonic terms.[15] To overcome the image of thought, therefore, the image must be destroyed. This is Deleuze's essential iconoclasm and the task he assigns to philosophy: to displace the idea of what thinking is. Deleuze writes:

[C]onceptual philosophical thought has as its implicit presupposition a pre-philosophical and natural Image of thought, borrowed from the pure element of common sense. According to this image, thought has an affinity with the true; it formally possesses the true and materially wants the true. It is in terms of this image that everybody knows and is presumed to know what it means to think.[16]

The image of thought relies on a series of pre-existing 'postulates' that exist prior to thinking.

Philosophy must therefore generate 'A new image of thought – or rather, a liberation of thought from those images which imprison it.'[17] How, then, to free thought from the dogmatic image of thought that occurs prior to thinking? Deleuze gives us an important clue, drawing an analogy with modernist painting's shift towards abstraction: 'The theory of thought is like painting: it needs that revolution which took art from representation to abstraction. This is the aim of a theory of thought without image.'[18] In painting's withdrawal from the demands of mimesis, it was gradually freed from the constraints of imitation. Importantly, this shift contained a lesson for philosophy seeking to undertake thinking prior to the image, language and representation.

How does Deleuze's call to overcome the image of thought relate to Didi-Huberman? On several occasions, Didi-Huberman has spoken of his desire to pursue a non-dogmatic approach to the study of images. In a 2002 interview with Elie During, following the publication of *L'image survivante*, Didi-Huberman explicitly identified the proto-Deleuzian impulse in Warburg's *Mnemosyne Atlas*: 'Warburg n'aurait pas déplu à Gilles Deleuze –, c'est produire une "image de pensée".'[19] ('Warburg would not have displeased Gilles Deleuze – it produces an "image of thought".') Like Deleuze, Didi-Huberman was interested in challenging orthodox conventions. If art history is organised through a series of pre-existing conventions, these conventions predetermine outcomes. In an earlier interview with Robert Maggiori, Didi-Huberman declared:

Grosso modo, je m'intéresse à l'image en ce qu'elle fait bouger les assises de la représentation, c'est-à-dire notre *idée* de la représentation … Ce qui me fascine souvent, c'est la façon dont une image est capable d'inventer … des configurations qui, littéralement, défient la pensée. Voilà pourquoi j'ai moins l'impression de porter un 'regard philosophique' sur les images … que de me rendre au pouvoir qu'a

l'image – si elle est forte – de bouleverser, donc de faire littéralement
recommencer la pensée elle-même, sur tous les plans.[20]
Grosso modo, I am interested in the image in that it moves the
foundations of representation, that is to say our *idea* of representation … What often fascinates me is the way an image is capable of
inventing… configurations that, literally, defy thought. This is why
I have less an impression of projecting a 'philosophical gaze' onto
images, than of handing myself over to the power that the image
has – if it is strong – to upset, that is, to literally *make thought itself
start over*, on all levels.

There are two important points to recognise in this passage. The first is
Didi-Huberman's desire to displace pre-existing ideas of what representation can possibly be. From his earliest research, Didi-Huberman has
sought to pursue alternative modes of representation that depart from
classic understandings of mimesis. How, then, to escape the idealism,
or the *a priori* philosophical commitment that implicitly inhabits the
discipline? If the image is predetermined by discourse itself, how can
it be dismantled from the disciplinary framework preceding it? To
reframe this problematic in Deleuzian terms: disciplinary conventions
blind the art historian to an actual image itself. If the methodology
determines our approach, how may we perceive the image prior to its
theorisation? How to overturn the theory or methodology preceding
the image? Didi-Huberman cautions: 'we must always, even in the most
transparent of pragmatisms, take into account automatic philosophical models or their vestiges, in other words the always masked and
transfigured presence of initial schemas and thought choices.'[21] Like
Deleuze, Didi-Huberman is committed to a line of inquiry seeking
to overturn the pre-existing image that determines the structure of
thought. This is one of the central questions raised in *Confronting
Images*: can images be liberated from a discourse that exists prior to
their existence, a discourse that seeks to distort the image, bending it 'to
this ideal, imagines it, sees it, or rather foresees it – in short, it informs
and invents it in advance.'[22]

The second point in the conversation with Maggiori establishes Didi-
Huberman's proximity to Deleuze. Let's return to Deleuze's conclusion
at the end of *Cinema 2*: 'Cinema's concepts are not given in cinema. And
yet they are cinema's concepts, not theories about cinema.'[23] Rather than
using philosophy to illustrate ideas about cinema, cinema is positioned

in terms of Deleuze's broader inquiry into the creation of a 'new image of thought'. Images no longer 'represent' or 'imitate' reality, but are capable of actively constructing thought. Didi-Huberman is trying to avoid importing a pre-existing 'philosophical gaze' and simply apply it to illustrate his discussion of images. Instead he is attempting to recommence with thought itself, what it means to think free from disciplinary conventions that predetermine thought and outcomes. This challenge is considered by Didi-Huberman as 'unthinkable in positivist terms – consisting of not-grasping the image, of *letting oneself be grasped by it instead: thus of letting go of one's knowledge about it*'.[24] Only once this predetermined knowledge has been abandoned, is it possible to begin thinking anew.

Didi-Huberman's argument is more than a deconstructionist gesture aimed at recovering the image from its subordination to text. Instead, he tries to approach the image free from the conventions that implicitly determine art history's discursive frameworks. We are now in a better position to return to his observation: 'Montage is the art of producing this form that thinks'. For Didi-Huberman, the potential of montage resides in reimagining the discipline, beyond its linguistic and logocentric biases. Didi-Huberman writes, 'Beyond the model of the graphic or cinematographic process as such, we ought to conceive of montage as doing for the field of images what signifying difference did for the field of language in the post-Saussurian conception.'[25] To be clear, this is an epistemological shift, according to Didi-Huberman, on par with the impact of Derridean deconstruction.

How, then, does a deeply visual tradition rethink its dependence on representation and imitation? How to overcome the image of thought? Deleuze's answer is the encounter. He writes, 'Something in the world forces us to think. This something is an object not of recognition but a fundamental *encounter*.'[26] What is this encounter Deleuze speaks of? A genuine encounter is a shock or jolt, forcing a rupture and breaking with convention. As opposed to the representation, which reinforces the same, conventional habits of thought, the affective force of the encounter forces us to think otherwise, to develop a new image of thought. Like Deleuze, Didi-Huberman points to the power of the artistic encounter to alter pre-existing thought. In a discussion with François Noudelmann, he outlined the importance of the experience or encounter before Fra Angelico's *marmi finti* in the San Marco convent:

D'emblée, c'est l'expérience qui m'a mobilisé, parce que l'expérience, avec la surprise philosophique qui la caractérise, commence toujours par mettre en question tout ce que l'on croyait penser jusque-là. L'expérience modifie la matière même du penser.[27] Firstly, it is the experience that got me going, because the experience, with the philosophical surprise that characterises it, always starts by calling into question everything that we thought we knew until then. Experience changes the very stuff of thinking.

The encounter functions as a type of limit experience, forcing a reconfiguration of principles inherited from the discipline. Didi-Huberman frames this in Deleuzian terms: 'I had to give up … that very old postulate, the most widely shared no doubt and also the least considered in the history of classical art, that claims that figurative painting imitates things by imitating their visible aspect.'[28] This was the discourse that has understood all representation as a mimetic copy since the Renaissance.

Montage as an epistemological tool

Deleuze's critique of the image of thought holds important implications for what philosophy can be. Philosophy now demands a new approach that is non-dogmatic and non-systematic. Didi-Huberman responds to Deleuze's challenge, reaching back to the historical avant-garde practices of the early twentieth century, where he detects a sensibility eschewing recognition and imitation through the widespread use of montage. Importantly, from *Images in Spite of All* onwards, montage becomes a key operative principle in his writing. For Didi-Huberman, montage is an exemplary form of intervention. Montage is antimimetic, therefore aligned with his critique of idealist formulations of representation. Moreover, montage is discontinuous. It can jolt, reconfigure and reassemble. Montage cuts through existing knowledge structures, refusing to allow anything to settle.

Didi-Huberman returns us to a historical moment where it is possible to detect a pre-Deleuzian strain or sentiment. Importantly, Didi-Huberman forces us to recognise the Benjaminian thrust in Deleuze's writing. Benjaminian motifs such as crystals and monads feature frequently in Deleuze's writing; however, to the best of my knowledge, Deleuze makes no explicit references to Benjamin. Foreshadowing

Deleuze's concerns, Benjamin's criticism of idealist philosophy may be detected as early as 1924 in his extraordinary reconsideration of German baroque theatre, *The Origin of German Tragic Drama*. The 'basic task of philosophy', Benjamin argues, is 'the representation of ideas'.[29] Benjamin's 'idea' is understood in Leibnizian terms as a 'monad', again directly anticipating Deleuze. Furthermore, Benjamin uncannily anticipates Deleuze's call for the philosopher to create concepts, freed from the rigidity of pre-existing ideas, arguing, 'Whereas the concept is a spontaneous product of the intellect, ideas are simply given to be reflected upon. Ideas are pre-existent.'[30] Benjamin's distinction between the concept and the idea is akin to the self-generative capacity of cinema to create concepts.

Montage was an important concept for the modernist avant-garde, and Walter Benjamin theorised the effects of montage as a form of shock or interruption throughout his writing in the 1920s and 1930s. For Benjamin, shock was understood in Marxist terms, as a necessary pre-condition for the disruption of the anaesthetising effects of late capitalism. Like Deleuze, Benjamin privileged the shock of the encounter as a means for thought renewal freed from existing postulates. This mechanism of shock is constantly at play and adopts slightly different inflections over the course of his writing. Consider, for example, Benjamin's essay on Baudelaire, where he argues that 'Baudelaire placed the shock experience at the very centre of his artistic work.'[31] Later, in *The Arcades Project*, Benjamin makes a similar observation:

> In Baudelaire's theory of art, the motif of shock comes into play not only as a prosodic principle. Rather, this same motif is operative wherever Baudelaire appropriates Poe's theory concerning the importance of surprise in the work of art. – From another perspective, the motif of shock emerges in the 'scornful laughter of hell' which rouses the startled allegorist from his brooding.[32]

Furthermore, Benjamin's thought intersects with Deleuze on the subject of the Proustian *mémoire involontaire* and its capacity to surprise and jolt the reader from their normative everyday state. Benjamin observes that 'The true reader of Proust is constantly jarred by small shocks.'[33] The conjunction between the shock of the encounter and montage is made clear in Deleuze's *Cinema* books. Deleuze writes that 'Montage is in thought the "intellectual process" itself, or that which, under the shock, thinks the shock.'[34] Here, Deleuze was able to crystallise this new non-representational image of thought in terms of cinema. Cinema consists of images, but the image is not understood in Platonic terms, as a mimetic copy. The image is what cinema thinks with, as thought itself is a creation. The visual images of crystals, shocks, jolts and aberrations converge in Benjamin's final text, the 'Theses on the Philosophy of History', where Benjamin writes 'Thinking involves not only the flow of thoughts, but their arrest as well. Where thinking stops in a configuration pregnant with tensions, it gives that configuration a shock, by which it crystallizes into a monad.'[35]

The requisite jolt required to disrupt normative experience is extended to the dialectical image in Benjamin's *The Arcades Project*. Here the dialectical image undertakes a certain 'caesura in the movement of thought'.[36] Benjamin emphasises the disruption performed by the dialectical image, writing, 'The dialectical image is an image that emerges suddenly, in a flash.'[37] Returning to Deleuze's challenge issued in *Difference and Repetition*, Benjamin's dialectical image does not depend on memory or recognition, but is the result of a 'fundamental encounter'.[38] Benjamin's dialectical image is not understood by Didi-Huberman in figurative or representational terms. As Didi-Huberman argued in *Devant le temps*, the dialectical image is a *crystal of time*:

> Pourquoi une image? Parce que l'image désigne, chez Benjamin, tout autre chose qu'une imagerie, une *picture*, une illustration figurative. L'image est d'abord un *cristal de temps*, la forme, construite et flamboyante tout à la fois, d'un choc fulgurant.[39]
>
> Why an image? Because the image designates, in Benjamin, anything but a collection of images, a *picture*, a figurative illustration. The image is firstly a *crystal of time*, it takes the form, both constructed and brilliant at the same time, of a dazzling shock.

The 'dazzling shock' Didi-Huberman evokes in this passage is reminiscent of Deleuze's emphasis on the shock of the encounter. This marks an enormous shift in Didi-Huberman's own intellectual development. The meta-psychoanalytic frameworks that characterised Didi-Huberman's earliest work give way to the 'masters of montage':[40] Aby Warburg, Carl Einstein, Walter Benjamin, Georges Bataille and Bertolt Brecht.

It is critical to recognise that montage must be understood as a philosophical achievement in its own right. Didi-Huberman is close to Gilles

Deleuze's principle that philosophy creates concepts. Deleuze writes that 'philosophy is a discipline that is just as inventive, just as creative as any other discipline, and it consists in creating or inventing concepts. Concepts do not exist ready-made in a kind of heaven waiting for some philosopher to come grab them. Concepts have to be produced.'[41] Montage produces, not simply reproduces an existing idea.

Montage is privileged by Didi-Huberman for its epistemological capacity to reconfigure thought and knowledge. Unlike other theorists of the avant-garde such as Peter Bürger, who located the origins of montage specifically in the *papiers collés* of Pablo Picasso and Georges Braque, Didi-Huberman instead identifies a broad cross-disciplinary impulse incorporating art, cinema and literature.[42] Soviet filmmaker and theorist Sergei Eisenstein asserted that the theoretical possibilities of montage could theoretically extend well beyond cinema to encompass all art forms: '[T]he montage principle in films is only a sectional application of the montage principle in general, a principle which, if fully understood, passes far beyond the limits of splicing bits of film together.'[43] Crucially, Eisenstein stressed that the possibilities of montage could theoretically extend well beyond cinema to encompass all art forms. By electing not to restrict his discussion to Soviet avant-garde cinema, Didi-Huberman retrieves the general principles of the procedure itself, emphasising the shock or juxtaposition between individual parts to generate new lines of thought. Out of the collision, something new is created. At no point does Didi-Huberman get drawn into a detailed discussion of montage, preferring to concentrate on its epistemological capabilities as a mode of disruption. As a result, he places himself at risk of flattening the concept, ignoring the form's individual nuances, complexities and mutations as it was taken up in other geographies.

Focusing on montage as a tool or mechanism for producing knowledge, Didi-Huberman is not far from Foucault here. In his essay, 'Nietzsche, Genealogy and History', Foucault underscored the necessity for discontinuous modes of knowledge, arguing: 'History becomes "effective" to the degree that it introduces discontinuity into our very being ... knowledge is not made for understanding; it is made for cutting.'[44] Whereas traditional historical approaches promoted long, interrupted periods of history, strung together by causal succession, the 'new' history was distinguished by discontinuities, gaps, ellipses, interruptions and displacements. Didi-Huberman has taken this remark seriously and moved the notion of montage as an epistemological 'cut' to the fore of his enquiry. In a recent interview discussing Foucault's legacy, Didi-Huberman declared that 'I could work with that command (epistemic, but also literary, ethical, and political) for years.'[45]

Didi-Huberman identifies a broad montage impulse deployed across an array of unconventional mediums in the 1920s and 1930s. Consider, for example, his analysis of Georges Bataille's journal *Documents* in *La resemblance informe ou le gai savoir visuel selon Georges Bataille*.[46] Founded and edited between 1929 and 1930, *Documents* consisted of a mere fifteen issues. Despite its extremely short shelf life, the journal has grown in stature in recent decades. Bataille introduced the notorious *informe* or formless in *Documents* no. 7, as part of the *dictionnaire critique*, and the concept has become significant for art historians and theorists seeking to rethink modernist genealogies. Rosalind Krauss and Yve-Alain Bois have done much to elaborate the notion of the *informe* and it was the subject of their 1997 exhibition at the Georges Pompidou Centre in Paris.[47] Krauss and Bois argued that the *informe* comprised the following four features, or characteristics: 'base materialism' (the work's material nature, and the use of 'low' or 'unprecious' materials), 'horizontality' (against verticality and the work's historic mode of address), 'pulse' and 'entropy' (the disintegration of matter).

Didi-Huberman advances an altogether different argument based on his repositioning of montage as an epistemological principle. To develop this line of thought he points to Bataille's familiarity with Eisenstein's theorisation of montage. During Eisenstein's trip to Paris in 1930, Bataille attended his public lecture at the Sorbonne.[48] Didi-Huberman argues that Eisenstein's visit and lecture left a lasting impression on Bataille that went as far as influencing his editorial and design decisions concerning the overall visual look and feel of *Documents*. Didi-Huberman points to the montage effect of the curious juxtapositions Bataille created between images and text. Didi-Huberman's close reading of the physical design and layout of the pages in *Documents* brings the journal into dialogue with other roughly contemporaneous avant-garde montage projects, Warburg's *Mnemosyne Atlas* and Benjamin's *The Arcades Project*. Take, for example, the juxtaposition between dissident Surrealist photographer Jacques-André Boiffard's images of a big toe juxtaposed with Bataille's essay 'Le gros orteil' ('The Big Toe'). In this piece, published in *Documents* no. 6, Bataille argued that despite being the most *human* part of the human body, the big toe is nevertheless perceived as *spit*: 'Mais quel que soit le rôle joué dans son érection par son pied, l'homme, qui a la tête légère, c'est-à-dire élevée vers le ciel et les choses du ciel, le regarde comme un crachat sous prétexte qu'il a ce pied dans la boue.'[49] ('But whatever the role that his foot plays in keeping him upright, man, who is lightheaded, in other words a head raised to the heavens and heavenly things, sees it as spit, on the pretext that he has this foot in the mud.')

In his reading of Bataille's article, Didi-Huberman alerts the reader to the jarring collision between text and image, which is akin to the experience generated by montage. Accompanying Bataille's article are three full-page photographic images taken by Boiffard. By selecting three photographs of a big toe, Bataille chooses not to represent other aspects of the article such as his comparison between the toe and other parts of the body. The effect of the close-up is startling. Boiffard's toe takes on monstrous proportions, silhouetted against a black background and abstracted from its original context. By presenting the toe in the tradition of portraiture, Didi-Huberman observes that the toe literally becomes anthropomorphic. Working within the conventions of portraiture, Bataille inverts the hierarchy between the ideal and the abject. If the layout of the journal promotes a juxtaposition between images and text, the effect is ultimately epistemological, designed to disrupt. Emphasising the anti-mimetic possibilities of montage, *Documents* is conceived by Didi-Huberman in cinematic terms, as a 'certain *art des ressemblances* – un certain art des rapprochements, des montages, des frottements, des attractions d'images'[50] ('certain *art of resemblances* – a certain art of comparing, of montages, of frictions, of attractions of images'). For Didi-Huberman, the journal's goal was to put mimesis under pressure by presenting a fractured or *torn* version of mimesis by way of montage.

If Eisenstein is helpful for theorising a broad understanding of montage beyond cinema, Didi-Huberman's greatest intellectual debt lies with Aby Warburg's incomplete project, the *Mnemosyne Atlas*. Didi-Huberman has written two books and curated three exhibitions exploring the legacy of Aby Warburg and the *Mnemosyne Atlas*. He first discussed *Mnemosyne* in *L'image survivante*, but it was in *Atlas ou le gai savoir inquiet* that he dedicated a full examination to the epistemological possibilities of the atlas.[51] The *Mnemosyne Atlas* was conceived by Warburg in 1924 and remained unfinished at his death in 1929. It consisted of about a thousand images pinned over seventy-nine panels covered in black fabric. Dismantled with the Warburg Library's evacuation from Hamburg to London, it exists today only as a series of photographs. Warburg's objective, according to Didi-Huberman, was to visually demonstrate how certain visual motifs from antiquity 'survive' and recur in visual modes. By mapping out his ideas in arrangements of images, the atlas allowed Warburg the flexibility to pursue his ideas visually with a freedom not afforded by the written text. Rejecting a linear structure, the image configurations could be continually changed around, altered, photographed and dismembered, only for another series of images to be repositioned, explored, documented and dismantled (Figure 19).

Didi-Huberman is quick to differentiate the atlas from its cousins the encyclopaedia and the archive, observing, 'But there is a difference which for me is capital: the atlas proceeds by cutting, by incisive choices, by montage and successive re-montages.'[52] Akin to *The Arcades Project*, an atlas refuses to be 'read' in the sense one would read a novel or an essay from first page to last. Its point of entry is random, and the pathway through is not linear or predetermined. The atlas does not behave systematically like the encyclopaedia or exhaustively like the archive. It makes no claim to exhaustive knowledge. Instead, the atlas 'chooses'. From the 25,000 photographic reproductions available in Warburg's personal image library, the *Mnemosyne Atlas* only consisted of 1,000 carefully selected images. Didi-Huberman resists the temptation to construct an image-by-image reconstruction.

For Didi-Huberman, the atlas is an exemplary form of montage driven by the imagination:

> It is a tool, not for the logical exhaustion of possibilities given, but for the inexhaustible opening up to possibilities that are not yet given. Its principle, its motor, is none other than the *imagination*.[53]

As opposed to knowledge that is predetermined, imagination is active, it 'cuts across', and is anti-representational. Imagination then, in Didi-Huberman's hands, is not a passive reflection, bound to imitation and recollection. Instead, imagination is connected to the production and generation of knowledge. Didi-Huberman writes: 'Imagination is not a withdrawal to the mirages of a single reflection, as is too often thought. It is instead a construction and a *montage* of various forms placed in correspondence with one another.'[54] To support this active understanding of the imagination, Didi-Huberman draws from

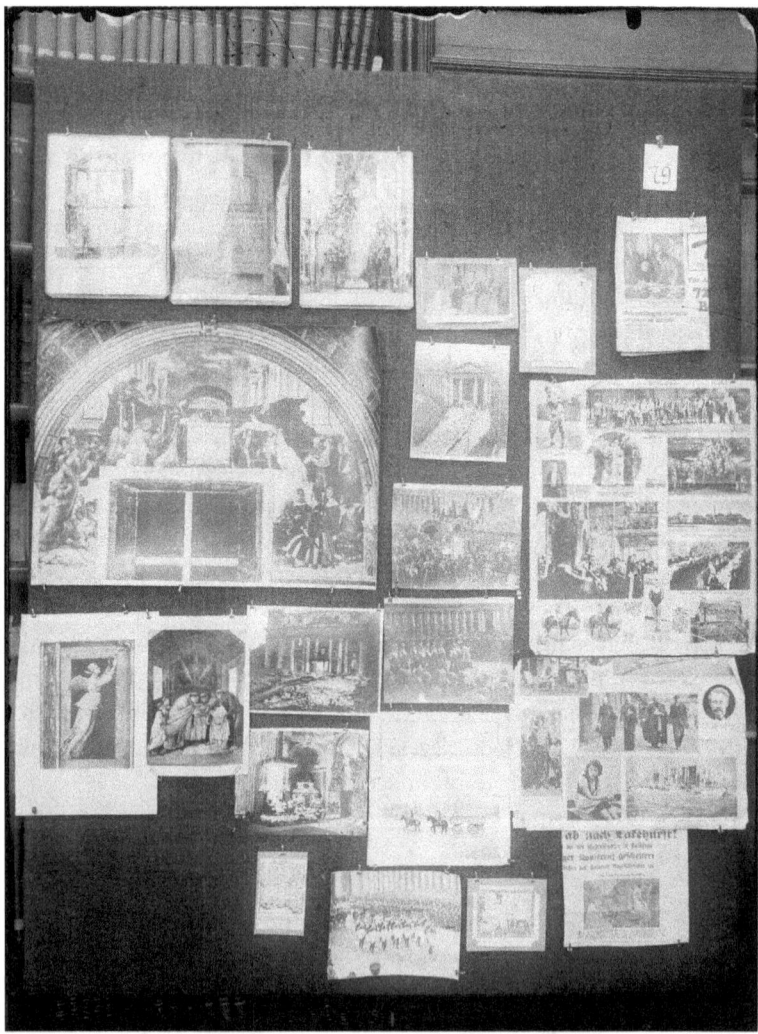

Figure 19 Aby Warburg, *Bilderatlas Mnemosyne* (1927–29), plate 79

Charles Baudelaire's essay on Edgar Allan Poe. In an important passage, Baudelaire observed:

> Imagination is not fantasy, nor is it sensibility, difficult though it would be to conceive of an imaginative man who was not sensitive. Imagination is a virtually divine faculty that apprehends immediately,

by means lying outside philosophical methods, the intimate and secret relations of things, the correspondences and analogies.[55]

It is in the 'intimate and secret relations', the 'correspondences' and 'analogies' that Didi-Huberman detects a montage impulse in Baudelaire's understanding of imagination. At first glance, Didi-Huberman's interest in the atlas is part of the broader surge of art-historical concern with the archive following the publication of Derrida's *Archive Fever*.[56] In line with Foucault's thinking, the atlas is understood as a form of 'cutting'. Unlike the archive, the atlas makes no claim to exhaustive knowledge. In comparison to the encyclopaedia or archive, *Mnemosyne* is unruly and refuses to adhere to pre-existing axioms or rules. Its combinations are theoretically endless, and with every new grouping of images, fresh possibilities and structures of thought are revealed.

The *Mnemosyne Atlas*, in Warburg's hands, refuses to conform to pre-existing art-historical classificatory systems. Again, Didi-Huberman is not far from Foucault here. Foucault begins the *The Order of Things* by drawing on Borges's arrangement of animals found in an old Chinese encyclopaedia. It was not the odd juxtapositions in Borges's description that struck Foucault. Instead, it was the deep structures of knowledge that frame what is and what can be thinkable: '[T]he exotic charm of another system of thought, is the limitation of our own, the stark impossibility of thinking *that*.'[57] Borges's cataloguing schema made no sense under existing organisational frameworks. These epistemes are products of deeply internalised principles that predetermine how we make sense of things. Foucault's point is clear: different classificatory systems exist, beyond European taxonomies and systems for grouping and ordering.

The form of montage in *Mnemosyne* is more than the result of an artistic process. Didi-Huberman resists the temptation to assemble an image-by-image reconstruction as this would impose a closed reading on the panels.[58] Like cinema, the *Mnemosyne Atlas* provides art history with a new means of creating concepts that displace its earlier human-centred universals. Warburg's *Mnemosyne* serves as a springboard for how new ideas are created through montage and juxtaposition. The montage effect does not illustrate pre-existing ideas and concepts, but constantly generates new lines of inquiry between the constellations of images. We can recognise here Didi-Huberman's commitment to Deleuze's call to overcoming the image of thought:

> Warburg expresses in his atlas a fundamental *complexity* – of an anthropological order – that was neither to be synthesised (through a unifying concept) nor described exhaustibly (in an integral archive), nor classed from A to Z (in a dictionary). Warburg's atlas does not perform according to a pre-axiomatic structure. It is not predictable in its outcome.[59]

Didi-Huberman is also rallying against Ernst Gombrich's claim that the *Atlas* is a 'large work of synthesis'.[60] The atlas remains resolutely unsynthesised, unfinished and forever incomplete. Didi-Huberman accentuates the axiomatic openness of the images, and their ability to be constantly rearranged. Eschewing a fixed and immobile illustration of ideas, the *Atlas* is in a permanent state of *becoming*. Thinking has to free itself from the fixed foundations of Man as the subject. In its capacity to conjure unforeseen relations and give form to previously unnoticed affinities, montage, Didi-Huberman argues, is a 'procedure capable of putting into movement new "thought spaces"'.[61] The atlas is dynamic. No longer dependent on the illusionism of mimetic forms, montage brings Didi-Huberman's work directly into dialogue with Deleuze's claim that cinema generates its own concepts. It is through montage and collision of images that new dialogues and new relationships are created. This results in a shift or displacement in the source or origin of knowledge. No longer located in the subject, the atlas itself is a visual form of knowledge. The atlas 'thinks', performing its own philosophical and epistemological project.

This chapter has charted Didi-Huberman's final update in an ongoing critique of representation that commenced in his earliest writings. Whilst explicit references to Deleuze are rare in his writing, it is possible to trace Didi-Huberman's commitment to rethinking the discipline of art history beyond the idealism that has shaped it since birth. Didi-Huberman's deep commitment to displacing the image preceding thought extends the previous generation's critique of mimesis. What is at stake here is no longer representation, but epistemology. The terms of the debate are shifted from aesthetics to knowledge. No longer trapped in a pre-existing or 'dogmatic' relation to representation, images are now capable of generating knowledge, of thinking.

Notes

1 Didi-Huberman, *Images in Spite of All*, 138.

2 Alfred Gell, *Art and Agency: An Anthropological Theory* (Oxford: Clarendon Press, 1998); Bill Brown, *Other Things* (Chicago: University of Chicago Press, 2016); Mitchell, *Picture Theory*; Moxey, 'Visual Studies and the Iconic Turn'.

3 Barthes, *Camera Lucida*, 38. Also see Jacques Rancière, 'The Pensive Image', in *The Emancipated Spectator*, trans. Gregory Elliott (London: Verso, 2009), 107–32. Rancière writes, 'Things become complicated when we say of an image that it is pensive. An image is not supposed to think' (107).

4 Hanneke Grootenboer, 'The Pensive Image: On Thought in Jan van Huysum's Still Life Paintings', *Oxford Art Journal*, 34:1 (2011), 13–30; Hanneke Grootenboer, 'Introduction "The Thought of Images"', *Image [&] Narrative*, no. 18 (2007), www.imageandnarrative.be/inarchive/thinking_pictures/grootenboer.htm.

5 Lacan, *The Four Fundamental Concepts*, 109.

6 Jean-Paul Sartre, *Nausea*, trans. Robert Baldick (London and New York: Penguin Modern Classics, 2000), 22.

7 *Ibid.*.

8 Foucault, *The Order of Things*, 387.

9 Foucault, *The Archaeology of Knowledge*, 12–16.

10 See Didi-Huberman, *Confronting Images*, 85–138.

11 Gilles Deleuze, *Proust and Signs: The Complete Text*, trans. Richard Howard (Minneapolis: University of Minnesota Press, 2000), 94.

12 Gilles Deleuze, *Desert Islands and Other Texts, 1953–1974*, trans. Michael Taormina (Cambridge, MA: MIT Press, 2004), 139.

13 Foucault, *The Order of Things*, 324.

14 Gilles Deleuze, *Difference and Repetition*, trans. Paul Patton (New York: Columbia University Press, 1994), 132.

15 Deleuze's anti-Platonism is well documented. See, for instance, Paul Patton, 'Anti-Platonism and Art', in Constantin V. Boundas and Dorothea Olkowski (eds), *Gilles Deleuze and the Theatre of Philosophy* (New York: Routledge, 1994), 141–56; Martin Crowley, 'Deleuze on Painting', *French Studies*, 67:3 (2013), 371–85.

16 Deleuze, *Difference and Repetition*, 131.

17 *Ibid.*, xvi–xvii.

18 *Ibid.*, 276.

19 Georges Didi-Huberman, 'Aby Warburg, l'histoire de l'art à l'âge des fantômes', interview by Élie During, *Artpress*, 277 (2002), 20.

20 Didi-Huberman, 'Des gammes anachroniques'. Didi-Huberman's emphasis.
21 Didi-Huberman, *Confronting Images*, 124.
22 *Ibid.*, 87.
23 Deleuze, *The Time-Image*, 269.
24 Didi-Huberman, *Confronting Images*, 16. Didi-Huberman's emphasis.
25 Didi-Huberman, *Images in Spite of All*, 121.
26 Deleuze, *Difference and Repetition*, 139. Deleuze's emphasis.
27 Didi-Huberman, 'Image, matière: immanence', 91
28 Didi-Huberman, *Fra Angelico*, 2.
29 Benjamin, *The Origin of German Tragic Drama*, 34.
30 *Ibid.*, 30.
31 Walter Benjamin, 'On Some Motifs in Baudelaire', in Hannah Arendt (ed.), *Illuminations*, ed. trans. Harry Zohn (New York: Schocken Books, 2007), 163.
32 Benjamin, *The Arcades Project*, 383.
33 Benjamin, 'The Image of Proust', 208.
34 Deleuze, *Cinema 2: The Time-Image*, 153.
35 Benjamin, 'Theses on the Philosophy of History', 262–3.
36 Benjamin, *The Arcades Project*, 475.
37 *Ibid.*, 473.
38 Deleuze, *Difference and Repetition*, 139.
39 Didi-Huberman, *Devant le temps*, 241.
40 Didi-Huberman, *Images in Spite of All*, 152.
41 Gilles Deleuze, *Two Regimes of Madness: Texts and Interviews 1975–1995*, trans. Ames Hodges and Mike Taormina (New York: Semiotext(e), 2006), 313.
42 Peter Bürger, *Theory of the Avant-Garde*, trans. Michael Shaw (Manchester: Manchester University Press, 1984), 73. The notion of montage's origins being located in the cubist practices of Picasso and Braque is shared by John Willet, *Art and Politics in the Weimar Period: The New Sobriety, 1917–1933* (New York: Pantheon Books, 1978).
43 Sergei Eisenstein, 'Word and Image', in *The Film Sense*, trans. Jay Leyda (Cleveland, OH and New York: Meridian Books, 1957), 36.
44 Michel Foucault, 'Nietzsche, Genealogy, History', in Donald F. Bouchard (ed.), *Language, Counter-Memory, Practice*, trans. Donald F. Bouchard and Sherry Simon (Ithaca, NY: Cornell University Press, 1977), 88.
45 Didi-Huberman, 'Knowing When to Cut', 84.
46 Georges Didi-Huberman, *La ressemblance informe ou le gai savoir visuel selon Georges Bataille* (Paris: Macula, 1995).

47 See Yve-Alain Bois and Rosalind Krauss, *Formless: A User's Guide* (New York: Zone Books, 1997).

48 On Eisenstein's recollections of the lecture, see Sergei Eisenstein, *Immoral Memories*, trans. Herbert Marshall (Boston: Houghton Mifflin, 1983), 91–5.

49 Georges Bataille, 'Le gros orteil', in Denis Hollier (ed.), *Œuvres complètes*, vol. 1 (Paris: Gallimard, 1970), 200.

50 *Ibid.*, 18.

51 See Georges Didi-Huberman, *L'image survivante: histoire de l'art et temps des fantômes selon Aby Warburg* (Paris: Les Éditions de Minuit, 2002), 452–505; Didi-Huberman, *Atlas ou le gai savoir inquiet.*

52 Georges Didi-Huberman, 'Atlas: comment remonter le monde?', interview by Catherine Millet, *Artpress*, 373 (2012), 49.

53 Didi-Huberman, *Atlas: How to Carry the World on One's Back?*, 15.

54 Didi-Huberman, *Images in Spite of All*, 120.

55 Charles Baudelaire, 'Further Notes on Edgar Poe', in *Selected Writings on Art and Artists*, trans. P. E. Charvet (Cambridge: Cambridge University Press, 1981), 199.

56 See Jacques Derrida, *Archive Fever: A Freudian Impression*, trans. Eric Prenowitz (Chicago: University of Chicago Press, 1996); Okwui Enwezor, *Archive Fever: Uses of the Document in Contemporary Art* (New York and Göttingen: International Center of Photography, 2008).

57 Foucault, *The Order of Things*, xv.

58 For a close reconstruction of plates 78 and 79 see, for example, Charlotte Schoell-Glass, 'Aby Warburg's Late Comments on Symbol and Ritual', *Science in Context*, 12:4 (1999), 621–42.

59 Didi-Huberman, *Atlas: How to Carry the World on One's Back?*, 19.

60 E. H. Gombrich, *Aby Warburg: An Intellectual Biography* (London: The Warburg Institute, 1970), 282.

61 Didi-Huberman, *Atlas: How to Carry the World on One's Back?*, 182.

Conclusion

Is it possible to be consistent without being dogmatic? Or predictable, without succumbing to stereotype? In *Passés cités par JLG*, Didi-Huberman demonstrates that it is. Wholly dedicated to the work of the French filmmaker Jean-Luc Godard, the text draws together many of the distinctive strains distinguishing Didi-Huberman's thought. Consider, for example, his discussion of part IB, 'Une histoire seule', in Godard's *Histoire(s) du cinéma* (1989–98). Godard shows a still image from D. W. Griffith's *Way Down East* (1920), where Lillian Gish is lying exhausted on an ice floe in a river (Figure 20). The still of Gish is replaced with a close-up from André Brouillet's 1887 painting, *Un leçon clinique à la Salpêtrière* (Figure 21). Laid over the top is Godard's voice, which enquires: 'But what is the difference between Lillian Gish on her ice floe and Augustine at Salpêtrière?'

The arc of Gish's body, lying on the ice, evokes images of Charcot's favourite patient Augustine and her hysterical back arch documented in the photographic archive that formed the *Iconographie photographique de la Salpêtrière* (Figure 22). Didi-Huberman describes the sequence in the following terms:

[C]'est vouloir souligner la fécondité heuristique, l'exubérance potentielle de tout montage. C'est y voir un *mouvement centrifuge* d'associations productrices d'idées nouvelles, d'hypothèses, de fantaisies imaginatives, mais aussi de savoirs authentiques: un libre geste pour multiplier les figures, les combiner en 'phrases' douées à la fois de rigueur quant à la connaissance (Griffith contemporain de Charcot, Charcot proche, via Albert Londe, de la cinématographie) et d'intensité quant à la passion ou, du moins, quant au désir (Lilian Gish offerte au vent comme au regard de ses cinéphiles, Augustine offerte à l'*aura hysterica* comme au regard de ses médecins),[1]

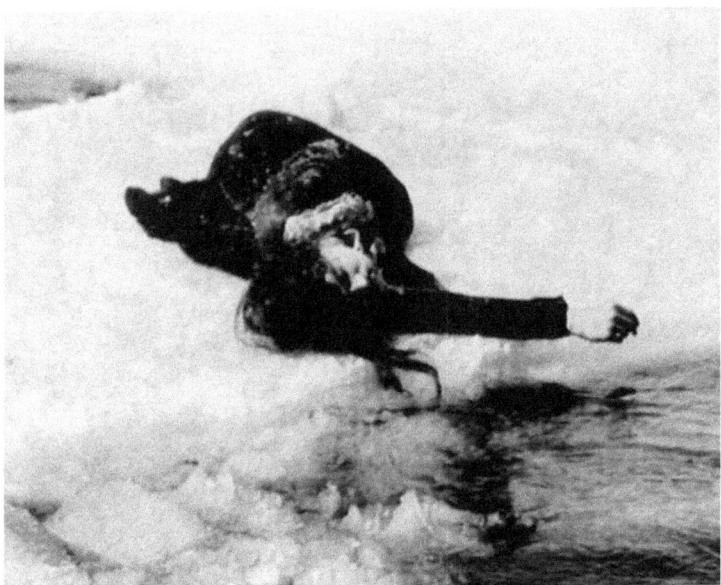

Figure 20 Jean-Luc Godard, *Histoire(s) du cinéma*, 1988–98, episode 1B, 'Une histoire seule'

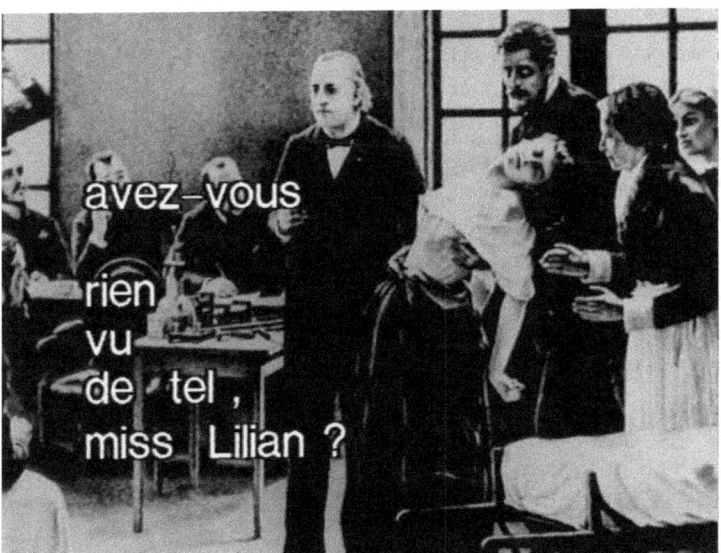

Figure 21 Jean-Luc Godard, *Histoire(s) du cinéma*, 1988–98, episode 1B, 'Une histoire seule'

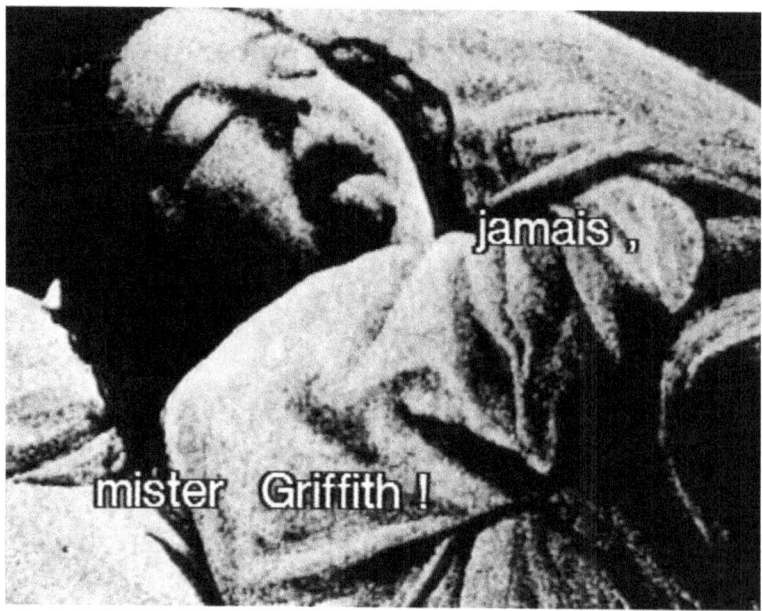

Figure 22 Jean-Luc Godard, *Histoire(s) du cinéma*, 1988–98, episode 1B, 'Une histoire seule'

> I]t is to emphasise the heuristic fecundity, the potential exuber-
> ance of all montage. It is a centrifugal movement of associations
> producing new ideas, hypotheses, imaginative fantasies, but also
> authentic knowledge: a free gesture to multiply the figures, to com-
> bine them into 'statements' simultaneously endowed with rigour as
> to knowledge (Griffith contemporary of Charcot, Charcot close, via
> Albert Londe, to cinematography) and with intensity as to passion
> or, at least, to desire (Lillian Gish offered to the wind as she is to the
> gaze of her cinephiles. Augustine offered to the hysterical aura she is
> to the gaze of her doctors).

Didi-Huberman's account of Godard's montage reminds us just how consistent his project is. Didi-Huberman incorporates key moments that have defined his intellectual development: from Charcot's invention of hysteria and Augustine's hysterical 'performances', to Warburg's formulation of *Nachleben* and the idea that extreme emotional gestures survive through time.

To approach Didi-Huberman from an archaeological perspective reveals his engagement with some of the most important currents of twentieth century French intellectual history: structuralism, poststructuralism and deconstruction. He has sought disciplinary renewal by reinventing its styles, techniques and theoretical orientations. Furthermore, it is particularly important to recognise the contextual influence of the École des hautes études en sciences sociales on the formation of Didi-Huberman's concerns. His early work must be measured in relation to the critique of representation initiated by his colleagues, Louis Marin and Hubert Damisch. Didi-Huberman broadly extends this critique, by shifting the terms of engagement beyond language to the sensual, material image.

To trace the contours of a discipline, to examine its occlusions and silences amounts to only half of Didi-Huberman's project. It is not enough to sustain an ongoing critique of idealism, as this fails to satisfy Foucault's original challenge issued in *The Archaeology of Knowledge*, 'This epistemological mutation of history is not yet complete.'[2] The challenge for the archaeologist of thought is to formulate epistemological renewal, developing new theoretical orientations and modes of thinking. The task assigned by Foucault to the new history is 'to develop its own theory: how is one to specify the different concepts that enable us to conceive of discontinuity (threshold, rupture, break, mutation, transformation)?'[3] What, then, are the consequences of an 'archaeological method' for art history? How to reframe a discipline in terms of discontinuity? Didi-Huberman's transformations are clear: contrary to the modern episteme inaugurated by Vasari, Didi-Huberman assembles a heterogeneous constellation of theorists including Walter Benjamin, Aby Warburg and Georges Bataille. Against *a priori* conditions of knowledge, he proposes an exploratory 'knowledge through images' derived from Benjamin's and Warburg's great experimental montage projects of the 1920s and 1930s. In opposition to Hegelian lines of continual and progressive development, he introduces Warburg and the eternal return. Undermining Vasari's emphasis of opticality, Didi-Huberman retrieves a materialist mode of contact through the *empreinte*. In contrast to Erwin Panofsky's iconological formulation of images as the illustration of words, the image becomes Deleuzian, capable of pursuing and undertaking its own theoretical and philosophical project, and generating new modes of thought.

Didi-Huberman has sought to regenerate art-historical thinking. This finds its most visible form in his retrieval of montage from the twentieth-century avant-garde. Montage, like idealism, is notoriously overdetermined. It can encompass John Heartfield's photomontages, Sergei Eisenstein's montages and Dziga Vertov's intervals. For Clement Greenberg, montage as collage amounted to a supreme form of flatness. Montage gave visual form to *Nachleben* in Aby Warburg's *Mnemosyne Atlas*. Walter Benjamin explored the literary possibilities of montage in his enormous collection of quotations and aphorisms in *The Arcades Project*. Georges Bataille applied lessons learned from Eisenstein in the juxtaposition of word and text in the journal *Documents*. How, then, can montage be anything more than a quaint dream of the historical avant-garde? To push the question even further, how is it possible to imagine a contemporary relevance for montage practices? For Didi-Huberman, montage is an exemplary form of intervention. Importantly, it is anti-mimetic, therefore aligned with his critique of idealist formulations of representation. Furthermore, in an accordance to history and knowledge being organised around Foucault's call for discontinuity and disjuncture, montage can jolt, shock, reconfigure and reassemble. Montage cuts through existing knowledge structures, refusing to allow anything to settle. Montage allows for the recommencement of thought.

In his reactivation of montage as a tool for intervention, Didi-Huberman mobilises historically long-standing Marxist debates concerning the effectiveness of representation, particularly montage. Georg Lukács memorably condemned montage as little more than a monotonous 'one-dimensional technique'. Lukács wrote:

> The details may be dazzlingly colourful in their diversity, but the whole will never be more than an unrelieved grey on grey. After all, a puddle can never be more than dirty water, even though it may contain rainbow tints.[4]

Fast-forward to the postmodernism of the 1980s and 1990s. Against a generation defined by Fredric Jameson's postmodern 'depthlessness' and historical pastiche, Didi-Huberman reinvests in the image's critical capacity *to take a position* (*prendre une position*). Underpinning this is Didi-Huberman's belief that images *count*. They actively shape our realities. Montage is carefully retrieved by Didi-Huberman from the historical avant-garde to deliver a mode of representation wholly aligned with an archaeological gambit of discontinuity and rupture. This is not a nostalgic revival on Didi-Huberman's part. Instead, it suggests that perhaps we still belong to that era. In Warburgian terms, we might say that the past has returned to haunt the present with a certain intensity. To return to my opening question: is it possible to be consistent without being dogmatic? In the recently published *Aperçues*, Didi-Huberman proves that even after a forty-year career, it is.[5] Taking an enormous step away from what we would recognise as 'conventional' academic writing, *Aperçues* is his most ambitious departure from mainstream art-history writing to date. Didi-Huberman's proclivity for montage now directs his own writing style as the gap between form and expression closes. Divided into four sections, the text consists of almost 200 fragments. All the fragments are dated, but not organised chronologically. As a result, the text eschews being organised into a linear or teleological narrative. Instead, *Aperçues* is an unruly montage, akin to Walter Benjamin's *The Arcades Project*. In *Aperçues*, fragments collide and juxtapose, refusing to settle into a predictable narrative. Like *The Arcades Project* there is no singular point of entry. The fragments behave like a kaleidoscope, as Didi-Huberman's gaze is restless, shifting and constantly varying. This eclectic collection of intimate thoughts and memories, combined with research notes and observations, self-consciously draws attention to the traditions and conventions that continue to determine art-historical writing.

'Aperçues' is derived from the verb *apercevoir*, which means *to catch sight*, or *to catch a glimpse of*. The noun 'aperçu' is usually configured in the masculine. Didi-Huberman, however, feminises the noun by adding an 'e'. He distances himself from the masculine noun: 'Je n'aime pas que l' "aperçu" soit au masculin, il évoque alors quelque chose comme un résumé, une table des matières, un programme.' ('I don't like the fact that "aperçu" is masculine, it then suggests something like an overview, a table of contents, a programme.') Instead, an 'aperçue' – in the feminine – is 'plus belle et plus étrange'[6] ('is stranger and more beautiful'). Didi-Huberman's long-held mistrust towards language and its violence towards non-literary sign systems is therefore articulated through the *aperçues* in feminine plural form. By emphasising the shift from the gaze (*le regard*) to the glimpse (*aperçues*), Didi-Huberman stresses the incomplete, fragmentariness of the glimpse and hints of an evacuation of authority, an abdication of a desire to control the image. The fragment is an exemplary literary device for capturing in language the image's fragility, without lapsing into the conventional power relationship that privileges the authorial voice of the art historian.

In *Aperçues*, Didi-Huberman has mobilised montage as a form of art writing. To write in an aphoristic manner is certainly not new. Didi-Huberman acknowledges Charles Baudelaire as 'le grand maître de l'aperçue'[7] ('the grand master of the glimpse'). His decision to utilise the fragment has a historical echo, and it is possible to reach beyond Benjamin and Baudelaire, to the Jena Romantics who extolled the importance of the fragment as a literary form. The fragment is experimental, incomplete and subjective. As Philippe Lacoue-Labarthe and Jean-Luc Nancy observed, the fragment 'does not pretend to be exhaustive'.[8] Instead, it is partially *incomplete*: '[T]he fragment-project does not operate as a program or prospectus but as the immediate projection of what it nonetheless incompletes.'[9] The fragment does not contribute to an overall homogeneous programme, yet as Lacoue-Labarthe and Nancy indicate, this sense of fragmentary incompletion suggests an ineffable wholeness. Didi-Huberman confirms this: 'Je ne désire pourtant ni dresser le système des singularités multiples où se dessinerait un physionomie de ma sensibilité, ni écrire un roman du personnage que mes expériences de regard finiraient par dessiner.'[10] ('However, I have no desire either to organise these multiple singularities into a system that would provide an outline of my sensitivity, or to write a novel around the character that my visual experiences would end up drawing.') The fragmentary form allows Didi-Huberman to destabilise narrative structure, and any sense of temporal continuity. The fragments rub and collide, eluding notions of totality, while paradoxically reaffirming Didi-Huberman's eschewal of the totalising effect of homogenising systems such as structuralism, iconology and the Hegelian dialectic.

Reaching back further in French literary history, Lacoue-Labarthe and Nancy link the fragment to the essayistic tradition initiated by sixteenth-century statesman and philosopher Michel de Montaigne (1533–92). Montaigne developed a new style of writing and a new approach to nonfiction: 107 essays collected in three volumes of the *Essais*, published in 1580 and subject to two revisions: in 1588 and again in 1595.[11] With the 'essay', derived from the French verb *essayer*, to try or attempt, Montaigne instigated an experimental literary genre that sought to test and search for new literary forms. Montaigne considered the essay to be the ideal form for the trying out of new ideas, his own subjectivity and of broader observations of society. Importantly, Montaigne was the first to identify the notion of uncertainty as a valid mode of writing against the orthodoxy of traditional scholarship: 'The scholars distinguish and mark off their ideas more specifically and in detail. I, who cannot see beyond what I have learned from experience, without any system, present my ideas in a general way, and tentatively.'[12] Uncertainty was therefore linked to the form of the essay, and Montaigne returned to the theme through the *Essais*. In another famous passage, he distanced himself from the authorial voice of the scholar: 'Determining and knowing, like giving, appertains to rule and mastery; to inferiority, subjection, and apprenticeship appertains enjoyment and acceptance.'[13] Montaigne's theorisation and practice of writing, combined with the question of self and subjectivity, have ensured that his insights have enduring relevance for contemporary essayists.[14]

Didi-Huberman takes up Montaigne's theme of uncertainty in *Aperçues*. If the measure of historical truth was the confidence of the all-knowing, complete subject, Didi-Huberman exploits the essay form to problematise the authorial voice. Didi-Huberman moves in and through the text, and the boundaries between fact and fiction become blurred and unstable. The formality of third person gives way to the intimacy of first person: this is the Didi-Huberman who mourns, desires and loves. As readers, we are never entirely sure where the boundaries lie. Didi-Huberman shifts in tone and register as the fragments collide. Unusually, Didi-Huberman's dry sense of humour comes to the fore as he quips, 'On ne choisit pas sa famille'[15] ('We do not choose our family') in relation to Gerhard Richter's 1965 painting of his Uncle Rudi.

In one fragment, Didi-Huberman questions the authorial self in relation to the authority connoted by the word 'selon' (according to). He observes, 'Il faudrait savoir employer le mot *selon* sans avoir à dire "selon moi".' ('It would be necessary to know how to use the word *according to* without having to say "according to me".') He continues, 'C'est une manie de philosophes depuis Platon ... Cela s'appelle académisme, voire dogmatisme.'[16] ('It has been a mania of philosophers since Plato ... It is called academism, even dogmatism.') Instead, Didi-Huberman turns to the *Dictionnaire historique de la langue française* and retrieves older meanings of the term that have fallen into disuse: work, risk and modesty.[17]

From its very inception, the essay evaded rigid definitions. Montaigne ruminated, 'How often and perhaps how stupidly have I extended my book to make it speak of itself!'[18] The broad characteristics of the essay, however, are generally agreed upon: the essay affords a flexibility that traditional academic writing does not. Essayistic writing has come to indicate a work that expresses ideas in a relaxed, even playful way. The essay tends to be contrasted with conventional styles of nonfiction writing. It is typically a mode of writing particularly well suited to an exploratory testing or the trying out of new ideas. These ideas are often revisited, reconfigured and reworked. Drawing together these two interconnected literary traditions, the fragment and the essay, I argue that Didi-Huberman is deliberately working in the essayistic form because of its self-conscious distance from art-writing conventions. The essay is endlessly open, unfinished and incomplete. The examples of Didi-Huberman's essayistic writing are many and varied and span the breadth of his career as the format was ideally suited to testing new ideas: from his 1990s series of monographs considering the work of Simon Hantaï, Giuseppe Penone, James Turrell, through to his collaboration with filmmaker Maria Kourkouta and writer Nikki Giannari in *Passer, quoi qu'il en coûte*, Didi-Huberman has explored different forms and styles of art writing.[19]

Theodor Adorno's essay 'The Essay as Form' is helpful to understanding the essay's challenge to the orthodoxy of form. Adorno argued, '[t]he essay shies away from the violence of dogma'[20] and 'suspends the traditional concept of method'.[21] Moreover, concepts in the essay do not build in a linear manner, but instead 'interweave as if in a carpet'.[22] The fragments in *Aperçues* simultaneously look forwards and backwards. It is possible to identify embryonic 'sketches' that have been fully developed in his longer book projects over the past decade. The fragments also look backwards, reiterating long-standing concerns that have preoccupied him from the start of his career. Didi-Huberman's own personal recollections come to the fore: he will juxtapose fragments describing the death of his mother with delicate descriptions of the Tuscan countryside when he was conducting his research for *Fra Angelico*.[23]

Adorno's insights are particularly relevant, as Didi-Huberman began his career rallying against the latent positivism in art history. The 'aperçue devient alors une pratique d'écriture intermittente, mon "petit" genre littéraire dispersé-rapide, multiforme et sans projet, en marge ou en traverse de mes "grandes" recherches obstinées-patientes'[24] ('the glimpse thus becomes an intermittent writing practice, my "minor" rapidly dispersed literary genre, multiform and with no overarching schema, marginal to, or cutting across my "major" obstinate-patient research'). The fragment has long been recognised as a literary form in its own right. It still retains, however, an element of subversion. By evoking the notion of a 'minor' literary genre, Didi-Huberman gestures towards Deleuze and Guattari's proposal in their book on Kafka: minor literature agitates within the body of that literary tradition. They write: 'We might as well say that minor no longer designates specific literatures but the revolutionary conditions for every literature within the heart of what is called great (or established) literature.'[25] Deleuze and Guattari make the point that minor literature does not take place elsewhere, separate and distinct from major literature. Instead, minor literature functions as an internal operation from within, such as Kafka electing to write in German. By implication, this is Didi-Huberman's argument: the essay disrupts art-historical writing from within.

Aperçues is a poignant reminder that writing is not neutral or transparent. Instead, art-history writing exists as a series of literary conventions. As Hayden White demonstrated so eloquently, historians produce narratives, much in the same way as authors produce fiction. These narratives place constraints on how historians interpret the past. While the discipline's gaze and objects of study might have expanded since the 1980s, the literary form of art history has not visibly altered in the ensuing decades. Even following in the wake of the 'new' and 'radical' art history, the discipline remains committed to carefully developed arguments supported by judiciously collected facts. Art historians have generally been reluctant to pursue alternative literary genres, and tend to err safely on the side of objective facts and a deliberate bracketing of self. T. J. Clark's extended mediation on the practice of writing and Michael Ann Holly's haunting lament on melancholy as a central trope for art writing stand as notable exceptions.[26] Didi-Huberman recently discussed Foucault's style of writing and its enduring influence on his own practice: 'it was almost always beautiful. It was *written*. I think that art history is also a literary discipline … Foucault, Derrida, and Deleuze knew that perfectly well: doing philosophy means writing because there are literary choices.'[27] Didi-Huberman's comments are important, because they remind us that the practice of art history is a *literary* discipline. Ultimately, it is an art historian's duty of care:

Décrire, ne serait-ce que décrire. Pour cela déjà il faut en être passé par toutes les grandes décisions de la pensée et de l'écriture. Avoir sollicité le style, le bon style, je veux dire celui qui parvient au minuscule miracle de *toucher l'image*.[28]

To describe, just to describe. For this one has to have already moved through all the great decisions of thought and writing. To have sought out the style, the right style, by which I mean the one that achieves the tiny miracle of *touching the image*.

Notes

1 Didi-Huberman, *Passés cités par JLG*, 41–2.
2 Foucault, *The Archaeology of Knowledge*, 11.
3 *Ibid.*, 5.
4 Georg Lukács, 'Realism in the Balance', in *Aesthetics and Politics* (London: NLB, 1977), 43.
5 Georges Didi-Huberman, *Aperçues* (Paris: Les Éditions de Minuit, 2018).
6 *Ibid.*, 18.
7 *Ibid.*, 19.
8 Philippe Lacoue-Labarthe and Jean-Luc Nancy, *The Literary Absolute*, trans. Philip Barnard and Cheryl Lester (Albany: SUNY Press, 1988), 42.
9 *Ibid.*, 43.
10 Didi-Huberman, *Aperçues*, 18.
11 Michel de Montaigne, *The Complete Essays of Montaigne*, trans. Donald M. Frame (Stanford, CA: Stanford University Press, 1958).
12 *Ibid.*, 824.
13 *Ibid.*, 785.
14 For an excellent account of the shifting historical reception of Montaigne's formulation of subjectivity, see Richard L. Regosin, 'Montaigne and His Readers', in Denis Hollier (ed.), *A New History of French Literature* (Cambridge, MA: Harvard University Press, 1989), 248–53.
15 Didi-Huberman, *Aperçues*, 237.
16 *Ibid.*, 262.
17 *Ibid.*, 262–4.
18 Montaigne, *The Complete Essays*, 818.
19 Didi-Huberman, *L'étoilement*; Georges Didi-Huberman, *Être crâne: lieu, contact, pensée, sculpture* (Paris: Les Éditions de Minuit, 2000); Georges Didi-Huberman, *L'homme qui marchait dans la couleur*

(Paris: Les Éditions de Minuit, 2001); Georges Didi-Huberman and Niki Giannari, *Passer, quoi qu'il en coûte* (Paris: Les Éditions de Minuit, 2017).

20 Theodor Adorno, 'The Essay as Form', *New German Critique*, 32 (1984), 158.

21 *Ibid.*, 159.

22 *Ibid.*, 160.

23 Didi-Huberman, *Aperçues*, 124–6.

24 *Ibid.*, 18.

25 Gilles Deleuze and Félix Guattari, *Kafka: Toward a Minor Literature* (Minneapolis: University of Minnesota Press, 1986).

26 T. J. Clark, *The Sight of Death: An Experiment in Art Writing* (New Haven, CT: Yale University Press, 2006); Michael Ann Holly, *The Melancholy Art* (Princeton: Princeton University Press, 2013).

27 Didi-Huberman, 'Knowing When to Cut', 81. Didi-Huberman's emphasis.

28 Didi-Huberman, *Aperçues*, 38. Didi-Huberman's emphasis.

Bibliography

Adorno, Theodor, *Aesthetic Theory*, trans. Robert Hullot-Kentor (London and New York: Continuum, 2002).

——, 'The Essay as Form', *New German Critique*, 32 (1984), 151–71.

——, *Prisms*, trans. Samuel and Shierry Weber (Cambridge, MA: MIT Press, 1981).

Agamben, Giorgio, *Remnants of Auschwitz: The Witness and the Archive*, trans. Daniel Heller-Roazen (New York: Zone Books, 1999).

Alberti, Leon Battista, *On Painting*, trans. Cecil Grayson (London: Penguin Books, 2004).

Alloa, Emmanuel, 'The Most Sublime of All Laws: The Strange Resurgence of a Kantian Motif in Contemporary Image Politics', *Critical Inquiry*, 41:2 (2015), 367–89.

Alpers, Svetlana, *The Art of Describing: Dutch Art in the Seventeenth Century* (Chicago: University of Chicago Press, 1983).

——, 'Interpretation without Representation, or, The Viewing of *Las Meninas*', *Representations*, 1 (1983), 30–42.

Alpers, Svetlana, Emily Apter, Carol Armstrong, Susan Buck-Morss, Tom Conley, Jonathan Crary, Thomas Crow *et al.*, 'Visual Culture Questionnaire', *October*, 77 (1996), 25–70.

Aquinas, Thomas, *Summa Theologica*, trans. Fathers of the English Dominican Province (London: Burns & Oates, 1947).

Arasse, Daniel, *Le détail. Pour une histoire rapprochée de la peinture* (Paris: Flammarion, 1996).

Bal, Mieke, *The Mottled Screen: Reading Proust Visually*, trans. Anna-Louise Milne (Stanford: Stanford University Press, 1997).

——, *Quoting Caravaggio: Contemporary Art, Preposterous History* (Chicago: University of Chicago Press, 1999).

Balzac, Honoré de, *The Unknown Masterpiece*, trans. Richard Howard (New York: New York Review of Books, 2001).

Barolsky, Paul, *Why Mona Lisa Smiles and Other Tales by Vasari* (University Park: Pennsylvania State University Press, 1991).

Barthes, Roland, *Camera Lucida*, trans. Richard Howard (London: Flamingo, 1984).

Bataille, Georges, 'Le gros orteil', in Denis Hollier (ed.), *Œuvres complètes*, vol 1 (Paris: Gallimard, 1970), 200–4.

Batchen, Geoffrey, *Burning with Desire: The Conception of Photography* (Cambridge, MA: MIT Press, 1999).

Baudelaire, Charles, 'Further Notes on Edgar Poe', in *Selected Writings on Art and Artists*, trans. P. E. Charvet (Cambridge: Cambridge University Press, 1981), 188–208.

Baugh, Bruce, *French Hegel: From Surrealism to Postmodernism* (New York: Routledge, 2003).

Belting, Hans, *The Invisible Masterpiece*, trans. Helen Atkins (Chicago: University of Chicago Press, 2001).

——, *Likeness and Presence: A History of the Image Before the Era of Art*, trans. Edmund Jephcott (Chicago: University of Chicago Press, 1994).

Benjamin, Walter, *The Arcades Project*, trans. Rolf Tiedemann (Cambridge, MA: Belknap Press of Harvard University Press, 1999).

——, 'The Crisis of the Novel', in Michael W. Jennings, Howard Eiland and Gary Smith (eds), *Walter Benjamin: Selected Writings*, vol. 2: *1927–1934*, trans. Rodney Livingstone *et al.* (Cambridge, MA: Belknap Press of Harvard University Press, 1999), 299–304.

——, 'The Image of Proust', in Hannah Arendt (ed.), *Illuminations*, trans. Harry Zohn (New York: Schocken Books, 2007), 201–15.

——, 'On Some Motifs in Baudelaire', in Hannah Arendt (ed.), *Illuminations*, trans. Harry Zohn (New York: Schocken Books, 2007), 155–200.

——, *The Origin of German Tragic Drama*, trans. John Osborne (London: Verso, 1998).

——, 'The Storyteller: Observations on the Works of Nikolai Leskov', in Howard Eiland and Michael W. Jennings (eds), *Walter Benjamin: Selected Writings*, vol. 3: *1935–1938*, trans. Edmund Jephcott, Howard Eiland *et al.* (Cambridge, MA: Belknap Press of Harvard University Press, 2002), 143–66.

——, 'Theses on the Philosophy of History', in Hannah Arendt (ed.), *Illuminations*, trans. Harry Zohn (New York: Schocken Books, 2007), 253–64.

Bloch, Ernst, *Aesthetics and Politics* (London: NLB, 1977).

Boehm, Gottfried, and W. J. T. Mitchell, 'Pictorial versus Iconic Turn: Two Letters', *Culture, Theory and Critique*, 50:2 (2009), 103–21.

Bois, Yve-Alain, and Rosalind Krauss, *Formless: A User's Guide* (New York: Zone Books, 1997).

Bonne, Jean-Claude, 'Art et image', in Jacques Revel and Nathan Wachtel (eds), *Une école pour les sciences sociales: de la VIe section à l'Ecole des hautes études en sciences sociales* (Paris: Les Éditions du Cerf, 1996), 353–65.

Botella, César, and Sárah Botella, 'Authors' Introduction to the English Edition', in *The Work of Psychic Figurability: Mental States without Representation*, trans. Andrew Weller (London and New York: Routledge with the Institute of Psychoanalysis, 2004), 1–13.

Bourneville, D. M., and P. Regnard, *Iconographie photographique de la Salpêtrière: service de M. Charcot* (Paris: Aux Bureaux du Progrés Médical, 1877–80).

Boyne, Roy, 'Foucault and Art', in Paul Smith and Carolyn Wilde (eds), *A Companion to Art Theory* (Oxford: Blackwell, 2002), 337–48.

Bredekamp, Horst, *Image Acts: A Systematic Approach to Visual Agency*, trans. Elizabeth Clegg (Berlin and Boston: De Gruyter, 2018).

Brown, Adam, *Judging 'Privileged' Jews: Holocaust Ethics, Representation, and the 'Grey Zone'* (New York and Oxford: Berghahn Books, 2013).

Brown, Bill, *Other Things* (Chicago: University of Chicago Press, 2016).

Bryson, Norman, *Calligram: Essays in New Art History from France* (Cambridge: Cambridge University Press, 1988).

Bürger, Peter, *Theory of the Avant-Garde*, trans. Michael Shaw (Manchester: Manchester University Press, 1984).

Cennini, Cennino d'Andrea, *The Craftsman's Handbook*, trans. Daniel V. Thompson (New York: Dover Publications, 1954).

Chaouat, Bruno, 'In the Image of Auschwitz', *Diacritics*, 36:1 (2007), 86–96.

Chare, Nicholas, and Dominic Williams (eds), *Testimonies of Resistance: Representations of the Auschwitz-Birkenau Sonderkommando* (New York and Oxford: Berghahn Books, 2019).

Cheetham, Mark A., Michael Ann Holly and Keith P. F. Moxey (eds), *The Subjects of Art History: Historical Objects in Contemporary Perspectives* (Cambridge: Cambridge University Press, 1998).

Chéroux, Clément (ed.), *Mémoire des camps: photographies des camps de concentration et d'extermination Nazis, 1933–1999* (Paris: Marval, 2001).

Cherry, Deborah, 'Art History, Visual Culture', *Art History*, 27:4 (2004), 479–93.

Clark, T. J., *The Sight of Death: An Experiment in Art Writing* (New Haven, CT: Yale University Press, 2006).

Crary, Jonathan, *Techniques of the Observer: On Vision and Modernity in the Nineteenth Century* (Cambridge, MA: MIT Press, 1992).

Crowley, Martin, 'Deleuze on Painting', *French Studies*, 67:3 (2013), 371–85.

Cunningham, Valentine, *Reading after Theory* (Oxford: Blackwell, 2001).

Damisch, Hubert, *Fenêtre jaune cadmium, ou, les dessous de la peinture* (Paris: Seuil, 1984).

——, *Théorie du /nuage/: pour une histoire de la peinture* (Paris: Éditions du Seuil, 1972).

——, *A Theory of /Cloud/: Toward a History of Painting*, trans. Janet Lloyd (Stanford, CA: Stanford University Press, 2002).

Davila, Thierry, and Pierre Sauvanet (eds), *Devant les images: penser l'art et l'histoire avec Georges Didi-Huberman* (Paris: Les Presses du Réel, 2011).

Davis, Colin, *After Poststructuralism: Reading, Stories and Theory* (New York: Routledge, 2006).

de Baecque, Antoine, 'Interview with László Nemes, *Son of Saul*', *Rendez Vous* (2015).

De Cauwer, Stijn, and Laura Katherine Smith, 'Critical Image Configurations', *Angelaki*, 23:4 (2018), 1–2.

Dekoninck, Ralph, 'Art History in France: A Conflict of Traditions', in Matthew Rampley, Thierry Lenain, Hubert Locher, Andrea Pinotti, Charlotte Schoell-Glass and C. J. M. (Kitty) Zijlmans (eds), *Art History and Visual Studies in Europe: Transnational Discourses and National Frameworks* (Leiden: Brill, 2012), 315–33.

Deleuze, Gilles, *Cinema 2: The Time-Image*, trans. Hugh Tomlinson and Robert Galeta (London and New York: Continuum, 1989).

——, *Difference and Repetition*, trans. Paul Patton (New York: Columbia University Press, 1994).

——, *Nietzsche and Philosophy*, trans. Hugh Tomlinson (New York: Bloomsbury, 2006).

——, 'Plato and the Simulacrum', *October*, 27 (1983), 45–56.

——, *Proust and Signs: The Complete Text*, trans. Richard Howard (Minneapolis: University of Minnesota Press, 2000).

——, *Two Regimes of Madness: Texts and Interviews 1975–1995*, trans. Ames Hodges and Mike Taormina (New York: Semiotext(e), 2006).

Deleuze, Gilles, and Félix Guattari, *Kafka: Toward a Minor Literature* (Minneapolis: University of Minnesota Press, 1986).

——, *A Thousand Plateaus: Capitalism and Schizophrenia*, trans. Brian Massumi (Minneapolis: University of Minnesota Press, 1987).

Derrida, Jacques, *Archive Fever: A Freudian Impression*, trans. Eric Prenowitz (Chicago: University of Chicago Press, 1996).

——, 'Différance', in *Margins of Philosophy*, trans. Alan Bass (Chicago University of Chicago Press, 1982), 1–28.

——, 'The Double Session', in *Dissemination*, trans. Barbara Johnson (London and New York: Bloomsbury, 1981), 187–315.

——, 'Economimesis', *Diacritics*, 11:2 (1981), 3–25.

——, 'From Restricted to General Economy: A Hegelianism without Reserve', in *Writing and Difference*, trans. Alan Bass (London and New York: Routledge, 1978), 317–50.

——, *Memoirs of the Blind: The Self-Portrait and Other Ruins*, trans. Pascale-Anne Brault and Michael Naas (Chicago: University of Chicago Press, 1993).

——, *Of Grammatology*, trans. Gayatri Spivak (Baltimore: Johns Hopkins University Press, 1976).

——, *Positions*, trans. Alan Bass (London: Athlone Press, 1987).

——, *The Truth in Painting*, trans. Geoff Bennington and Ian McLeod (Chicago: University of Chicago Press, 1987).

Descombes, Vincent, *Modern French Philosophy*, trans. L. Scott-Fox and J. M. Harding (Cambridge: Cambridge University Press, 1980).

Didi-Huberman, Georges. 'Aby Warburg, l'histoire de l'art à l'âge des fantômes', Interview by Élie During, *Artpress*, 277 (2002), 18–24.

——, *Aperçues* (Paris: Les Éditions de Minuit, 2018).

——, 'Appendix: The Detail and the *Pan*', in *Confronting Images: Questioning the Ends of a Certain History of Art*, trans. John Goodman (University Park: Pennsylvania State University Press, 2005), 228–72.

——, 'L'art de ne pas décrire. Une aporie du détail chez Vermeer', *La Part de l'Œil*, 2 (1986), 102–19.

——. 'Atlas: comment remonter le monde?', Interview by Catherine Millet, *Artpress*, 373 (2012), 48–55.

——, *Atlas: How to Carry the World on One's Back?* (Madrid: Museo Nacional Centro de Arte Reina Sofía, 2011).

——, *Atlas, or the Anxious Gay Science*, trans. Shane B. Lillis (Chicago: University of Chicago Press, 2018).

——, *Atlas ou le gai savoir inquiet*, L'œil de l'histoire 3 (Paris: Les Éditions de Minuit, 2011).

——, *Bark*, trans. Samuel E. Martin (Cambridge, MA: MIT Press, 2017).

——, *Ce que nous voyons, ce qui nous regarde* (Paris: Les Éditions de Minuit, 1992).

——, *Confronting Images: Questioning the Ends of a Certain History of Art*, trans. John Goodman (University Park: Pennsylvania State University Press, 2005).

——, 'La couleur de chair ou le paradoxe de Tertullien', *Nouvelle Revue de Psychanalyse*, 35 (1987), 9–49.

——. 'Des gammes anachroniques', Interview by Robert Maggiori, *Plaquette du Journal Libération* (November 2000), 8.

——, *Devant le temps: histoire de l'art et anachronisme des images* (Paris: Les Éditions de Minuit, 2000).

——, 'Dialogue sur le symptôme (avec Patrick Lacoste)', *L'Inactuel*, 3 (1995), 191–226.

——, *Écorces* (Paris: Les Éditions de Minuit 2011).

——, *L'empreinte* (Paris: Éditions du Centre Georges Pompidou, 1997).

——. 'En ordre dispersé', *Trivium*, no. 1 (2008). http://journals.openedition. org/trivium/351.

——, *L'étoilement: Conversation avec Hantaï* (Paris: Les Éditions de Minuit, 1998).

——, *Être crâne: lieu, contact, pensée, sculpture* (Paris: Les Éditions de Minuit, 2000).

——, 'Ex-Voto: Image, Organ, Time', *L'Esprit Créateur*, 47:3 (2007), 7–16.

——, *Ex-voto: image, organe, temps* (Paris: Bayard, 2006).

——, *The Eye of History: When Images Take Positions* trans. Shane B. Lillis (Cambridge, MA: MIT Press, 2018).

——, *Fra Angelico: Dissemblance and Figuration*, trans. Jane Marie Todd (Chicago: University of Chicago Press, 1995).

——, *Fra Angelico: dissemblance et figuration* (Paris: Flammarion, 1990).

——. 'Georges Didi-Huberman: "… Ce qui rende le temps lisible, c'est l'image"', Interview by Susana Nascimento Duarte and Maria Irene Aparício, *Cinema: Journal of Philosophy and the Moving Image*, 1 (2010), 118–33.

——, *L'homme qui marchait dans la couleur* (Paris: Les Éditions de Minuit, 2001).

——. 'Image, matière: immanence', Interview by François Noudelmann, *Rue Descartes*, 38 (2002), 86–99.

——, *L'image survivante: histoire de l'art et temps des fantômes selon Aby Warburg* (Paris: Les Éditions de Minuit, 2002).

——, *Images in Spite of All: Four Photographs from Auschwitz*, trans. Shane B. Lillis (Chicago: University of Chicago Press, 2008).

——, *Images malgré tout* (Paris: Les Éditions de Minuit, 2003).

——, ' " Imaginum pictura … in totum exoleuit": début de l'histoire de l'art et fin de l'époque de l'image', *Critique* 52:586 (1996), 138–50.

——, 'The Index of the Absent Wound (Monograph on a Stain)', *October*, 29 (1984), 63–81.

——, 'L'indice de la plaie absente (monographie d'un tache)', *Traverses*, 30–31 (1984), 151–63.

——, *Invention de l'hystérie. Charcot et l'iconographie photographique de la Salpêtrière* (Paris: Macula, 1982).

——, *Invention of Hysteria: Charcot and the Photographic Iconography of the Salpêtrière*, trans. Alisa Hartz (Cambridge, MA: MIT Press, 2003).

——, 'Knowing When to Cut', in François Caillat (ed.), *Foucault Against Himself* (Vancouver: Arsenal Pulp Press, 2015), 77–109.

——, 'La matière inquiète (plasticité, viscosité, étrangeté)', *Lignes*, 1 (2000), 206–23.

——, 'The Molding Image: Genealogy and the Truth of Resemblance in Pliny's *Natural History*, Book 35, I-7', in Costas Douzinas and Lynda

Nead (eds), *Law and the Image: The Authority of Art and the Aesthetics of Law* (Chicago: University of Chicago Press, 1999), 71–88.

——, 'Of Images and Ills', *Critical Inquiry*, 42:3 (2016), 439–72.

——, 'Opening Up an Anachronistic Point of View', in Ruth Pelzer-Montada (ed.), *Perspectives on Contemporary Printmaking: Critical Writing since 1986* (Manchester: Manchester University Press, 2018), 184–95.

——, 'Ouvrir les camps, fermer les yeux', *Annales. Histoire, Sciences Sociales* 61:5 (2006/5), 1011–49.

——, *Passés cités par JLG*, L'œil de l'histoire 5 (Paris: Les Éditions de Minuit, 2015).

——, *La peinture incarnée* (Paris: Les Éditions de Minuit, 1985).

——, *Peuples en larmes, peuples en armes*, L'œil de l'histoire 6 (Paris: Les Éditions de Minuit, 2016).

——, *Peuples exposés, peuples figurants*, L'œil de l'histoire 4 (Paris: Les Éditions de Minuit, 2012).

——, *Quand les images prennent position*, L'œil de l'histoire 1 (Paris: Les Éditions de Minuit, 2009).

——, *Remontages du temps subi*, L'œil de l'histoire 2 (Paris: Les Éditions de Minuit, 2010).

——, *La ressemblance informe ou le gai savoir visuel selon Georges Bataille* (Paris: Macula, 1995).

——, *La ressemblance par contact: archéologie, anachronisme et modernité de l'empreinte* (Paris: Les Éditions de Minuit, 2008).

——, *Sortir du noir* (Paris: Les Éditions de Minuit, 2015).

——, *Soulèvements* (Paris: Gallimard/Jeu de Paume, 2016).

——, *Sur le fil* (Paris: Les Éditions de Minuit, 2013).

——, *The Surviving Image: Phantoms of Time and Time of Phantoms*, trans. Harvey L. Mendelsohn (University Park: Pennsylvania State University Press, 2017).

Didi-Huberman , Georges, and Niki Giannari, *Passer, quoi qu'il en coûte* (Paris: Les Éditions de Minuit, 2017).

Dreyfus, Hubert L., and Paul Rabinow, *Michel Foucault: Beyond Structuralism and Hermeneutics*, 2nd edn (Chicago: University of Chicago Press 1983).

Dumoulin, O., 'Anachronisme', in A. Burguière (ed.), *Dictionnaire des sciences historiques* (Paris: Presses Universitaires de France, 1986).

Eagleton, Terry, *After Theory* (New York: Basic Books, 2003).

Eisenstein, Sergei, *Immoral Memories*, trans. Herbert Marshall (Boston: Houghton Mifflin, 1983).

——, 'Word and Image', in *The Film Sense*, trans. Jay Leyda (Cleveland, OH and New York: Meridian Books, 1957), 3–65.

Elkins, James, and Robert Williams, *Renaissance Theory* (New York: Routledge, 2008).

Enwezor, Okwui, *Archive Fever: Uses of the Document in Contemporary Art* (New York and Göttingen: International Center of Photography, 2008).

Febvre, Lucien, *The Problem of Unbelief in the Sixteenth Century: The Religion of Rabelais*, trans. Beatrice Gottlieb (Cambridge, MA: Harvard University Press, 1985).

Fink, Daniel A., 'Vermeer's Use of the Camera Obscura: A Comparative Study', *Art Bulletin*, 53:4 (1971), 493–505.

Flower, Harriet, I., *Ancestor Masks and Aristocratic Power in Roman Culture* (Oxford: Clarendon Press, 1996).

Foster, Hal, Yve-Alain Bois, Rosalind Krauss, Benjamin H. D. Buchloh and David Joselit, *Art since 1900: Modernism, Antimodernism, Postmodernism* (London and New York: Thames and Hudson, 2004).

Foucault, Michel, *The Archaeology of Knowledge*, trans. A. M. Sheridan Smith (London and New York: Routledge, 1989).

——, *The Archaeology of Knowledge; and The Discourse on Language*, trans. A. M. Sheridan Smith (New York: Pantheon Books, 1972).

——, *The Birth of the Clinic: An Archaeology of Medical Perception*, trans. A. M. Sheridan Smith (London and New York: Routledge, 1989).

——, 'Nietzsche, Genealogy, History', in Donald F. Bouchard (ed.), *Language, Counter-Memory, Practice: Selected Essays and Interviews*, trans. Donald F. Bouchard and Sherry Simon (Ithaca, NY: Cornell University Press, 1977), 139–64.

——, *The Order of Things: An Archaeology of the Human Sciences*, trans. Anonymous (New York: Vintage, 1994).

——, 'Theatrum Philosophicum', in Donald F. Bouchard (ed.), *Language, Counter-Memory, Practice: Selected Essays and Interviews*, trans. Donald F. Bouchard and Sherry Simon (Ithaca, NY: Cornell University Press, 1977), 165–98.

Fourcade, Dominique, 'Hantaï, an Exhibition', in *Simon Hantaï* (Paris: Éditions du Centre Pompidou 2013), 19–186.

Freedberg, David, *The Power of Images: Studies in the History and Theory of Response* (Chicago: University of Chicago Press, 1989).

Freud, Sigmund, 'Charcot', in James Strachey, Anna Freud, Alix Strachey and Alan Tyson (eds), *The Standard Edition of the Complete Psychological Works of Sigmund Freud Vol. III (1893)*, trans. James Strachey (London: The Hogarth Press, 1962), 11–24.

——, 'The Development of Symptoms', in *A General Introduction to Psychoanalysis*, trans. G. Stanley Hall (New York: Horace Liveright, 1920), 311–27.

——, *A General Introduction to Psychoanalysis*, trans. G. Stanley Hall (New York: Horace Liveright, 1920).

——, 'Inhibitions, Symptoms and Anxiety', in James Strachey, Anna Freud, Alix Strachey and Alan Tyson (eds), *The Standard Edition of the Complete Psychological Works of Sigmund Freud Vol. XX (1925–1926)*, trans. James Strachey (London: The Hogarth Press, 1959), 75–176.

——, 'The Interpretation of Dreams', in James Strachey, Anna Freud, Alix Strachey and Alan Tyson (eds), *The Standard Edition of the Complete Psychological Works of Sigmund Freud Vol. IV (1900)*, trans. James Strachey (London: The Hogarth Press, 1953).

——, 'Letter from Freud to Fliess, January 3, 1899', in *The Complete Letters of Sigmund Freud to Wilhelm Fliess, 1887–1904*, ed. and trans. Jeffrey Moussaieff Masson (Cambridge, MA: Belknap Press of Harvard University Press, 1985), 338–9.

Fried, Michael, 'Art and Objecthood', *Artforum*, 5:10 (1967), 12–23.

——, *Art and Objecthood: Essays and Reviews* (Chicago: University of Chicago Press, 1998).

Gell, Alfred, *Art and Agency: An Anthropological Theory* (Oxford: Clarendon Press, 1998).

Gilson, Étienne, '*Regio Dissimilitudinis* de Platon à Saint Bernard de Clairvaux', *Medieval Studies*, 9:1 (1947), 108–30.

Godard, Jean-Luc, 'La légende du siècle', *Les Inrockuptibles*, 170 (1998), 20–8.

Gombrich, E. H., *Aby Warburg: An Intellectual Biography* (London: The Warburg Institute, 1970).

——, *Art and Illusion: A Study in the Psychology of Pictorial Representation* (London: Phaidon Press, 1960).

——, 'The Father of Art History', in *Tributes: Interpreters of Our Cultural Tradition* (Oxford: Phaidon, 1984), 51–69.

——, 'Julius von Schlosser', *Burlington Magazine for Connoisseurs*, 74:431 (1939), 98–9.

Greenberg, Clement, 'Modernist Painting', in Gregory Battcock (ed.), *The New Art: A Critical Anthology* (New York: Dutton, 1973), 66–77.

Greffrath, Krista R., 'Proust et Benjamin', in Heinz Wismann (ed.), *Walter Benjamin et Paris* (Paris: Les Éditions du Cerf, 1986), 113–31.

Grootenboer, Hanneke. 'Introduction: "The Thought of Images"', *Image [&] Narrative*, no. 18 (2007). www.imageandnarrative.be/inarchive/thinking_pictures/grootenboer.htm.

——, 'The Pensive Image: On Thought in Jan van Huysum's Still Life Paintings', *Oxford Art Journal*, 34:1 (2011), 13–30.

Gutting, Gary, *Michel Foucault's Archaeology of Scientific Reason* (Cambridge: Cambridge University Press, 1989).

Halliwell, Stephen, *The Aesthetics of Mimesis: Ancient Texts and Modern Problems* (Princeton and Oxford: Princeton University Press, 2002).

Hegel, G. W. F., *Lectures on the Philosophy of History*, trans. J. Sibree (London: Bell, 1878).

Heidegger, Martin, 'Nietzsche's Overturning of Platonism', in *Nietzsche: Volumes One and Two*, trans. David Farrell Krell and Joan Stambaugh (San Francisco: HarperSanFrancisco, 1961), 200–10.

Hirsch, Marianne, 'The Generation of Postmemory', *Poetics Today*, 29:1 (2008), 103–28.

Holly, Michael Ann, *The Melancholy Art* (Princeton: Princeton University Press, 2013).

——, *Panofsky and the Foundations of Art History* (Ithaca, NY: Cornell University Press, 1984).

Jameson, Fredric, *Postmodernism, or, The Cultural Logic of Late Capitalism* (Durham, NC: Duke University Press, 1991).

Johnson, Christopher D., *Memory, Metaphor, and Aby Warburg's Atlas of Images* (Ithaca, NY: Cornell University Press, 2012).

Kant, Immanuel, *Critique of Pure Reason*, trans. Paul Guyer and Allen Wood (Cambridge: Cambridge University Press, 1998).

Keilbach, Judith, 'Photographs, Symbolic Images, and the Holocaust: On the (Im)possibility of Depicting Historical Truth', *History and Theory*, 48:2 (2009), 54–76.

Kelsey, R. E., and B. Stimson, *The Meaning of Photography* (Williamstown, MA: Sterling and Francine Clark Art Institute, 2008).

Krauss, Rosalind, 'Notes on the Index', in *The Originality of the Avant-Garde and Other Modernist Myths* (Cambridge, MA: MIT Press, 1985), 196–210.

——, 'A View on Modernism', in *Perpetual Inventory* (Cambridge, MA: MIT Press, 2013), 115–28.

Lacan, Jacques, *The Four Fundamental Concepts of Psychoanalysis*, trans. Alan Sheridan (New York and London: W. W. Norton, 1998).

——, *The Seminar of Jacques Lacan, Book III: The Psychoses (1955–1956)*, trans. Russell Grigg, ed. Jacques-Alain Miller. (New York: W. W. Norton, 1997).

Lacoue-Labarthe, Philippe, and Jean-Luc Nancy, *The Literary Absolute*, trans. Philip Barnard and Cheryl Lester (Albany: SUNY Press, 1988).

Landau, David, 'Vasari, Prints and Prejudice', *Oxford Art Journal*, 6:1 (1983), 3–10.

Landau, David, and Peter Parshall, *The Renaissance Print: 1470–1550* (New Haven, CT and London: Yale University Press, 1994).

Lanzmann, Claude, 'Holocauste, la répresentation impossible', *Le Monde*, 3 March 1994, 1, 7.

——. 'Le monument contre l'archive?', Interview by Régis Debray, Daniel Bougnoux, Claude Mollard *et al.*, *Les Cahiers de Médiologie*, 11 (2001), 271–9.

Leśniak, Andrzej, 'Images Thinking the Political: On the Recent Works of Georges Didi-Huberman', *Oxford Art Journal*, 40:2 (2017), 305–18.

Levi, Primo, *The Drowned and the Saved*, trans. Raymond Rosenthal (London: Penguin Books, 1988).

Lichtenstein, Jacqueline, and Elisabeth Decultot, 'Mimesis', in Barbara Cassin, Emily Apter, Jacques Lezra and Michael Wood (eds), *Dictionary of Untranslatables*, trans. Emily Apter, Jacques Lezra and Michael Wood (Princeton: Princeton University Press, 2014), 659–75.

Loraux, Nicole, 'Éloge de l'anachronisme en histoire', *Le Genre Humain*, 27 (1993), 23–39.

Lotringer, Sylvère, and Sande Cohen, *French Theory in America* (New York: Routledge, 2001).

Lukács, Georg, 'Realism in the Balance', in *Aesthetics and Politics* (London: NLB, 1977), 28–59.

Lunn, Eugene, *Marxism and Modernism: An Historical Study of Lukács, Brecht, Benjamin, and Adorno* (Berkeley: University of California Press, 1984).

Lyotard, Jean-François, *The Differend: Phrases in Dispute* (Minneapolis: University of Minnesota Press, 1988).

Marin, Louis, 'Des noms et des corps dans la peinture: marginalia au *Chef-d'œuvre inconnu*', in *Autour du 'Chef-d'œuvre inconnu' de Balzac* (Paris: École nationale supérieure des arts décoratifs, 1985), 45–60.

——, *Des pouvoirs de l'image: gloses* (Paris: Éditions du Seuil, 1993).

Mayor, A. Hyatt, 'The Photographic Eye', *Metropolitan Museum of Art Bulletin*, 5:1 (1946), 15–26.

Michaud, Philippe-Alain, *Aby Warburg and the Image in Motion*, trans. Sophie Hawkes (New York: Zone Books, 2004).

——, *Aby Warburg et l'image en mouvement* (Paris: Macula, 1998).

Mitchell, W. J. T., *Iconology: Image, Text, Ideology* (Chicago: University of Chicago Press, 1986).

——, *Picture Theory: Essays on Verbal and Visual Representation* (Chicago: University of Chicago Press, 1994).

——, *What Do Pictures Want? The Lives and Loves of Images* (Chicago: University of Chicago Press, 2005).

Montaigne, Michel de, *The Complete Essays of Montaigne*, trans. Donald M. Frame (Stanford, CA: Stanford University Press 1958).

Moxey, Keith, 'Art History's Hegelian Unconscious', in Mark A. Cheetham, Michael Ann Holly and Keith P. F. Moxey (eds), *The Subjects of Art History: Historical Objects in Contemporary Perspectives* (Cambridge: Cambridge University Press, 1998), 25–51.

——, 'Visual Studies and the Iconic Turn', *Journal of Visual Culture*, 7:2 (2008), 131–46.

——, *Visual Time: The Image in History* (Durham: Duke University Press, 2013).

Nagel, Alexander, and Christopher S. Wood, *Anachronic Renaissance* (New York: Zone Books, 2010).

——, 'Toward a New Model of Renaissance Anachronism', *Art Bulletin*, 87:3 (2005), 403–15.

Nancy, Jean-Luc, 'The Deconstruction of Monotheism', in *Dis-Enclosure: The Deconstruction of Christianity*, trans. Bettina Bergo, Gabriel Malenfant and Michael B. Smith (New York: Fordham University Press, 2008), 29–41.

——, 'Forbidden Representation', in *The Ground of the Image*, trans. Jeff Fort (New York: Fordham University Press, 2005), 27–50.

——, 'On Dis-enclosure and its Gesture, Adoration', in Alena Alexandrova, Ignaas Devisch, Laurens Ten Kate and Aujke van Rooden (eds), *Retreating Religion: Deconstructing Christianity with Jean-Luc Nancy* (New York: Fordham University Press, 2012), 304–43.

——, 'Visitation: Of Christian Painting', in *The Ground of the Image*, trans. Jeff Fort (New York: Fordham University Press, 2005), 108–25.

Pagnoux, Elizabeth, 'Reporter photographe à Auschwitz', *Les Temps Modernes*, 56:613 (2001), 84–108.

Panofsky, Erwin, 'The History of Art as a Humanistic Discipline', in *Meaning in the Visual Arts* (Harmondsworth: Penguin Books, 1970), 23–50.

——, *Idea: A Concept in Art Theory*, trans. Joseph J. S. Peake (New York: Harper & Row, 1968).

Patton, Paul, 'Anti-Platonism and Art', in Constantin V. Boundas and Dorothea Olkowski (eds), *Gilles Deleuze and the Theatre of Philosophy* (New York: Routledge, 1994), 141–56.

Pelzer-Montada, Ruth, *Perspectives on Contemporary Printmaking: Critical Writing since 1986* (Manchester: Manchester University Press, 2018).

Perl, Eric, 'Pseudo-Dionysius the Areopagite', in Lloyd P. Gerson (ed.), *The Cambridge History of Philosophy in Late Antiquity* (Cambridge: Cambridge University Press, 2010), 767–87.

Pic, Muriel (ed.), 'Qu'est-ce que s'orienter dans les images?', *Europe*, 1069 (2018), 3–173.

Plato, *The Republic*, trans. Desmond Lee, 2nd edn (London: Penguin Classics, 1987).

Pliny the Elder, *Natural History*, trans. H. Rackham, vol. 35 (Cambridge, MA: Harvard University Press, 1952).

Podro, Michael, *The Critical Historians of Art* (New Haven, CT and London: Yale University Press, 1982).

Pollock, Griselda, *Vision and Difference: Feminism, Femininity and Histories of Art* (London and New York: Routledge, 2003).

Pope-Hennessy, John, *Fra Angelico* (London: Phaidon, 1952).

Prendergast, Christopher, *The Triangle of Representation* (New York: Columbia University Press, 2000).

Pseudo-Dionysius, 'The Celestial Hierarchy', in *Pseudo-Dionysius: The Complete Works*, trans. C. Luibhéid and P. Rorem (New York: Paulist Press, 1987), 143–92.

——, *Pseudo-Dionysius: The Complete Works*, trans. C. Luibhéid and P. Rorem (New York: Paulist Press, 1987).

Rampley, Matthew, 'Introduction', in Matthew Rampley, Thierry Lenain, Hubert Locher, Andrea Pinotti, Charlotte Schoell-Glass and C.J.M. (Kitty) Zijlmans (eds), *Art History and Visual Studies in Europe: Transnational Discourses and National Frameworks* (Leiden: Brill, 2012), 1–13.

——, *The Remembrance of Things Past: On Aby M. Warburg and Walter Benjamin* (Wiesbaden: Otto Harrassowitz, 2000).

Rancière, Jacques, 'Are Some Things Unrepresentable?', in *The Future of the Image*, trans. Gregory Elliot (London: Verso, 2007), 109–38.

——, 'Le concept d'anachronisme et la vérité de l'historien', *L'Inactuel*, 6 (1996), 53–68.

——, 'The Pensive Image', in *The Emancipated Spectator*, trans. Gregory Elliott (London: Verso, 2009), 107–32.

Rees, A. L., and Frances Borzello (eds), *The New Art History* (London: Camden Press, 1986).

Regosin, Richard L., 'Montaigne and His Readers', in Denis Hollier (ed.), *A New History of French Literature* (Cambridge, MA: Harvard University Press, 1989), 248–53.

Rochlitz, Rainer, 'Walter Benjamin: une dialectique de l'image', *Critique*, 431 (1983), 287–319.

Rose, Sven-Erik, 'Auschwitz as Hermeneutic Rupture, Differend, and Image *malgré tout*: Jameson, Lyotard, Didi-Huberman', in David Bathrick, Prager Brad and Richardson Michael D. (eds), *Visualizing the Holocaust* (Rochester, NY: Camden House, 2008), 114–37.

Ross, Christine, *The Past is the Present, It's the Future Too: The Temporal Turn in Contemporary Art* (New York: Bloomsbury, 2012).

Rubin, Patricia Lee, *Giorgio Vasari: Art and History* (New Haven, CT: Yale University Press, 1995).

Saint, Nigel, 'Georges Didi-Huberman: Images, Critique and Time', in Nigel Saint and Andy Stafford (eds), *Modern French Visual Theory: A Critical Reader* (Manchester: Manchester University Press, 2013), 219–38.

Sartre, Jean-Paul, *Being and Nothingness: An Essay on Phenomenological Ontology*, trans. Hazel E. Barnes (London: Methuen, 1957).

——, *Nausea*, trans. Robert Baldick (London and New York: Penguin Modern Classics, 2000).

Saxton, Libby, *Haunted Images: Film, Ethics, Testimony and the Holocaust* (London and New York: Wallflower Press, 2008).

Schlosser, Julius von, 'History of Portraiture in Wax', in *Ephemeral Bodies: Wax Sculpture and the Human Figure* (Los Angeles: Getty Research Institute, 2008), 171–303.

Schneller, Katia, 'Sur les traces de Rosalind Krauss: la réception française de la notion d'index, 1977–1990', *Études Photographiques*, 21 (2007), 123–43.

Schoell-Glass, Charlotte, 'Aby Warburg's Late Comments on Symbol and Ritual', *Science in Context*, 12:4 (1999), 621–42.

Schrift, Alan D., *Nietzsche's French Legacy: A Genealogy of Poststructuralism* (New York and London: Routledge, 1995).

Smith, Terry, *What is Contemporary Art?* (Chicago: University of Chicago Press, 2012).

Spencer, John R., 'Spatial Imagery of the Annunciation in Fifteenth Century Florence', *Art Bulletin*, 37:4 (1955), 273–80.

Tagg, John, *The Burden of Representation: Essays on Photographies and Histories* (London: Macmillan, 1988).

Tiedemann, Rolf, 'Dialectics at a Standstill', in Walter Benjamin, *The Arcades Project*, trans. Howard Eiland and Kevin McLaughlin (Cambridge, MA: Belknap Press of Harvard University Press, 1999), 929–45.

Tylor, Edward B., *Primitive Culture: Researches into the Development of Mythology, Religion, Language, Art and Custom*, vol. 1, 3rd US from 2nd UK edn (New York: Henry Holt and Company, 1889).

Urmson, J. O., *The Greek Philosophical Vocabulary* (London: Duckworth, 1990).

Vasari, Giorgio, *Lives of the Artists*, trans. George Bull, vol. 1 (London: Penguin Books, 1987).

Veyne, Paul, 'Foucault Revolutionizes History', in Arnold I. Davidson (ed.), *Foucault and His Interlocutors* (Chicago: University of Chicago Press, 1997), 146–82.

Vinci, Leonardo da, *Leonardo on Painting: An Anthology of Writings by Leonardo da Vinci, with a Selection of Documents Relating to His Career as an Artist* (New Haven, CT and London: Yale University Press, 1989).

Wajcman, Gérard, 'De la croyance photographique', *Les Temps Modernes*, 56:613 (2001), 47–83.

Warburg, Aby, 'The Art of Portraiture and the Florentine Bourgeoisie (1902)', in *The Renewal of Pagan Antiquity: Contributions to the Cultural History of the European Renaissance* (Los Angeles: Getty Research Institute for the History of Art and the Humanities, 1999), 185–221.

——, 'Dürer and Italian Antiquity (1905)', in *The Renewal of Pagan Antiquity: Contributions to the Cultural History of the European Renaissance* (Los Angeles: Getty Research Institute for the History of Art and the Humanities, 1999), 553–8.

——, 'The Emergence of the Antique as a Stylistic Ideal in Early Renaissance Painting (1914)', in *The Renewal of Pagan Antiquity: Contributions to the Cultural History of the European Renaissance* (Los Angeles: Getty Research Institute for the History of Art and the Humanities, 1999), 271–3.

Willet, John, *Art and Politics in the Weimar Period: The New Sobriety, 1917–1933* (New York: Pantheon Books, 1978).

Wittkower, Rudolf, *The Sculptor's Workshop: Tradition and Theory from the Renaissance to the Present* (Glasgow: University of Glasgow Press, 1974).

Wollaston, Isabel, 'Emerging from the Shadows? The Auschwitz Sonderkommando and the "Four Women" in History and Memory', *Holocaust Studies: A Journal of Culture and History*, 20:3 (2014), 137–70.

Zimmerman, Laurent (ed.), *Penser par les images: autour des travaux de Georges Didi-Huberman* (Nantes: Cécile Defaut, 2006).

Index

Note: page numbers in *italic* refer to illustrations. Didi-Huberman works are indexed by title under 'Didi-Huberman, works of'.

Adorno, Theodor
and Holocaust discourse 126, 127, 130, 136
'The Essay as Form' 170
Agamben, Giorgio 126
Alberti, Leon Battista 11, 59, 60, 63, 101
Alpers, Svetlana 6, 26, 54
anachronism
Aby Warburg and 82–8
Didi-Huberman's understanding of 69, 70–1, 74, 78, 93, 116
the *empreinte* and 99–100, 104, 110, 112
Gilles Deleuze and 90–1
Lucien Febvre's caution against 72
mémoire involontaire and 80–2, 150
recuperation of by Jacques Rancière and Nicole Loraux 73
Walter Benjamin and 78–82
see also Didi-Huberman, works of, *Devant le temps*; Didi-Huberman, works of, *L'image survivante*
Angelico, Fra
Annunciation with Saint Peter Martyr (*c.* 1440–44) 14–15, *15*, 28
Didi-Huberman's case study on 57–64, 82, 91

Madonna delle Ombre (*Madonna of the Shadows*) (*c.* 1450) 57–9, *58*, 70, 82
Noli me tangere (1438–50) 115
Anonymous, *Death of Orpheus*, detail of vase from Nola (*c.* 475–50 BC) 84, *87*
Anonymous, Northern Italian, *Death of Orpheus* (*c.* 1470–80) 84, *86*
Anonymous, Venice, *Death of Orpheus*, 1497, woodcut from Ovid, *Metamorphoses* 84, *86*
Aquinas, Thomas 18, 114–15, 116–17
Arasse, Daniel 7, 54–5, 56
archaeology *see* Foucault, Michel, *Archaeology of Knowledge, The*
art history
discipline of 1
renewal of 4
Auschwitz-Birkenau *see* Didi-Huberman, works of, *Images malgré tout*; Didi-Huberman, works of, *L'oeil de l'histoire*; Holocaust, discourse; Holocaust, photographs

Bachelard, Gaston 75
Bal, Mieke 67n12, 74
Balzac, Honoré de, *Le chef-d'oeuvre inconnu* (*The Unknown Masterpiece*) (1831) 33–5

Barthes, Roland 5, 6, 113
    Camera Lucida 49, 143
Bataille, Georges, Didi-Huberman's
    engagement with 2, 5–6, 18–19,
    78, 151, 153–4, 165, 166
Batchen, Geoffrey 25
Baudelaire, Charles 92, 150,
    156–7, 168
Baugh, Bruce 77
Baxandall, Michael 6, 8, 72
Bazin, André 113, 130
Belting, Hans 12, 34–5
Benjamin, Walter 127
    Arcades Project, The (1927–40)
        90, 91–2, 97n73, 150, 151, 153,
        166, 167
    attitude towards neo-Hegelian
        historiography 81
    'Crisis of the Novel, The'
        (1930) 137
    Didi-Huberman's engagement
        with 2, 71, 78–82, 93, 137–9,
        149–51, 153, 165, 166,
        167, 168
    Origin of German Tragic Drama,
        The (1924/25) 78–9, 150
    'Storyteller, The: Observations on
        the Works of Nikolai Leskov'
        (1936) 138
    'Theses on the Philosophy of
        History' 81, 151
Blanchot, Maurice 5, 6
Boehm, Gottfried 7
Boiffard, Jacques-André 153, 154
Bois, Yve-Alain 7, 94n22, 153
Bonnefoy, Yves 8
Botella, César and Sárah 43
Boyne, Roy 25
Brecht, Bertolt 127, 151
Bredekamp, Horst 12
Breton, André 100
Brouillet, André, *Un leçon clinique à*
    la Salpêtrière (1887) 162, *163*
Brown, Bill 142

Brunelleschi, Filippo 55, 59
Bryson, Norman 8
Buchloh, Benjamin H. D. 7, 94n22
Bürger, Peter 152

camera obscura 53–4, 136
Canguilhem, Georges 75
Careri, Giovanni 7
Charcot, Jean-Martin 14–16, 25,
    37–9, 162–3, *163*, *164*
Chastel, André 7
Cheetham, Mark A. 8
Clark, T. J. 8, 171
Crary, Jonathan 25

Damisch, Hubert 7, 14, 45n37, 54–6,
    143, 165
de Baecque, Antoine 131, 135
Dekoninck, Ralph 8
Deleuze, Gilles 5–6, 10, 19, 22n43,
    24, 76, 88–9, 171
    Cinema 2: The Time-Image 90, 144,
        147–8, 150–1
    Didi-Huberman's engagement
        with 71, 83, 90–91, 93, 143,
        146–52, 158–9, 165, 171
    Difference and Repetition (1968)
        88, 144–5, 145–6, 151
    on Nietzsche 71, 88–9, 90, 145
Derrida, Jacques 5–6, 10, 67n31, 76,
    78, 80, 103–4, 143
    Archive Fever 157
    Didi-Huberman's engagement
        with 14, 17, 24, 29, 43, 48–9,
        56, 60, 63, 99, 102, 103, 104,
        113–14, 117, 157, 171
    and *différance* 80, 104
    Of Grammatology (1976) 56,
        63, 103
    Memoirs of the Blind: The
        Self-Portrait and Other Ruins
        (1993) 102
    reading of Rousseau 56, 63
Descartes, René 19, 48, 145

Descombes, Vincent 76
detail, the 54, 56
Didi-Huberman, works of
  Aperçues (2018) 167–8, 169–71
  Bark (2011) 137
  Devant l'image (Confronting Images) (1990) 16–17, 24, 28, 34, 36, 43, 48, 59, 66n2, 69, 144, 147
  Devant le temps (2000) 3, 17, 69–70, 72, 90, 94n10, 151
  L'étoilement: conversation avec Hantaï 100, 118n11
  Fra Angelico (1990) 17, 57–9, 170
  L'image survivante (The Surviving Image: Phantoms of Time and Time of Phantoms) (2017) 1, 10, 17, 18, 77, 82–3, 146, 154
  Images in Spite of All (2008) 18–19, 126, 129, 132, 133, 139n2, 142, 149
  Images malgré tout (2003) 18, 125–6
  L'invention d'hystérie (Invention of Hysteria) (2003) 14–15, 24, 25, 37, 38
  Mémoire des camps (exhibition, Hôtel de Sully, Paris, 2001) 18, 121, 127
  L'oeil de l'histoire (The Eye of History) 4, 18, 121, 126
  Passer, quoi qu'il en coûte (2017) 170
  Passés cités par JLG (2015) 162
  peinture incarnée, suivi de 'Le chef-d'oeuvre inconnu' de Balzac, La (1984) 33–4, 36, 49, 51, 56
  Sortir du noir (2015) 135, 136, 137
Différance see Derrida, Jacques, and *différance*
dissemblance 17, 48, 59, 60–6, 103, 115, 116

dreams, interpretation of *see* Freud, Sigmund, and dreams, interpretation of
Dreyfus, Hubert L. 26–7
Duchamp, Marcel 98, 99, 113
Dürer, Albrecht
  Death of Orpheus (1494) 84, *85*
During, Elie 146

EHESS (École des hautes études en sciences sociales), art history at 1, 7, 45n37, 48, 54–5, 56, 165
Einstein, Carl 151
Eisenstein, Sergei 152, 153, 154, 166
Elkins, James 4
empreinte (the imprint) 18, 98–120, 165
  definition of 98–9
  encounter, shock of the 148–9, 150–1

Febvre, Lucien 72
Fink, Daniel A. 53–4
Fliess, Wilhelm 40
Foster, Hal 7, 94n22
Foucault, Michel 75, 76–7, 78, 118n25, 143, 145
  Archaeology of Knowledge, The 16, 24–7, 75, 118n25, 144, 165
  Birth of the Clinic, The: An Archaeology of Medical Perception 25, 27
  concept of the modern subject 13–14
  on Deleuze 10
  Didi-Huberman's engagement with 4, 5–6, 14, 15–16, 24–8, 31, 43, 71, 75, 152–3, 157, 165–6, 171
  Invention of Madness, The 25
  'Nietzsche, Genealogy and History' 152
  Order of Things, The 13, 25–6, 145, 157

Freedberg, David 12, 111
Freud, Sigmund
    Didi-Huberman's engagement
        with 6, 24, 33–4, 37, 38, 39,
        42, 43, 69
    and dreams, interpretation of 38,
        40–3, 47n64
    and symptom formation 33,
        36–43, 77–8, 80
Fried, Michael 6, 11, 74

Gell, Alfred 142
German Institute of Art History 1
Ghirlandaio, Domenico 109–10
Giannari, Nikki 170
Gilson, Étienne 61
Giotto 30, 109
Gish, Lillian 162, 164
Godard, Jean-Luc
    Histoire(s) du cinéma
        (1989–98) 162
    and representation of the
        Holocaust 129–30
Gombrich, Ernst 82, 111, 158
Goodman, John 43, 66n2
Greenberg, Clement 11, 73–4,
    99, 166
Griffith, D. W., *Way Down East*
    (1920) 162, 164
Grootenboer, Hanneke 143
Guattari, Félix 22n43, 171
Gunthert, André 7
Gutting, Gary 27

Halliwell, Stephen 9
Hantaï, Simon 100–2, 118n11, 170
Heartfield, John 166
Hegel, Georg Wilhelm Friedrich
    Didi-Huberman's engagement
        with 6, 39, 71, 72–8, 88, 92–3,
        165, 168
    master-slave dialectic 51
    narrative of progress 2, 3, 110
Heidegger, Martin 32–3

Holly, Michael Ann 8, 19, 171
Holocaust
    discourse 3–4, 18–19, 124–41
    photographs 121–5, *122, 123, 124,*
        125, 142
Hyppolite, Jean 76

Iconographie photographique de
    la Salpêtrière 14–15, 37–8,
    162, 164
    see also Charcot, Jean-Martin
idealism
    art history's privileging of 17, 18,
        29, 102, 103, 147
    definition of 2–3, 29
    see also Kant, Immanuel; Krauss,
        Rosalind; Panofsky, Erwin;
        Vasari, Giorgio
imitation 2, 9–10, 28, 31, 34–5, 62–3,
    83, 89, 116, 146
    see also Angelico, Fra; *empreinte*
        (the imprint); mimesis
index, the 62, 70, 99–100,
    111, 113–17

Jameson, Fredric 128, 166
Joselit, David 94n22

Kafka, Franz 171
Kant, Immanuel 16–17, 29, 31–3, 43,
    51, 59–60, 126
    Heidegger on 32–3
Kourkouta, Maria 170
Krauss, Rosalind 7, 74–5, 94n22, 99,
    113, 115, 153
Kristeva, Julia 8

Lacan, Jacques 24, 51, 112
    Seminar XI 143
Lacoste, Patrick 36–7, 57
Lacoue-Labarthe, Philippe 168
Lanzmann, Claude 126, 137
    Shoah (1985) 127–8, 129–30, 131,
        135, 139

Leśniak, Andrzej 4
Londe, Albert 163, 164
Loraux, Nicole 73
Lotringer, Sylvère 5
Lukács, Georg 127, 166
Lyotard, Jean-François 5, 126

Maggiori, Robert 146, 147
Maldiney, Henri, Didi-Huberman's
    studies with 14
Mansfield, Elizabeth 34
Marin, Louis 7, 8, 14, 54–5, 165
mémoire involontaire 80–2, 150
Michaud, Philippe-Alain 3
Michelangelo 30, 107, 109
mimesis
    definition and conflation with
        representation 2, 9, 31, 34
    Didi-Huberman on 17, 28–30,
        33–5, 36–7, 40, 42, 43, 55–7,
        62–4, 147, 154
    see also pan, le; wax
Mitchell, W. J. T. 7, 8, 12, 142
montage 18–19, 22n43, 89–93
    as an epistemological tool
        149–59
    see also Benjamin, Walter; Nemes,
        László, *Saul Fia (Son of Saul)*
        (2015); Warburg, Aby
Montaigne, Michel de
    Essais (1580/1588/1595) 6,
        168–70
Moxey, Keith 3, 8, 13, 74, 142

Nagel, Alexander 3, 74
Nancy, Jean-Luc 64–5, 66, 116,
    126, 168
Nemes, László, *Saul Fia (Son of Saul)*
    (2015) 128–39, *132, 133*
'New Art History' 8
Nietzsche, Friedrich 9–10, 13, 71, 76,
    83, 88, 89, 90, 145
    Heidegger on 32
Noudelmann, François 75, 148

Pagnoux, Elizabeth 126
pan, le 17, 48, 49–57, *50, 52, 53,* 62,
    65–6, 69, 91, 103, 112
    definition of 49, 66n2, 66n4
    see also symptom, the, material
        status as *le pan*
Panofsky, Erwin 8, 16–17, 19, 25, 26,
    29, 43, 54
    Didi-Huberman's engagement
        with 30–1, 32, 33, 36, 48, 59, 72,
        144, 165
    Warburg's influence on 82
Peirce, Charles Sanders 111, 113,
    114, 115
Penone, Giuseppe 98, 170
Pia, Secondo 113–14
Plato and Platonism 29, 34–5, 48, 55,
    61, 145–6, 169
    dependence of art history on 17
    forms, ideas, images and mimesis
        3, 9–11, 35, 40, 89, 105, 151
    Heidegger's critiques of 32–3
    Kant and 31–2
Pliny the Elder 107–8, 111
Pollock, Griselda 8, 26
Pollock, Jackson 70, 71, 91, 100
Pontormo, Jacopo, *Visitation*
    (1528–29) 65
Pope-Hennessy, John 59
poststructuralism 2, 5, 8, 9–10, 165
    see also Deleuze, Gilles; Derrida,
        Jacques; Foucault, Michel
Poussin, Nicholas 143
Prendergast, Christopher 9
presencing 17, 36, 48, 57, 64, 65–6
Proust, Marcel
    À la recherche du temps perdu 49,
        67n12, 80
    mémoire involontaire 80–2, 150
Pseudo-Dionysius the Areopagite 61,
    64, 68n39, 91

Rabinow, Paul 26–7
Rampley, Matthew 32

Rancière, Jacques 73, 126
  Emancipated Spectator, The 159n3
Raphael 30
repetition 84, 88–9
representation
  definition and contestation 2, 9–19
  see also Holocaust, discourse;
    imitation; mimesis, definition
    and conflation with
    representation
Resnais, Alain, *Nuit et Brouillard*
  (1956) 129, 130
Riegl, Aloïs 84–5, 102–3
Ross, Christine 74
Rousseau, Jean-Jacques, Derrida's
  reading of 56, 63

Saint, Nigel 3
Salpêtrière hospital *see* Charcot,
  Jean-Martin
Sartre, Jean-Paul
  Being and Nothingness (1957)
    111, 112
  Nausea (1937) 143
Sassetti, Francesco 109–10
Saussure, Ferdinand de 39, 55,
  63, 104
Saxton, Libby 128
Schlosser, Julius von, *History
  of Portraiture in Wax*
  (1910) 110–11
Smith, Terry 74
Sontag, Susan 113
Spencer, John R. 59
Spielberg, Steven, *Schindler's List*
  (1993) 129
Strachey, James, translation of
  Freud 43
symptom, the
  Didi-Huberman and the
    aesthetics of 33, 36–43, 77–80,
    90–1, 93
  material status as *le pan* 49,
    53, 62, 69

see also Angelico, Fra; *empreinte*
  (the imprint)

Tagg, John 25
Théâtre National de Strasbourg,
  Didi-Huberman as
  playwright at 14
Tiedemann, Rolf 97n73
time, Didi-Huberman's
  understanding of
  and anti-Hegelianism 71, 73–8, 81,
    83, 85, 87, 88, 89, 92, 93
  and the influence of Aby
    Warburg 82–9
  and the influence of Walter
    Benjamin, 78–82
  and interrogation of the temporal
    models underpinning art's
    history 69–75
  and montage 89–93
Todd, Janie Marie 66n2
Turrell, James 170
Tylor, Edward Burnett 83–4

Vasari, Giorgio
  Didi-Huberman's critique of
    16–17, 18, 27–8, 28–9, 31,
    33, 43, 57, 59, 87–8, 105–8,
    116, 165
  *Lives of the Most Eminent Painters,
    Sculptors, and Architects* (1550/
    1568) 30, 105, 106, 108, 116
  von Schlosser's critique of 110–11
Velázquez, *Las Meninas*
  (1656) 25–6
Vermeer, Jan
  Lacemaker, The (c. 1669–70) 51–4,
    52, 53, 57, 112
  *View of Delft from the Rotterdam
    Canal* (1658–60) 49, 50
Vertov, Dziga 166
Veyne, Paul 26
Vinci, Leonardo da 30, 105–6
visual culture studies 8

Wajcman, Gérard 126–7
Warburg, Aby 1, 109
  Bilderatlas Mnemosyne
    (*Mnemosyne Atlas*) (1927–29)
    10–11, *11*, 13, 22n43, 90,
    146, 153, 154–5, *156*,
    157–8, 166
  departure from Hegelianism 83,
    85–6, 88
  Didi-Huberman's engagement
    with 2, 3, 12–13, 32, 71, 78,
    82–9, 93, 165

and *Nachleben* 12, 17–18, 83–4,
    85–6, 87–8, 90, 93, 164, 166
and *Pathosformel* 12, 83, 84,
    87–8, 89
wax 99, 106–12
White, Hayden 171
Whiteread, Rachel 98
Winckelmann, Johann Joachim
    84, 87–8
Wittkower, Rudolf 109
Wölfflin, Heinrich 74, 84–5
Wood, Christopher 3, 74

EU authorised representative for GPSR:
Easy Access System Europe, Mustamäe tee 50,
10621 Tallinn, Estonia
gpsr.requests@easproject.com

www.ingramcontent.com/pod-product-compliance
Lightning Source LLC
Chambersburg PA
CBHW070316190526
45169CB00005B/1648

*9 7 8 1 5 2 6 1 6 7 1 0 1 *